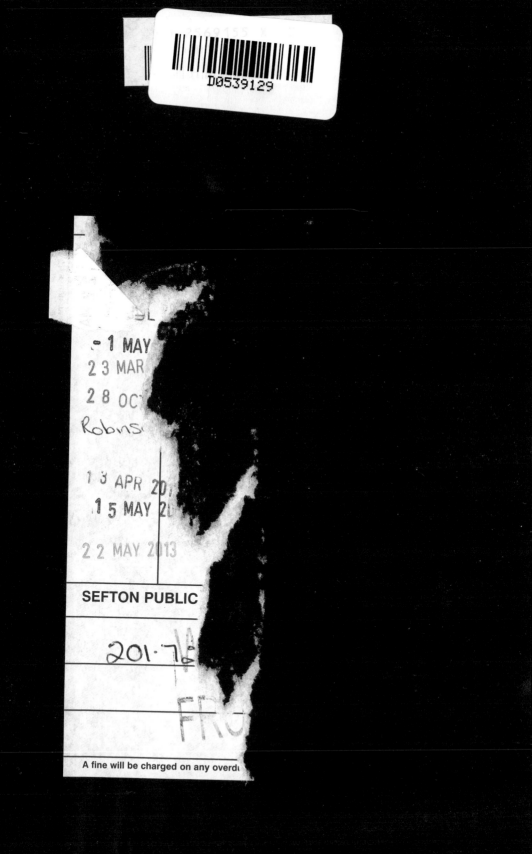

THE MIGHTY & THE ALMIGHTY

Also by Madeleine Albright

Madam Secretary

THE MIGHTY

&

THE ALMIGHTY

Reflections on

Power, God, and

World Affairs

MADELEINE ALBRIGHT
with Bill Woodward

MACMILLAN

Dedicated to those of every nation and faith
who defend liberty, build peace, dispel
ignorance, fight poverty, and seek justice.

First published in Great Britain 2006 by Macmillan
an imprint of Pan Macmillan Ltd
and simultaneously in United States by HarperCollins*Publishers*
Pan Macmillan, 20 New Wharf Road, London N1 9RR
Basingstoke and Oxford
Associated companies throughout the world
www.panmacmillan.com

ISBN-13: 978-1-4050-9160-2
ISBN-10: 1-4050-9160-6

1 3 5 7 9 8 6 4 2

A CIP catalogue record for this book is available from
the British Library.

Printed and bound in Great Britain by
Mackays of Chatham plc, Chatham, Kent

Contents

———⟨⟩———

Part Two

Cross, Crescent, Star

Part Three

Final Reflections

Preface to UK Edition

In December 2005, I joined mourners in London at historic St. Margaret's church, Parliament's official house of worship. The occasion was a memorial service for Robin Cook, who had served as foreign secretary during my own years as secretary of state. Four months earlier, Robin had collapsed while hiking in the Scottish highlands with his wife Gaynor. Two years before that, he had resigned from the British government because he could not support the invasion of Iraq.

Robin Cook did not profess faith in God, but neither would he have objected to his life being celebrated in a church; he was, it is said, a Presbyterian atheist. At the service, Tony Blair offered a reading from Luke. Gaynor recited the passage in Micah foretelling the day—still awaited—when nations "shall beat their swords into plowshares, and their spears into pruning hooks." Gordon Brown called Cook "the greatest parliamentarian." I offered my own recollections, including Robin's and my participation in what we called "the X-mins," a group of former foreign ministers from Europe, Canada and the United States. A crowd of more than 850, representing countries from across the globe, jammed the pews. For a moment, the strains of debating public policy were set aside, but only for a moment, because the same questions of principle that caused Robin Cook to break with his party's leadership have caused larger divisions in Europe and America, and between the Bush administration and its many critics in every part of the world.

On one side, there are those who see the invasion of Iraq as a necessary response to 9/11, an event perceived as so shocking that it transformed the rules of war, justified wide-scale exceptions to legal due process and granted to America a license to defend itself when, where, and however its leaders see fit. On the other side, there are those (myself included) who see international terrorism as a global danger that can best be defeated through vigorous cooperation among old friends and steadfast allegiance to long-settled standards of human rights and law. The military has a role in this struggle, but the decisive battlefield will be one of ideas.

Debates over strategy and tactics are, of course, common enough, even in time of war. What is different now is the resurgent role of religion. Many Europeans, including some supporters of the Iraq invasion, are uncomfortable with the religious themes embedded in President Bush's rhetoric, not least his assertion that God intended for him to become president. Quite a number of Americans share this discomfort. Students of history recognize all too well the dangers posed by political leaders who see themselves as God's surrogates.

The present controversy has fed generalizations about Europe's secularity and America's religiosity; the reality, of course, is more complex. America has not become a theocracy; Europe is far from godless. It is true, though, that the average European is more cautious about mixing religion and politics than the average American, and less likely to equate religion with morality. Unlike Europe, the United States has never experienced a major religious war, nor has it ever been ruled by the church. For most Americans, the connotations of religion are manifestly positive. The missionary impulse, though inherited from Europe, flourishes today far more in the new world than the old.

When I have the opportunity to travel around Europe and America, I often find myself attempting to explain one to the other. I feel as if I am in a time warp, stuck in the era a century or two ago when Europe looked down on America as uncivilized and Americans saw Europeans as effete. This is not something I expected when I left government service in 2001. I thought at the time that the Trans-Atlantic partnership was in good shape, notwithstanding disagreements over such matters as trade subsidies and bio-genetic foods. Hubert Vedrine, the French foreign minister, may have criticized America as a "hyperpower," but when a crisis of bloodletting arose in Kosovo, the United States and France stood together with the rest of Europe to stop it.

The Mighty and the Almighty is, in some senses, a plea for greater understanding between Europe and the United States, between the political right and left, between the religious and secular, and among those of varying faiths. It argues that our differences, though important, mean little compared to the common humanity that binds us. That may seem a platitude but it *must* be recognized and acted on. Efforts to escape or deny it have long been a cause of repression and war.

Enhanced understanding, though, is not sufficient. Policy mistakes cannot be excused simply because the motives behind them can be explained. Those in power must be held accountable for the consequences of their decisions even when their intentions are for the best. Countries cannot afford leaders who are too often wrong; nor can the world. I believe that the unilateralists are wrong and that 9/11 did far more to validate the relevance of the Trans-Atlantic partnership—and the institutions of alliance and law that support that partnership—than to render it or them obsolete. I agree with Robin Cook's observation in his resignation speech that "history will be astonished at the diplomatic miscalculations" that took place after 9/11 and before the invasion of Iraq.

Nostalgia about the state of U.S.–European relations during the cold war can be overdone. There were always disagreements, tensions and jealousies. There was also, however, a core belief that, though we were on different sides of the Atlantic, we were on the same side in responding to the transcendent issues of the day. I draw strength from my conviction that this shared belief has not lost its power, and that it will be restored to full health by those we choose to lead us in years to come.

Madeleine K. Albright
2006

Introduction

by William J. Clinton,
forty-second president of the United States

During the time she was secretary of state, the world learned what I already knew: Madeleine Albright is unafraid to take on hard issues or to speak her mind. In *The Mighty and the Almighty*, she writes with uncommon frankness and good sense about America's international role, religion, ethics, and the current divided and anxious state of the world. To my knowledge, no former secretary of state has written anything similar. It is an unexpected book, drafted against the advice of friends who worried that these topics could not be discussed without stepping on toes. In my experience, the only way to avoid stepping on toes is to stand still. Madeleine Albright is the embodiment of forward movement.

After our initial conversation about this project, I called Madeleine to discuss it further, not knowing at the time where she was. It turned out that she was in Gdańsk, Poland, commemorating the twenty-fifth anniversary of Solidarity, the democracy movement that ended the cold war and brought freedom to Central and East Europe. When I rang,

Madeleine was standing in a crowd that included the former Czech president Václav Havel and the current presidents of Ukraine and Poland. She passed the phone around, and I had an unforeseen but welcome chance to catch up with some old friends. Meanwhile, Madeleine placed a bouquet of flowers as a memorial to Solidarity and attended a three-hour open-air mass in celebration of freedom. I had caught her at a moment and in a place where God and democracy were together at center stage. One theme of this book, and a source of continuing controversy in public life, concerns the relationship between the two.

"The core of democracy," wrote Walt Whitman, "is the religious element. All the religions, old and new, are there." I expect we have all come across people who would embrace the first of Whitman's sentences while ignoring the second, rendering both without meaning. At their best, religion and democracy each respect the equality and value of every human being: all of us stamped with the Creator's image, each endowed with certain inalienable rights. These doctrines sit next to one another comfortably; they are unifying and inclusive. Problems arise when we try to place our own interpretation ahead of Whitman's, arguing that those sharing our particular understanding of the universe are more worthy than others. To have faith is to believe in the existence of absolute truth. It is quite another thing to assert that imperfect human beings can be in full possession of this truth, or that we have a political ideology that is fully true and allows us to penalize, coerce, or abuse those who believe differently.

The Constitution of the United States created something truly new: a system of government in which the highest trust is placed not in the top officials, who are hemmed in by an ingenious system of checks and balances, but in the people as a whole. Among the limitations our founders placed on those in government was that they could not establish an official state religion, or abridge the right of anyone to worship freely. The founders understood from history that the concentration of political and religious authority in the same hands could be toxic.

We know, of course, that the power of faith is often exploited by those seeking to enhance their own power at the expense of others. In the Balkans, Slobodan Milošević talked much about defending Christian Europe, but his real interest was in using religion and extreme divisiveness to fortify his hold on power. Osama bin Laden poses as a defender of Islam, but his willingness to murder innocents, including other Muslims, is not a fair reading of the Quran and is disloyal to the tenets of that faith. In the wrong hands, religion becomes a lever used to pry one group of people away from another not because of some profound spiritual insight, but because it helps whoever is doing the prying.

Does this mean that policy makers should try to keep religion walled off from public life? As Madeleine Albright argues, the answer to that question is a resounding no. Not only shouldn't we do that; we couldn't succeed if we tried. Religious convictions, if they are convictions, can't be pulled on and off like a pair of boots. We walk with them wherever we go, the skeptics and atheists side by side with the devout. A president or secretary of state must make decisions with regard both to his or her own religious convictions and to the impact of those decisions on people of different faiths. However, as Madeleine points out, assessing that impact is no easy task.

During my visit to India in 2000, some Hindu militants decided to vent their outrage by murdering thirty-eight Sikhs in cold blood. If I hadn't made the trip, the victims would probably still be alive. If I hadn't made the trip because I feared what religious extremists might do, I couldn't have done my job as president of the United States. The nature of America is such that many people define themselves—or a part of themselves—in relation to it, for or against. This is part of the reality in which U.S. leaders must operate.

When radical imams try to subvert the thinking of alienated, disaffected young people, not all of whom are poor or lacking in education, by offering a supposed quick trip to paradise in return for the believers' willingness to kill civilians by blowing themselves up, how should we respond? We can try to kill and capture them, but we can't get them all. We can try to persuade them to abandon violence, but if our arguments have no basis in their own experience, we can't fully succeed. Our best chance is to work cooperatively with those in the Muslim world who are trying to reach the same minds as the radicals by preaching a more complete Islam, not a distorted, jagged shard.

I truly believe that this can be done, not by diluting spiritual beliefs but by probing their depths. The three Abrahamic faiths have more similarities than differences. Each calls for reverence, charity, humility, and love. None is fully revealed. The challenge for our leaders is to use what we have in common as a basis for defeating the most extreme elements and draining support for terror. Once people acknowledge their common humanity, it becomes more difficult for them to demonize and destroy each other. It is far easier to find principled compromise with one of "us" than with one of "them." Our religious convictions can help us erase the age-old dividing line. No job is more important, but as this book by Madeleine Albright makes clear, it is a job that—four and a half years after 9/11—we have barely begun.

—New York
February, 2006

Part One

God, Liberty, Country

One

The Mighty and the Almighty

———— ⚘ ————

I had watched previous inaugural addresses, but the first one I truly took in was John Kennedy's in 1961. My brother John, who was in junior high school, played the trumpet in the Denver police band and had been invited to Washington to march in the inaugural parade. It seems that everyone remembers the snow on the ground and how the glare of sunshine made it impossible for Robert Frost to read the poem he had composed for the occasion. The new president, hatless in the crystal-cold air, his breath visible, asked us to "ask not." It was the speech about "passing the torch" to another generation. I saw it on television—that is how I experienced all the inaugural addresses until 1993. Then, and again four years later, I watched President Clinton deliver his speeches from the balcony of the U.S. Capitol. The words combined with the crowds and the view of the Washington Monument brought out the sense of history and pride in the United States that has done so much to shape my view of the world.

•　　•　　•

The inaugural address provides an American president with a matchless opportunity to speak directly to 6 billion fellow human beings, including some 300 million fellow citizens. By defining his country's purpose, a commander in chief can make history and carve out a special place for himself (or perhaps, one day, herself) within it. On January 20, 2005, facing an audience assembled in the shadow of the Capitol, President George W. Bush addressed America and the world. From the first words, it was evident that both he and his speechwriters had aimed high. "It is the policy of the United States," he declared, "to seek and support the growth of democratic movements and institutions in every nation and culture, with the ultimate goal of ending tyranny in our world." He continued, "History has an ebb and flow of justice, but history also has a visible direction, set by liberty and the Author of Liberty." The president concluded that "America, in this young century, proclaims liberty throughout the world and to all the inhabitants thereof." He might have added that, in the Bible, God had assigned that same job, in the same words, to Moses.

The speech was vintage George W. Bush, one that his admirers would hail as inspirational and his detractors would dismiss as self-exalting. It was of a piece with the president's first term, during which he had responded to history's deadliest strike on U.S. soil, led America into two wars, roused passions among both liberals and conservatives, set America apart from its longtime European allies, aggravated relations with Arab and Muslim societies, and conveyed a sense of U.S. intentions that millions found exhilarating, many others ill-advised.

Within the United States, there are those who see the president as a radical presiding over a foreign policy that is, in the words of one commentator, "more than preemptive, it is theologically presumptuous; not only unilateral, but dangerously messianic; not just arrogant; but rather bordering on the idolatrous and blasphemous." The president's supporters suggest the contrary, that his leadership is ideally, even heroically, suited to the perils of this era and in keeping with the best traditions of America.

My own initial instinct, particularly when the president is trumpeting the merits of freedom, is to applaud. I firmly believe that democracy is one of humankind's best inventions: a form of government superior to any other and a powerful source of hope. I believe just as firmly in the necessity of American leadership. Why wouldn't I? When I was a little girl, U.S. soldiers crossed the ocean to help save Europe from the menace of Adolf Hitler. When I was barely in my teens, the American people welcomed my family after the communists had seized power in my native Czechoslovakia. Unlike most in my generation who were born in Central Europe, I had the chance to grow up in a democracy, a privilege for which I will forever be grateful. I take seriously the welcoming words at the base of the Statue of Liberty; and I have always wanted to think of America as an inspiration to people everywhere—especially to those who have been denied freedom in their own lands.

As appealing as President Bush's rhetoric may sometimes be, however, I also know that proclaiming liberty is far simpler than building genuine democracy. Political liberty is not a magic pill people can swallow at night and awaken with all problems solved, nor can it be imposed from the outside. According to the president, "Freedom is God's gift to everybody in the world." He told Bob Woodward, "As a matter of fact, I was the person who wrote the line, or said it. I didn't write it, I just said it in a speech. And it became part of the jargon. And I believe that. And I believe we have a duty to free people. I would hope we wouldn't have to do it militarily, but we have a duty."

These are uplifting sentiments, undoubtedly, but what

exactly do they mean? The president says that liberty is a gift to everybody, but is he also implying that God appointed America to deliver that gift? Even to raise that question is to invite others. Does the United States believe it has a special relationship with God? Does it have a divinely inspired mission to promote liberty? What role, if any, should religious convictions play in the decisions of those responsible for U.S. foreign policy? But perhaps we should begin by asking why we are even thinking about these questions, given America's constitutional separation between church and state. And haven't we long since concluded that it is a mistake, in any case, to mix religion and foreign policy? I had certainly thought so.

Although—as I learned late in life—my heritage is Jewish,* I was raised a Roman Catholic. As a child, I studied the catechism, prayed regularly to the Virgin Mary, and fantasized about becoming a priest (even a Catholic girl can dream). As I was growing up, my sense of morality was molded by what I learned in church and by the example and instruction of my parents. The message was drilled into me to work hard, do my best at all times, and respect the rights of others. As a sophomore at Wellesley College, I was required to study the Bible as history, learning the saga of ancient Israel in the same way as that of Greece or Rome.†

As an immigrant and the daughter of a former Czechoslovak diplomat, I was primarily interested in world affairs. I did not,

---

* A full discussion of the discovery of my Jewish heritage, including the shock of learning that three of my grandparents and a number of other family members had died in the Holocaust, is included in my autobiography, *Madam Secretary: A Memoir*, Miramax, New York, 2003, 235–249.

† Wellesley is a college for women. The school's motto is "Non ministrari sed ministrare": "Not to be ministered unto but to minister." My classmates and I used to joke that it really meant "Not to be ministers, but to be ministers' wives."

however, view the great issues of the day through the prism of religion—either my own or that of others. Nor did I ever feel secure enough about the depth of my religious knowledge to think I was in a position to lecture acquaintances about what they should believe. I did not consider spiritual faith a subject to talk about in public. For the generation that came of age when and where I did, this was typical. I am sure there were parts of America where attitudes were different, but the scholar Michael Novak got it right when he asserted in the early 1960s, "As matters now stand, the one word [that could not be used] in serious conversation without upsetting someone is 'God.' "

The star most of us navigated by in those years was modernization, which many took as a synonym for secularization. The wonders we celebrated were less biblical than technological: the space race, breakthroughs in medicine, the birth of nuclear power, the introduction of color television, and the dawn of the computer age. In the United States, the play and movie *Inherit the Wind* dramatized the triumph of science (the theory of evolution) over creationism (a literal interpretation of Genesis).* When we thought of Moses, the image that came to mind was Charlton Heston, in technicolor. Religious values endured, but excitement came from anticipating what our laboratories and researchers might come up with next. We Americans were not alone in our pragmatic preoccupations. Abroad, the

---

* This "triumph of science" did not arrive all at once and may not be permanent. Not until 1968 did it become legal to teach evolution in every part of the United States. More recently, there has been pressure from some church groups to teach "intelligent design" as an alternative to the theory of evolution. The idea behind intelligent design, as I understand it, is that the complexity of life proves that the world must have been created by an all-knowing supernatural force. I do not consider myself an expert on everything that should be taught in classrooms, but I do believe a clear distinction should be drawn between concepts that are derived from the scientific method and those that are not.

rising political tides were socialism and nationalism, as Africans and Asians freed themselves from their colonial overseers and began the task of building countries that could stand on their own.

In the early 1980s, I became a professor at Georgetown University. My specialty was foreign policy, about which such icons as Hans Morgenthau, George Kennan, and Dean Acheson theorized in almost exclusively secular terms. In their view, individuals and groups could be identified by the nations to which they belonged. Countries had governments. Governments acted to protect their nations' interests. Diplomacy consisted of reconciling different interests, at least to the point where wars did not break out and the world did not blow up. Foreign policy was commonly compared to a game of chess: cerebral, with both sides knowing the rules. This was a contest governed by logic; its players spoke in the manner of lawyers, not preachers. During my adult years, western leaders gained political advantage by deriding "godless communism"; otherwise, I cannot remember any leading American diplomat (even the born-again Christian Jimmy Carter) speaking in depth about the role of religion in shaping the world. Religion was not a respecter of national borders; it was above and beyond reason; it evoked the deepest passions; and historically, it was the cause of much bloodshed. Diplomats in my era were taught not to invite trouble, and no subject seemed more inherently treacherous than religion.

This was the understanding that guided me while I was serving as President Clinton's ambassador to the United Nations and secretary of state. My colleagues felt the same. When, in 1993, Professor Samuel Huntington of Harvard predicted that the era following the end of the cold war might well witness an interreligious "clash of civilizations," we did all we could to distance ourselves from that theory. We had in mind a future in which nations and regions would draw closer as democratic bonds grew stronger, not a world splitting apart along historic fault lines of culture and creed.

When fighting broke out in the Balkans, we urged each side to focus on the rights of the individual, not the competing prerogatives of religious groups. In 1998, after U.S. embassies in Kenya and Tanzania were bombed by terrorists, we published posters seeking information and offering a reward; these posters had the heading, "This is not about religion. This is not about politics. This is about murder, plain and simple." During the administration's marathon effort to find a basis for peace in the Middle East, President Clinton and I were fully aware of the religious significance of Jerusalem's holy places. We hoped, nevertheless, to devise a legal formula clever enough to quiet the emotions generated by the past. We asked and expected both sides to be realistic and settle for the best deal they could get.

We were living, after all, in modern times. The wars between Catholics and Protestants that had claimed the lives of one-third the population of Christian Europe had been brought to a close in 1648 by the Peace of Westphalia. Large-scale fighting between Christians and Muslims had ceased when, in 1863, the advance of the Ottoman Turks was halted at the gates of Vienna. I found it incredible, as the twenty-first century approached, that Catholics and Protestants were still quarreling in Northern Ireland and that Hindus and Muslims were still squaring off against each other in south Asia; surely, I thought, these rivalries were the echoes of earlier, less enlightened times, not a sign of battles still to come.

Since the terror attacks of 9/11, I have come to realize that it may have been I who was stuck in an earlier time. Like many other foreign policy professionals, I have had to adjust the lens through which I view the world, comprehending something that seemed to be a new reality but that had actually been evident for some time. The 1990s had been a decade of globalization and spectacular technological gains; the information revolution altered our lifestyle, transformed the workplace, and fostered the development of a whole new vocabulary. There was, however, another force at work. Almost everywhere, religious movements are thriving.

In many parts of Central and South America, Protestant evangelicals are contesting the centuries-old dominance of the Catholic Church. In China, authorities saddled with an obsolete ideology of their own are struggling to prevent burgeoning religious and spiritual movements from becoming a political threat. India's identity as a secular society is under challenge by Hindu nationalists. Throughout the former Soviet Union, long-repressed religious institutions have been reinvigorated. In Israel, Orthodox religious parties are seeking more influence over laws and society. Secular Arab nationalism, once thought to embody the future, has been supplanted by a resurgent Islam extending beyond Arab lands to Iran, Pakistan, central and southeast Asia, and parts of Africa. Christianity, too, is making remarkable inroads in Asia and Africa; ten of the world's eleven largest congregations are in South Korea, and the other is in Nigeria. A reawakening of Christian activism is also altering how we think about politics and culture in the United States. In contrast to Michael Novak's observation four decades ago, people now talk (and argue) about God all the time. Even in Europe, which seems otherwise exempt from the trend toward religious growth, the number of observant Muslims is rising quickly, and a new pope—named for Benedict of Nursia, the continent's patron saint—is determined to re-evangelize its Christian population.

What does one make of this phenomenon? For those who design and implement U.S. foreign policy, what does it mean? How can we best manage events in a world in which there are many religions, with belief systems that flatly contradict one another at key points? How do we deal with the threat posed by extremists who, acting in the name of God, try to impose their will on others? We know that the nature of this test extends back to pagan times and is therefore nothing new; what is new is the extent of damage violence can inflict. This is where technology has truly made a difference. A religious war fought with swords, chain mail, catapults, and battering rams is one thing. A war fought with high explosives against civilian targets is quite another. And the prospect of a nuclear bomb detonated by terrorists in purported service to the Almighty is a nightmare that may one day come true.

Leaving government service in 2001, I returned to an earlier love, the university classroom. At Georgetown, I teach one course a semester, alternating between graduates and under-graduates. At the beginning of each course, I explain to my students that the main purpose of foreign policy is to per-suade other countries to do what we want. To that end, a president or secretary of state has tools ranging from the blunt instrument of military force to the hard work of back-and-forth negotiations to the simple use of logical argument. The art of statecraft consists of finding the combination that produces the best results. That, in turn, requires a clear grasp of what matters most to those we are trying to influ-ence. For businesspeople, this translates into "knowing your customer." In world affairs, it means learning about foreign countries and cultures; at a time when religious passions are embroiling the globe, that cannot be done without taking religious tenets and motivations fully into account.

Increasingly, in the classes I teach and in discussions with friends and colleagues, I have solicited thoughts about the impact of religion on current events. At first most people are surprised, as if uncertain what to think; then they open up. My request leads not to one set of debates, but to many. It is a Rorschach test, revealing much about the preoccupations and anxieties of those who respond.

My students tend to equate religion with ethics and so frame their responses in moral terms. They want to know why the world is not doing more to alleviate poverty and disease, prevent genocide, and help developing countries compete in the global economy. After 9/11, quite a number were eager to join the military or the CIA, feeling a powerful urge to volunteer; but in most cases the feeling did not last. The war in Iraq created confusion about the wisdom of U.S. policy, and about whether America's goal was to lead the world or try to dominate it. The foreign students I teach are an eclectic group and therefore offer a mixed bag of opinions. They are most divided, not surprisingly, by questions of right and wrong in the Middle East.

My friends who are experts on foreign policy—a somewhat older group—are focused on the threat posed by religious extremists, including the possibility that terrorists will gain access to weapons of mass murder. They are alarmed, as well, about the gap in understanding that has opened between predominately Islamic societies and the West.

Arab leaders to whom I have spoken share this concern. They are upset, too, by the spread of what they consider to be false and damaging generalizations about Islam.

The religious scholars I have consulted are passionate about the need for political leaders to educate themselves in the varieties of faith and to see religion more as a potential means for reconciliation than as a source of conflict.

Political activists, not just Democrats, are agitated about the influence of the religious right on the White House and Congress; this is a subject also weighing on the minds of foreign diplomats.

My own reactions are grounded in my various identities, as a daughter of Czechoslovakia, an American who is intensely proud of her adopted country, and a former secretary of state. My hero when I was growing up was Tomáš Garrigue Masaryk, who founded modern Czechoslovakia in 1918. Masaryk was a major influence on the thinking of my father and—through him—on me. Unlike many religious people, who see humanism as an alternative to faith in God, Masaryk saw the two as linked. To him, religious faith meant showing respect for every person and being willing to help others. Masaryk did not think it was necessary to believe in God to be moral, but he did argue that religious faith, properly understood, did much to encourage and strengthen right behavior. I have similar views. It is a perversion of faith to turn religion into a source of conflict and hate; it also creates severe problems for America and for the world.

Growing up in the United States transformed me, despite having witnessed much turbulence at a tender age, into a confirmed optimist. As a young woman, I took my theme—but without irony—from Leonard Bernstein's adaptation of *Candide*: "Everything is for the best in this best of all possible worlds." All through my years of government service, I maintained a positive outlook. In the Clinton administration, we talked a lot about the twenty-first century and, characteristically, felt sure that America, with others, could find a solution to most problems. I still feel that way, but I worry that we have been making some serious and avoidable mistakes.

There are days now when it is hard to pick up a newspaper. I think the U.S. government has thoroughly botched its response to international terror, damaged America's reputation, and substituted slogans for strategy in promoting freedom. I willingly concede, however, the difficulty and complexity of the problems the Bush administration is facing. I have often said that those who have never held the highest jobs in government do not know how hard these jobs can be, and that those who retire from them tend to forget quickly. Critics have an obligation to be fair and to offer constructive ideas. That is the purpose of this book. Part One deals with America's position in the world and the role played by religion and morality in shaping U.S. foreign policy, both now and in the past. Part Two concentrates on troubled relationships between Islamic communities and the West. Part Three offers my thoughts about how U.S. foreign policy and religion can best intersect. In keeping with my nature, the chapters are aimed primarily at practical policy making—doing what works best. In keeping with the nature of religion, they are sometimes dominated by a parallel theme—doing what is right. Locating the convergence of the two is my ultimate goal, as it should be for the policy makers of a nation that has, from its earliest days, sought to be judged both by its prowess and by its ideals.

Two

"The Eyes of All People Are upon Us"

As a junior in high school, six years after my family arrived in this country, I took my first full course in U.S. history. In that simpler time, my classmates and I were taught a more uniformly positive view of America's past than many students learn now: a saga of freedom-loving men and women overcoming obstacles in which every crisis was capped by a happy ending. It was, to me, an amazing tale made more real by the place where we lived—Colorado. Out west, the states were bigger than many European countries; the mountains so high that we marveled at how the first settlers had ever been able to cross them. The history hooked me; it was one of the reasons I wanted so much to be accepted as an American. Looking back, I do not remember devoting many hours to the study of religion in the United States, but we did of course begin with the story of the earliest arrivals from Europe, the intrepid people who made a long and uncomfortable voyage in search of a place to practice their faith freely, without interference from the government.

• • •

Writing in his shipboard diary in 1630, John Winthrop, governor of the Massachusetts Bay Colony, imagined that the community he and his fellow Puritans were about to establish would be "as a Citty upon a Hill, [with] the eies of all people . . . uppon us."* The Puritans believed that, if God so willed, the new colony would become a model for how to live a righteous life. They came to the New World in order to escape God's judgment on the corrupt churches of Europe, find refuge from the poverty and overpopulation of England, and obey the divine command to spread the gospel.

Theirs was a society based on a certain understanding of God's will, dependent on God's favor, eager to enjoy the fruits of the earth, but careful not to become too attached to worldly goods. To protect their virtue, they excluded from their community those whose thinking did not conform to their own rigid ideas.

By the time of the American Revolution, the direct descendants of the Puritans were a small minority. Dutch Protestants had settled New York. William Penn had established his Society of Friends in Pennsylvania. Maryland had been founded by Catholics who were eventually overthrown by Protestants—a distant mirror of the English civil war. Virginia was led by planters who were well-versed—ironically, given that they owned slaves—in the latest European theories about the universal nature of human rights. America, already a magnet for immigrants, was populated by followers of many faiths and sects. Mindful of what religious strife had done to Europe

---

* Winthrop's phrase is derived from Matthew 5:14: "Ye are the light of the world. A city that is set on an hill cannot be hid." The passage was copied from a sermon, "A Model of Christian Charity," delivered by Winthrop on board ship before the Puritans' departure from England. Once in Massachusetts, Winthrop was considered something of a moderate. He opposed, for example, the suggestion of some Puritans that their women be required to wear veils.

and seeing echoes of it in their own colonial history, the founders embraced the concept of religious liberty. The new American Constitution provided, in Article VI, that "No religious Test shall ever be required as a Qualification to any Office or public Trust under the United States." The Bill of Rights went further, to prohibit both the official establishment of a religion and any abridgement of the right to worship. In this design, neither state nor church would be able to control or harm the other.

Until I began researching this book, I did not give much thought to the religious philosophy of America's founders; I considered them to be primarily political—not spiritual—theorists. They did, however, think deeply about religion. The early presidents, for example, were firm believers in a divine being, but not wedded to the finer points of church doctrine. George Washington, in his first inaugural address, acknowledged a debt to the divine by saying that America's every step "seems to have been distinguished by some token of providential agency." He pledged to repay that debt by ensuring that "the foundation of our national policy will be laid in the pure and immutable principles of private morality." More important, he set the pattern for future administrations through his scrupulous support for religious tolerance. Washington disclaimed any interest in whether people were "Mohametans, Jews or Christians of any sect, or Atheists." His sole concern was that they should have the right to exercise freedom of worship, expression, and thought. In 1790, in a letter to the Hebrew congregation of Newport, Washington wrote reassuringly, "The government of the United States gives to bigotry no sanction, to persecution no assistance."

America's founders were conscious that they were building something new and extraordinary—a system of government based on the rights and responsibilities of the individual. This was a concept that would influence political thinking around the world. Americans saw themselves as establishing a society superior in organization and morality to the decaying aristocracies of Europe. They compared themselves freely to the ancient Israelites as a people selected by providence to participate in the working out of a divine plan. Benjamin Franklin proposed that the great seal of the young country depict the Israelites crossing between the parted waters of the Red Sea, with Moses raising his staff and the pharaoh's troops about to be drowned.* Thomas Jefferson thought the seal should show the children of Israel in the wilderness, "led by a cloud by day and a pillar of fire at night." To Americans of the time, it seemed natural to associate their freedom with that earned by Moses, their bountiful new land with that promised to the Jews, and their commitment to the principle that "all men are created equal" with man's creation in the image of Abraham's God.

During the first decades of national independence, Americans' belief that their country had been the special recipient of God's favor grew apace. Despite periodic economic downturns and the sacking of the White House by the British in the War of 1812, the United States was vigorous and dynamic, bursting at the seams. The Louisiana Purchase, Lewis and Clark's expedition, the annexation of Texas, the discovery of gold in California—all pushed Americans relentlessly westward. As they moved, they built democratic institutions thought to be those of a model republic. The qualities of self-reliance, free enterprise, and

---

* Franklin was a particular champion of religious tolerance. In Philadelphia, he raised money for a public hall that would be available to any preacher from any faith. "Even if the Mufti of Constantinople were to send a missionary to preach Mohammedanism to us," he said, "he would find a pulpit at his service."

equal opportunity became the nation's creed. The spirit of the frontier may have been coarse, but it was also fired by energy and optimism. After observing Americans at work, worship, and play in the 1830s, Alexis de Tocqueville wrote, "America is a land of wonders, in which everything is in constant motion and every change seems an improvement. . . . No natural boundary seems to be set to the efforts of man; and in his eyes what is not yet done is only what he has not yet attempted to do." The historian George Bancroft, de Tocqueville's older contemporary, contended that the expression of popular will made possible by American democracy was intrinsically consistent with God's purpose. "Taming the frontier" meant extending the reach of civilization. The movement westward was ordained, in the words of the journalist John L. O'Sullivan, to fulfill America's "manifest destiny."*

Of course, not everyone interpreted the divine will in the same way. Some Native American religious leaders warned their followers not to expect any reward in the afterlife unless they rejected the immoral customs of the white man and returned to traditional ways. That meant forsaking alcohol and firearms, relying on the bow and arrow, and maintaining the spiritual beliefs of their ancestors. Among the traditionalists was Red Jacket, a Seneca chief who complained to a Christian missionary proselytizing among Indians: "Brother, you say there is but one way to worship and serve the Great Spirit. If there is but one religion, why do you white people differ so much about it? . . . We also have a religion. . . . It

---

* According to O'Sullivan (in *Democracy Review*, July 1845), America's claim to Oregon at the time was justified "by right of our manifest destiny to overspread and possess the whole of the continent which Providence has given us for the great experiment of liberative and federative self-government entrusted to us."

teaches us to be thankful for all the favors we receive, to love each other and to be united. We never quarrel about religion. Brother, we do not wish to destroy your religion or take it from you. We only want to enjoy our own."

The shameful treatment of Native Americans caused soul-searching among thoughtful people, but it was slavery that tore the country apart. Abolitionists and slave owners alike invoked God's name when pleading their cause. Southerners declared that slavery was sanctioned by the Bible; their opponents insisted that slavery was an abomination. In the Senate, the argument was taken up by John Calhoun, a slave-owning planter from South Carolina; and by Charles Sumner of Massachusetts, a liberal state then and now. Rather than try to reconcile slavery with the Declaration of Independence, Calhoun dared to denounce America's founding premise. "All men are not created," he insisted. "According to the Bible, only two, a man and a woman, ever were [created], and of these one was pronounced subordinate to the other. All others have come into the world by being born, and in no sense . . . either free or equal." As for Sumner, he took to the Senate floor in May 1856 to deliver a speech that lasted two full days. Referring to a pro-slavery legislator he declared:

> How little that senator knows himself or the strength of the [abolitionist] cause which he persecutes! He is but a mortal man; against him is an immortal principle. With finite power he wrestles with the infinite, and he must fall. Against him are stronger battalions than any marshaled by mortal arm—the inborn, ineradicable, invincible sentiments of the human heart; against him is nature in all her subtle forces; against him is God. Let him try to subdue these!

Through the tumultuous decades of expansion, war, and

economic booms and busts, there flowed the conviction that God was watchfully guiding America's course and fate. This belief remained widespread as the twentieth century approached and the country's energy and ambition moved beyond the now settled American frontier to the distant reaches of the Pacific. In 1898, explaining his administration's conquest of the Philippines, William McKinley told a group of Methodist clergymen:

> The truth is I didn't want the Philippines, and when they came to us, as a gift from the gods, I did not know what to do with them.... I walked the floor of the White House night after night until midnight; and I am not ashamed to tell you, gentlemen, that I went down on my knees and prayed Almighty God for light and guidance.... And one night it came to me.... There was nothing left for us to do but to take them all, and to educate the Filipinos, and uplift and civilize and Christianize them.

History would be far different if we did not tend to hear God most clearly when we think He is telling us exactly what it is we want to hear. McKinley liked to conceive of the expansion of American power as part of a divine plan, but although the war against Spain was successful and quick, consolidating control over the Philippines proved difficult and slow. Many Filipinos, even those long since "Christianized" by Catholic Spain, welcomed their liberators not with open arms but with arms of a deadlier kind. A rebellion against the U.S. occupation raged for four years, much to the puzzlement of many Americans. One leading newspaper said in an editorial, "It seems strange that the Filipinos—or so many of them—are bitterly opposed to our sovereignty. They must know it is likely to be a great improvement over former conditions. . . . Nevertheless they fight on. The situation is a depressing one from every point of view." By the time the resistance was ended, more than 100,000 of the islanders had died.

Was this imperialism? Not according to those most responsible for the policy. While campaigning to become McKinley's vice president, Theodore Roosevelt told an audience in Utah, "There is not an imperialist in the country that I have met yet." A leading Republican senator, Henry Cabot Lodge, offered this explanation: "I do not think there is any such thing as 'imperialism,' but I am clearly of the opinion that there is such a thing as 'expansion,' and that the United States must control some distant dependencies."

Whatever it was called, the missionary impulse was mixed with more worldly considerations. At the turn of the twentieth century, a young senator from Indiana, Albert Jeremiah Beveridge, became famous for an oration, "The March of the Flag," that he gave repeatedly in public appearances and on the Senate floor. "The Philippines are ours forever," exulted the senator, "and just beyond them are China's illimitable markets. We will not retreat from either. . . . We will not abandon one opportunity in the Orient. We will not renounce our part in the mission of our race, trustee under God, of the civilization of the world." Whatever else may be said, Beveridge did not lack ambition for his country. "Most future wars," he said, "will be conflicts for commerce. The power that rules the Pacific, therefore, is the power that rules the world. And, with the Philippines, that power is and will forever be the American Republic."

Such attitudes were typical of the time and should not be surprising to us. It was, after all, an age of exploration, acquisition, and zeal. The British had taken on what Kipling referred to as the "white man's burden" to spread Christianity and educational uplift to the Indian subcontinent and Africa. The

French were embarked on a *mission civilisatrice* to spread the benefits of their culture among Africans and Arabs. The Spanish, Belgians, Portugese, and Dutch all had overseas possessions. By taking the Philippines, the United States was in effect announcing its entry into the ranks of world powers.

Although most Americans welcomed their new status, some thought it hypocritical, based on a misreading of scripture and a misunderstanding of American ideals.

The historian Charles Francis Adams, great-grandson of the second president, remarked contemptuously:

> The clergymen have all got hold of the idea of Duty; we have a Mission; it is a distinct Call of the Almighty. They want to go out, and have this Great Nation [export] the blessings of Liberty and the Gospel to other Inferior Races, who wait for us, as for their Messiah;—only we must remember to take with us lots of shot-guns to keep those other Superior Races,—all wolves in sheep's clothing,—away from our flock. They would devour them;—but we won't. Oh no!—such ideas are "pessimistic"; you should have more faith in the American people!—Such cant!—It does make me tired.

Anti-imperialism leagues formed in many cities in the United States, but the American sense of mission still thrived, partly because it was embodied in more than gunboats and merchant ships. In increasing numbers, religious Americans found a calling to share their faith with those in distant lands. By the early 1900s, tens of thousands of American missionaries were established in foreign countries. They came from virtually every Christian denomination, with heavy representation from a movement that began in the United States, the Church of Jesus Christ of Latter-Day Saints, referred to commonly as the Mormons. The missionaries carried with them both the good news of the gospel and the democratizing influence of American values and culture. Missionaries were among the nation's first experts on foreign customs and the first to learn foreign languages. Their letters home heightened the interest of fellow parishioners in countries to which few Americans had previously given a thought. For the first time, people from places such as New York, Nebraska, and North Carolina began pressing Washington to recognize human rights (to protect the converted), support higher standards of commercial ethics (to prevent the exploitation of workers), and pursue a moral foreign policy (to protest the Chinese opium trade).

Separation of church and state rests on three "nos": no religious tests for public office, no established state religion, and no abridgement of the right to religious liberty. These principles are essential to America's democracy and to its identity as a nation; let us hope they are never breached. In expressing that wish, however, we must recognize that such a separation does not require and has not led to the removal of God from the civic life, currency, coinage, patriotic songs, or public rhetoric of the United States. This reality reflects both the depth of America's religious roots and a universal rule of practical politics: religion may be separated from government, but it is intimately connected to how leaders are judged. As Machiavelli wrote in 1505, "A prince . . . should seem to be all mercy, faith, integrity, humanity and religion. And nothing is more necessary than to seem to have this last quality."*

---

* It says something about the state of the Catholic Church in Machiavelli's time that the writer was offering his advice to Prince Cesare Borgia, whose father was Pope Alexander VI.

From the original George W. to the current one, every president has seen fit during his inaugural address to mention God in one context or another. Most have expressed gratitude for the blessings America has received. Many have suggested that God would continue to favor the United States as long as its policies were moral and just. Several have led the nation in prayer in time of national crisis. Some have found reason to discuss the nature of their religious faith in public settings. President Coolidge cited America's Christianity as proof of its good intentions ("The legions which she sends forth are armed, not with the sword, but with the cross") and proclaimed the Christianization of humanity as the country's national purpose ("The higher state to which she [America] seeks the allegiance of all mankind is not of human, but of divine origin").

Individuals, not nations, are said to be made in the image of God; but America's self-image has always been influenced by the feeling—faint at times and powerful at others—that it is the instrument of heaven. As President Ronald Reagan cautioned, "If you take away the belief in a greater future, you cannot explain America—that we're a people who believed there was a promised land; we were a people who believed we were chosen by God to create a greater world." Reagan did not specify how that world was to be created, but the answer most American leaders have given is "freedom."

In the Christian gospel, the kingdom of heaven is compared to a mustard seed and to yeast: little things that grow. Proponents of the American gospel have shown similar faith in democratic ideals. Shortly before his death, Jefferson wrote that the democratic system would spread across the globe "to some parts sooner, to others later, but finally to all." At first, Americans were confident that the merits of democracy were sufficiently obvious that others would adopt the system without any need for nudging by the United States. Through the nineteenth century, the country was in any case reluctant to involve itself very deeply in the affairs of others. After all, George Washington had warned against entering into permanent alliances, and John Quincy Adams had declared that America should be a well-wisher to freedom everywhere, but a defender only of her own. The twentieth century brought a new set of circumstances and imperatives. With first coal and then oil replacing wind as a source of power, transoceanic crossings became routine; next came airplanes. The world grew smaller, while America's interests expanded. In addition to the Philippines, the United States began to intervene closer to home, to protect economic interests and foster good governance in Cuba, Mexico, Haiti, Nicaragua, and the Dominican Republic. The country also found itself unable—despite strenuous efforts—to protect its security while remaining neutral in European conflicts. Confronted by the necessity of pulling Americans from their living rooms and dropping them into a cauldron of war thousands of miles across the sea, it was natural for U.S. leaders to define the stakes in the starkest terms.

"We shall fight for democracy," said Woodrow Wilson in his war message in 1917, "for the right of those who submit to authority to have a voice in their own governments, for the rights and liberties of small nations, for a universal dominion of right by such a concert of free peoples as shall bring peace and safety to all nations and make the world itself at last free." Following the war, he praised American troops for their victory: "These men were crusaders. They were not going forth to prove the might of the United States. They were going forth to prove the might of justice and right, and all the world accepted them as crusaders, and their transcendent achievement has made all the world believe in America as it believes in no other nation organized in the modern world."

Such claims may seem overblown from this distance, but to the people of many small nations at the time, they rang true. While European leaders were eagerly dividing postwar spoils in the Middle East and elsewhere, Wilson was championing democracy and the right of every nation to control its own fate. Largely because of his influence, an independent Czechoslovakia was born, with institutions patterned on America's. As a child, I was taught to think of Wilson as a hero who reflected the ideals of a country different from any other, a nation with immense power that nevertheless believed the world should be ruled not by the sword, but by law. Wilson was a stubborn man and not the best politician, but he did much to burnish America's reputation as a beacon of freedom and justice. It has become customary to mock his idealistic plan for a League of Nations, but his warning— that a second global war would be inevitable if America failed to join the League—proved sadly prescient.

That second war, fought heroically on two fronts, followed by the cold war against communism, secured America's standing as the world's foremost proponent of democracy. This role was memorably embodied in John Kennedy's inaugural promise to "pay any price, bear any burden, meet any hardship, support any friend, oppose any foe, to assure the survival and success of liberty." The poem that Robert Frost had prepared for the ceremony, but was unable to read, acknowledged the American mission:

> *We see how seriously the races swarm*
> *In their attempts at sovereignty and form.*
> *They are our wards we think to some extent*
> *For the time being and with their consent,*
> *To teach them how Democracy is meant.*
> *"New order of the ages" did we say?*
> *If it looks none too orderly today,*
> *'Tis a confusion it was ours to start*
> *So in it have to take courageous part.*

There are, of course, some who argue that any talk of an American mission on behalf of morality or democracy is dangerous nonsense. Overseas, it is well understood that America has high pretensions. It is not universally accepted, however, that the actions of the United States are based on calculations any more honorable than those of other nations. The leaders of every country boast; it is part of their job description. The difference with Americans, say the skeptics, is their tendency to believe their own rhetoric. In this opposing view, America is not an exception to anything; it is just another nation among many—albeit bigger and stronger. Americans may pretend or like to believe otherwise, so the argument runs, but our country responds to dangers and opportunities in the same manner and with the same degree of practical self-interest as others do. The purpose of any government's foreign policy is to protect its citizens' economic well-being and physical security; that our leaders have a tendency to camouflage narrow interests with rhetoric about universal values simply reflects their desire to appear better than they are, and to perpetuate the myth that America is special. Closer to home, George Kennan has warned that for Americans to see themselves "as the center of political enlightenment and as teachers to a great part of the rest of the world [is] unthought-through, vainglorious and undesirable."

My own inclination is to say "Bunk" to those who argue that America is not an exceptional country. I can point to the Declaration of Independence, the Constitution, the Bill of Rights, the Gettysburg Address, the role of the United States in two world wars, and the example of America's multiracial, multiethnic democracy and ask: what country can compare? A few are as big, some are as free, many have admirable qualities, but none has had the same overall positive influence on world history and none has been as clearly associated with opportunity and freedom.

Does this mean that I am among those who believe the United States has a mission to spread liberty across the globe? No. I am uncomfortable with such an idea, as if our country's purpose had been defined by some outside force—God, providence, nature, or history. I do, however, believe in the principle that much is expected from those to whom much has been given. The United States is a country of abundant resources, momentous accomplishments, and unique capabilities. We have a responsibility to lead, but as we fulfill that obligation we should bear in mind that liberty, at least in the sense of free will, is God's gift, not ours; it is also morally neutral. It may be used for any purpose, whether good or ill. Democracy, by contrast, is a human creation; its purpose is to see that liberty is directed into channels that respect the rights of all. As the world's most powerful democracy, America should help others who desire help to establish and strengthen free institutions. But, in so doing, we should remember that promoting democracy is a policy, not a mission, and policies must be tested on the hard ground of diplomacy, practical politics, and respect for international norms. Our cause will not be helped if we are so sure of our rightness that we forget our propensity, as humans, to make mistakes. Though America may be exceptional, we cannot demand that exceptions be made for us. We are not above the law; nor do we have a divine calling to spread democracy any more than we have a national mission to spread Christianity. We have, in short, the right to ask—but never to insist or simply assume—that God bless America.

Three

Good Intentions
Gone Astray:
Vietnam and the Shah

⎯⎯⎯ ⚓ ⎯⎯⎯

I attended college in the late 1950s, a time (I tell my students now) somewhere between the discovery of fire and
the invention of the handheld BlackBerry. For most
Americans, it was a time of moral clarity. With my father
writing books about the dangers of communism, I myself
had little trouble separating the global good guys from the
villains. There were few public quibbles, at least not in the
United States, when Vice President Nixon asserted that "We
are on God's side." A few weeks after I graduated, Nixon
engaged the blustery premier of the Soviet Union, Nikita
Khrushchev, in the so-called "kitchen debate" at an exhibit
of modern housewares in Moscow. The vice president
argued that the U.S. system was superior by pointing to the
high quality of American home appliances. This technological divide was more than matched, in 1961, by concrete
proof of a moral divide, the construction of the Berlin Wall
(or, as East German authorities preferred to call it, the
"Anti-Fascist Protection Wall"). Unlike the communists, the
free world had no need to erect barriers to keep its people

from escaping. The West, with the United States in the lead, was clearly winning the battle of ideas.

Then came Vietnam.

America's involvement in the war in southeast Asia, stretching from the early 1960s until the spring of 1973, muddied what had seemed so clear. This was a conflict in which no amount of courage on the part of American troops could produce victory. The containment of communism proved complicated in a region where nationalism and anti-imperial attitudes were readily exploited by charismatic leaders such as Ho Chi Minh of North Vietnam. The qualities of confidence and optimism that had contributed so much to America's rise to greatness steered its strategists wrong in Vietnam. Unused to failure, American leaders were unable to fathom how this tiny communist country could withstand the power they had unleashed against it. They misread the local culture; placed too much faith in corrupt, unpopular surrogates; and adopted a military strategy of gradual escalation that deepened our country's involvement without making a decisive difference on the battlefield. In the arena of world opinion, America's strength became a handicap; dramatic accounts of the massacre at My Lai and of Vietnamese children fleeing in terror from napalm made the United States appear more a bully than a champion of freedom.

It is startling how criticisms heard during the Vietnam era have a parallel in those uttered more recently about a different type of war, the invasion of Iraq by the United States. In 1965, Hans Morgenthau, whose classic writings on history and foreign policy I had studied at Wellesley, complained, "While normally foreign and military policy is based upon intelligence—that is, the objective assessment of the facts—the process is here reversed: a new policy has been decided upon, and intelligence must provide the facts to justify it." At Yale, twenty-two-year-old John Kerry warned his fellow graduates of the "serious danger of assuming the roles of policeman, prosecutor, judge and jury, all at one time, and then, rationalizing our way deeper and deeper into a hole of commitment that other nations neither understand nor support." The widely respected congressman Morris Udall of Arizona summed up the opinion of many when he declared bluntly that Vietnam was "the wrong war in the wrong place at the wrong time."

Certainly, the conflict divided America. Although Richard Nixon claimed that the "silent majority" of U.S. citizens supported the war, millions opposed it, often on moral grounds. Prominent religious leaders—such as Yale's William Sloane Coffin and Rabbi Abraham Joshua Heschel of the Jewish Theological Seminary—were among those raising their voices in opposition. Martin Luther King Jr. condemned the war for squandering resources needed to fight poverty, requiring African Americans to bear an unfair share of the risks, undermining the principle of nonviolence, and killing innocent Vietnamese. King also spoke of the damage done to America's standing in Europe and elsewhere: "Each day the war goes on the hatred increases in the hearts of the Vietnamese and in the hearts of those of humanitarian instinct. The Americans are forcing even their friends into becoming their enemies. The image of America will never again be the image of revolution, freedom and democracy, but the image of violence and militarism."

Opponents of the war had a partner in the movement for African American civil rights. Both causes were promoted with zeal from the pulpit, on college campuses, and in the streets. These movements soon spawned others: campaigns to advocate for women, protect the environment, combat world hunger, halt arms sales to repressive regimes, and increase respect for human rights. This activism constituted less a repudiation of the belief that America is an exceptional country, than a demand that the nation live up to its ideals. Protesters charged that the true spirit of America was being subverted by leaders who relied too much on force, practiced a double standard regarding human rights, and paid too little heed to world opinion. The critics felt vin-dicated when the threadbare moral fiber of the Nixon administration was exposed, leading to the unprecedented resignations first of the vice president, then of Nixon himself. The protesters also applauded when congressional investigators exposed the complicity of the CIA in propping up authoritarian governments and in carrying out political assassinations.

The tragic experience in Vietnam did not diminish America's commitment to fighting communism, but it did raise questions about how best to engage the battle. It also created a demand for more honest leadership. When Jimmy Carter, the little-known governor of Georgia, announced his campaign for the presidency in the election of 1976, he promised never to lie to the American people and to give them a government as good as they were. It was the right message for the time and Carter was elected. To my delight, the new president chose as his national security adviser Zbigniew Brzezinski, who was a leading theorist on world affairs and had been a professor of mine at Columbia University, where I had attended graduate school. Although Columbia had been a center of antiwar protests, neither Brzezinski nor I had joined them. We agreed that the war had been mismanaged, but we did not share the casual attitude exhibited by some protest leaders toward the dangers of communism. We believed firmly in America's goals for the cold war and thought it possible to develop a better approach to achieving them. When Brzezinski offered me a job on his staff, I joined an administration that would try to find the right balance between two moral demands: fighting communism effectively and showing consistent support for democratic principles and human rights.

We inherited a debate that had simmered throughout the cold war about how to confront communism most wisely. One side in this debate argued that America would be justified in using almost any means to defeat the threat posed by the Soviet bloc. If those means included aiding anticommunist dictators, so be it; that was still morally preferable to allowing Marxist revolutionaries to seize power, strangle freedom, and leave no hope of eventual reform. The other side in the debate insisted that America could best defeat communism by consistently upholding humanitarian principles. In this view, America would have nothing to fear if it placed itself solidly on the side of people struggling to improve their lives. The Carter administration sought to combine the merits of each argument. This required coming to terms with some internal differences. Brzezinski had no illusions about our struggle with the Soviet Union. He did not trust the Kremlin, and he felt that we had to be tough in our actions and policies. Carter was more idealistic; he wanted America to present a morally untainted image to the world. Both could agree, however, that we would be more successful in countering communism if we made respect for human rights a fundamental tenet of our foreign policy.

Four months after taking office, in a commencement speech at Notre Dame, President Carter explained our new approach. Although rejecting "simplistic moral maxims," he said that America had so much faith in democratic methods that it would no longer be tempted to use improper tactics at home or overseas:

Being confident of our own future, we are now free of that inordinate fear of Communism which once led us to embrace any dictator who joined us in that fear. For

too many years, we have been willing to adopt the
flawed and erroneous principles and tactics of our
adversaries, sometimes abandoning our own values for
theirs. We have fought fire with fire, never thinking
that fire is better quenched with water. This approach
failed, with Vietnam the best example of its intellectual
and moral poverty. But through failure, we have found
our way back to our own principles and values, and we
have regained our lost confidence.

The president's speech was welcomed as a breakthrough
by the groups that had blossomed during the Vietnamese
war as advocates of human rights and peace. They were further pleased when, for the first time, an assistant secretary
of state for human rights was appointed. Pursuant to a congressional mandate, the administration began preparing
annual reports chronicling the human rights practices of
countries receiving assistance from the United States. New
restrictions were placed on military training and arms sales
to friendly but authoritarian governments in such countries
as the Philippines, Argentina, El Salvador, Guatemala, and
Nicaragua. One dictator, however, escaped all such sanctions:
the shah of Iran.

The flamboyant Mohammad Reza Pahlavi had been
America's ally since 1953, the year the CIA engineered a
coup installing him as shah of Iran in place of an elected but
antiwestern prime minister. Once enthroned, the shah
proved himself both rigidly autocratic and an enthusiastic
modernizer. His "white revolution" won plaudits from the
West for reforming education, building roads, improving
health care, and expanding opportunities for women. The
Nixon administration had agreed to sell Iran virtually any

nonnuclear weapon that its government was willing to buy, expecting in return a regime that would serve as a bulwark of anticommunist stability.

For President Carter, the shah was an early test. A foreign policy based on human rights alone would have shunned such a dictator, whose secret police were well practiced in torture. Instead, the administration embraced him. Iran, with its abundant oil reserves and its strategic location along the northern banks of the Persian Gulf, was viewed as too great a prize to risk. This was a case in which both the president and Brzezinski agreed that the United States should allow its realistic side to prevail over its more idealistic instincts. We were, after all, engaged in a zero-sum game with the highest possible stakes. Washington and Moscow sat across from each other with the global chessboard between them. The world at the time was divided in two, or so we thought. It took awhile for the superpowers to realize that a bearded man in a long robe had sat down beside them and was already making moves of his own.

No one had paid attention in the 1960s when an obscure Iranian cleric, Ayatollah Ruholla Khomeini, was thrown out of his country for protesting against the "decadence" of the shah's regime. Few noticed when the exiled ayatollah began communicating with the Iranian population, using cassette tapes smuggled in from France. Nor was much concern expressed when, in November 1977, Khomeini's son was murdered by the shah's security forces. The following year, after the shah declared martial law, his troops opened fire on a crowd of unarmed demonstrators, killing 900. Alarmed at last, the United States assured the shah of its continuing support while urging him, in vain, to adopt reforms that might appease his opponents and restore calm.

Years later, in my classes, I was able to cite the next events as an example of what happens when our government is divided. The key decision makers at the White House, the National Security Council, the State Department, and the U.S. embassy in Tehran all had different sources of information, different understandings of what was going on, and different ideas about what to do. Until almost the end, the ambassador was convinced the shah could hold on to power. The State Department in Washington was preoccupied with finding a way to ease the monarch out and install, in his stead, a coalition of moderates. Brzezinski thought that the shah should use military force, if necessary, to put down the protests. Meanwhile, the CIA had little to contribute. At one crucial meeting, Stansfield Turner, then the agency's director, was asked for his assessment of the Iranians protesting against the shah. He replied that he did not have one: the shah had prohibited the CIA from talking to any political opponents of the regime. As a result, no overtures sponsored by the United States were ever made to Khomeini, and efforts by Khomeini's aides to contact U.S. officials were rebuffed. To the highest levels of American government, the Iranian insurgents were virtually anonymous—a band of religious reactionaries, whose membership and intentions were a mystery.

We were caught off-guard by the revolution in Iran for the simple reason that we had never seen anything like it. As a political force, Islam was thought to be waning, not rising. Everyone in the region was presumed to be preoccupied with the practical problems of economics and modernization. A revolution in Iran based on a religious backlash against America and the West? Other than a few fanatics, who would support such a thing?

Our experts failed to grasp either the depth of hostility toward the shah or the loyal following that the Muslim clerics could muster, even amid the rampant materialism of the late twentieth century. The policy makers compounded their error by assuming that the revolutionaries would be satisfied with getting rid of the shah and installing a democratic government. We learned soon enough that the Iranian uprising was not just a coup, a "regime change," or even a civil war, but a true political earthquake, like the revolutions of France or Russia. After the shah finally departed in January 1979, Ayatollah Khomeini seized power and the old security structures crumbled. Prisoners and jailers exchanged roles. A new view of the world was established as the official truth and, amazingly, that truth had nothing to do with either communism or democracy. It was a truth indifferent to both the economic needs of society and the political rights of the individual; a truth based instead on a narrow and inflexible interpretation of divine will.

The United States was not the only superpower at the time to undervalue the importance of religion. The leaders of the Soviet Union viewed the rupture in relations between Washington and Tehran as a strategic opportunity. Concerned since the time of the czars about the fractious populations along their southern border, they now saw a chance to invade Afghanistan (which they did in December 1979) without worry that Iran would provide a base from which America could respond. Although the Soviet leaders had little trouble establishing a puppet government, they failed to anticipate the anger their invasion would generate among Muslims not only in Afghanistan but throughout south Asia and the Arabian Peninsula. This hostility generated, in turn, a strategic opportunity for the United States. With Iran now off-limits, we turned to another of Afghanistan's neighbors, Pakistan. Following the logic of rivalries everywhere (the enemy of my enemy is my friend), we funneled large quantities of assistance through Pakistan to Muslim fighters who were determined to wage war against the Soviet infidels. Brzezinski felt it essential to make the Russians pay a high price for the invasion, which he saw as crossing a dangerous line in the way the cold war was conducted. Visiting Pakistan's border region, he declared to the Muslim warriors assembled there, "God is on your side." It took a decade, but the Afghans, with their allies, eventually pushed the invaders out and reclaimed their country. In contrast to Iran, the struggle in Afghanistan seemed an unqualified victory for the United States. Of course, we did not know then that many of the Muslim militants who fought so effectively against our shared enemy would one day redirect their anger—against us.

The experiences of the United States in Vietnam and Iran during the 1970s offer lessons that Americans would do well to recall today. The first is that we tend to think of ourselves more highly than others think of us. We were able over time to understand why so many Vietnamese fought the American presence in their country. But when we switched on our televisions in 1979 and 1980 and saw mobs of Iranians chanting, "Death to the United States," we encountered a level of hatred we could not comprehend. After all, Iran was not southeast Asia. We had sent no troops, nor had we dropped any bombs. We thought of ourselves as the defenders of freedom, the good guys, who had never meant this distant country any harm. The Iranians' frenzied outburst of anger seemed irrational; it had to be madness. How could people in their right mind refer to Uncle Sam as the "great Satan"?

That question leads directly to the second lesson: religion counts. To Muslims in Iran, the United States was intimately associated with a dictator who also shunned Islamic values. Thus the religious revolution was directed against both the shah and America. Because we underestimated the importance of tradition and faith to Iranian Muslims, we made enemies that we did not intend to make. Even the Vietnam War, primarily a struggle over political ideology and nationalism, had a religious component. From the outset, the anticommunist cause was undermined because the government in Saigon repressed Buddhism, the largest noncommunist institution in the country. Denied the right to display religious banners in celebration of the Buddha's birthday, worshippers rioted, prompting troops to shoot, a reaction that in turn provoked more riots. Several yellow-robed monks set themselves on fire in front of international news photographers, helping to turn local and world opinion against American policy. President Diem, whose government we were propping up, declared martial law and began arresting Buddhist leaders. Diem's sister-in-law made the disaster complete by publicly referring to the immolations as "a barbecue." This was hardly the way to win the hearts and minds of the Vietnamese people.

In 1977, a scholar of the Middle East, Bernard Lewis, wrote, "Westerners, with few exceptions, have ceased to give religion a central place among their concerns, and therefore have been unwilling to concede that anyone else could do so. For the progressive modern mind, it is simply not admissible that people would fight and die over mere differences of religion." For the Carter administration, this was a lesson learned the hard way. After the Iranian revolution, the president ordered a series of White House briefings by experts and scholars regarding the tenets and politics of Islam. The effort intensified after our embassy in Tehran was stormed and American diplomats were taken hostage. The briefings made little difference, however, because by then the popularity of the administration had dropped so low that it was defeated for reelection.

The third lesson is that even smart and well-meaning people can make moral assumptions that turn out wrong. The involvement of the United States in Vietnam began with noble intentions and little self-doubt; America would save the grateful South Vietnamese from the slavery of communism. When the war became a quagmire, the feeling grew that the moral course was to withdraw. Once that happened, activists celebrated. But the best of them grew somber when the corrupt, pro-western governments in South Vietnam and neighboring Cambodia were overthrown by regimes that imposed totalitarian rule in the former and created the killing fields of Pol Pot in the latter. America *in* Vietnam was a nightmare of body-counts, search-and-destroy missions, napalm, and endless predictions of a victory that never came. America *out* of Vietnam was a nightmare of a million boat people and a mountain of skulls.

In Iran, a comparable scenario has unfolded. The shah was a cruel and insecure leader who brutally repressed his opponents. When his hold on power began to slip, human rights activists accused the Carter administration of hypocrisy for continuing to support him. Many rejoiced when the monarch was brought down, but from any objective standpoint, the practices of Iran's successor governments with regard to human rights have been far worse than the shah's. In the first few years alone, thousands of people were executed for political dissent and "moral crimes." The shah's secret police were replaced by religious "guardians of the faith," who were even more ruthless. Hundreds of thousands of Iranians, including longtime opponents of the shah, had little choice but to follow him into exile. Today, more than a quarter century after the revolution, power in Iran remains in the hands of a small group of unelected mullahs.

Jimmy Carter, as much as any president before or since, thought that morality should be at the center of U.S. foreign policy. His commitment to human rights made me proud to serve in his administration. It also contributed mightily to the credibility of American leadership and to the eventual expansion of democracy in Latin America, Asia, Africa, and Central Europe. The president's convictions made the question of democratic values part of every deliberation on foreign policy, even though the final decisions sometimes gave more weight to other factors, as was the case in Iran. Our experience there showed how complex decisions about foreign policy can be. To maintain a hard line against one source of villainy (the communism of the Soviet Union) we stood too close to a second source (the repressive shah), thereby helping to open the way for the rise of a third (Ayatollah Khomeini).

Although I was not a senior policy maker at the time, I recall the sense of frustration we all felt as our assumptions proved wrong, our options narrowed, and the situation drifted out of control. Some critics said that we should have placed democratic values first and abandoned the shah much earlier. Others contended that we should have placed security interests first and backed the shah, with military force if necessary. In hindsight, it is always easy to identify mistakes whether of omission or commission. It is much harder to see clearly before the decisions are made, when the outcome is still in doubt and the players involved have yet to reveal their hands. In those circumstances, we need guidance, but for that—to whom, or to what, should we turn?

Four

The Question of Conscience

The opposition of Martin Luther King Jr. to the Vietnam War was but a minor part of his career and legacy. Fixed in his commitment to justice and nonviolence, he demanded a thorough reexamination of the moral foundation of American society and of its policies both at home and abroad. In countless appearances in crowded churches and assembly halls, his soaring voice thundered the challenge:

> Cowardice asks the question—is it safe? Expediency asks the question—is it politic? Vanity asks the question—is it popular? But conscience asks the question—is it right? And there comes a time when one must take a position that is neither safe, nor politic, nor popular; but one must take it because it is right.

Dr. King's rhetoric is compelling; it does, however, leave the impression that when decision makers gather around the table, they have in front of them a set of containers in which the options are clearly labeled "safe," "politic," "popular," or "right"—like individual dishes at a restaurant buffet.

As the examples of Vietnam and Iran suggest, this is rarely the case. To make smart decisions, U.S. leaders must begin with good information. When I was secretary of state, I started each day in my kitchen reading newspapers over a cup of coffee. By the time I arrived in my office on the seventh floor of the State Department, a packet of information from the department's Bureau of Intelligence and Research would be on my desk. The bureau's analysis was especially good on the history and diplomatic context of particular situations: who was doing what to whom, why, and since when. I read next a copy of the the President's Daily Brief (PDB). This was a highly classified document but on most days less than riveting. While I read, a representative of the CIA would stand by and watch, in case I had any questions or special requests.

The PDB was quite short; I studied it so that I would be sure what the president was being told. Then I waded through a longer version of the same material called the National Intelligence Daily, and after that I received a briefing on potential terrorist threats. Amid this wealth of data, one ingredient was almost always missing: certainty. If intelligence were a television set, it would be an early black-and-white model with poor reception, so that much of the picture was gray and the figures on the screen were snowy and indistinct. You could fiddle with the knobs all you wanted, but unless you were careful, what you would see often depended more on what you expected or hoped to see than on what was really there.

Still, the Clinton administration's foreign policy team had to make decisions; whether we were confident about how much we knew or not, events would not wait. Even relatively small decisions mattered, because once we began moving in a certain direction, it would be difficult to turn back. Decisions tended to build one upon another. We were conscious of this and so weighed our options carefully. Our first obligation was to protect the best interests of the American people. We had each also taken an oath to defend the Constitution and to execute faithfully the duties of our respective offices. But when—if ever—did our consciences come into play? Did we have a moral responsibility as well?

Dean Acheson was a brilliant but distinctly unsentimental man who had served as President Truman's secretary of state. In 1965, he wrote that "a good deal of trouble comes from the anthropomorphic urge to regard nations as individuals and apply to our own national conduct, for instance, the Golden Rule—even though in practice individuals rarely adopt it. The fact is that nations are not individuals; the cause and effect of their actions are wholly different."

Twenty years later, George Kennan argued, "The interests of a national society for which a government has to concern itself are basically those of its military security, the integrity of its political life, and the well-being of its people. These needs have no moral quality. . . . They are the unavoidable necessities of a national existence and therefore not subject to classification as either 'good' or 'bad.' "

The statements by Acheson and Kennan are classic expressions of a school of thought in foreign policy commonly referred to by academics as "realism." Realists caution against paying heed to moral considerations because such considerations may cause us to lose sight of how governments actually behave. When I studied this school of thought in college, I was also taught to consider nations as "rational actors" that could be counted on to behave solely in accordance with their interests. This mode of thinking, once considered persuasive, has lost popularity. Certainly, in an imperfect world, a completely altruistic foreign policy is not feasible; but to argue that the cause and effect of actions by states are "wholly different" from those of individuals is to lean too far in the other direction. After all, the policies of nations result from the decisions and actions of individuals.

As for Kennan's assertions, one might just as well say that our individual interests are to obtain food, shelter, and protection against external threats. These, too, are "unavoidable necessities" of existence and have no moral quality. But to secure those interests we must act, and when we do act, we leave ourselves open to moral judgment. Our needs do not automatically validate our means. This is true for individuals and for nations. It is one matter for me to protect myself from my neighbor by installing an alarm in my house, but quite another to knock him on the head with a crowbar. It is one thing for a government to raise an army to patrol its borders, quite another to dispatch that army to annihilate a neighboring population. A similar test applies to how we respond to the needs of others. The failure of the West to admit more Jewish refugees during World War II can hardly be classified as morally neutral.

When I was in government, I thought of myself neither as strictly a realist nor as strictly an idealist, but as a hybrid of the two. I saw government as a practical enterprise that had to operate in a messy and dangerous world, although the realist approach struck me as cold-blooded. I did not understand how we could possibly steer a steady course without moral principles to help guide us. What does this mean? To me, morality is measured by the impact of actions on lives. That is why I insisted as secretary of state on moving beyond the normal routine of diplomatic meetings. I wanted to see and hear from the people most affected by the decisions governments make.

To this end, I visited refugees, persons living with HIV/AIDS, families whose breadwinners had had limbs blown off by land mines, people struggling to recover from wounds inflicted by terrorist bombs, widows whose loved ones had been put to death because of their ethnicity, and mothers who lacked the means to feed their children. I remember, especially, holding a three-year-old girl in Sierra Leone. Her name was Mamuna; she wore a red jumper and played happily with a toy car using her one arm. A soldier had chopped the other arm off with a machete. I had, at the time, a grandchild about the same age. I could not comprehend how anyone could have taken a machete to that girl. Whom exactly did she threaten? Whose enemy was she?

At each stop, I wished I could have brought all of America with me. Given the opportunity to see the wretched conditions in which so many people must live, I was sure we would respond with urgency and generosity. I could not, of course, fit all of America into my plane, nor did I want to sound like a bleeding heart in describing the basis of our foreign policy. So as soon as I returned home, I would enumerate all the practical reasons Americans should care: because we had an interest in stability, in prosperous overseas markets, in strengthening the rule of law, in extending our influence, and in burnishing our reputation. But even as I presented these arguments, I felt that they should have been superfluous.

To illustrate why, I offer my favorite story about Abraham Lincoln: one day, when he was still a young lawyer riding from courthouse to courthouse in search of clients, he came across a pig struggling in vain to free itself from a bog. Lincoln paused for a moment, torn between sympathy for the pig and concern about what the mud might do to his new suit. He rode on. After about two miles, he turned back, unable to stop thinking about the animal and its plight. Arriving at the scene, he laid out some wood planks on which he descended into the bog, reaching the pig and hauling it out at great cost to his clothing. When asked why he had done all that for a pig, Lincoln replied, in essence, "I didn't do it for the pig; I did it for me—to take a pain out of my mind."

If Lincoln could recognize his self-interest in rescuing a pig at the cost of his suit, America should be able to see its stake in helping people to escape their own desperate circumstances. One of my father's deepest beliefs was that it is possible to ascribe characteristics to nations. Much of America's history has been driven by its sense of moral purpose. This is an essential part of its national identity. When that purpose is blurred, as it was in Vietnam, the country becomes divided and loses its capacity to inspire others. This had been the thinking behind Jimmy Carter's decision to emphasize human rights. It wasn't only a question of trying to do good; it was a way of reminding Americans of their true self-interest and of putting their country in a position of leadership on a matter vital to people everywhere.

To accept the principle that questions of morality should enter into judgments about foreign policy is to settle one question only to confront two others. How do we determine what is moral? And how much weight should we attach to morality in proportion to more obviously self-interested considerations?

To help answer these questions, Professor Michael Walzer, of Princeton, has identified four obligations, in order of descending importance. A country's first priority, according to Walzer, is to protect the life and liberty of its own citizens; if it fails to do that, it cannot put itself into a position to help others. A country's second duty is not to inflict harm. Its third is, when possible, to help people avoid man-made and natural disasters. Its fourth is to assist those who want aid in building better and less repressive political systems.

Another way to apply roughly the same concept is to

define as moral those actions that produce a net increase in what we associate with good: life, liberty, justice, prosperity, health, and peace of mind—as opposed to death, repression, lawlessness, poverty, illness, and fear. Even with this simple formula, trade-offs will be required. For example, to end a civil war, amnesty might be offered to members of an out-law militia in return for its demobilization and surrender of arms. Under this arrangement, the need for peace receives precedence over the ideal of justice. This is pragmatism. The test of whether an action is moral is not whether it conforms to some rigid principle, but whether it achieves (as best as we can assess) a moral result.

On some issues, the right path is clear, but on many, perhaps most, the relative morality of various options can be extremely hard to pin down.

Often, decisions must be made not only with incomplete information but also in the face of contradictory claims, bewildering uncertainties, and reassuring "truths" that shrink into half-truths the moment they are seriously tested. Although good and evil both exist, they tend to be mixed together, not separately packaged. This reality, a central theme of philosophy, drama, literature, art, and my child-hood catechism,* is often ignored in the sweeping rhetoric of political leaders. It has a habit of showing itself, however, when the talking stops and actions begin. That is when the gap between what we intend and what we actually accomplish can become painfully evident, clouding the distinction between wrong and right. For example, in 1991, after the Persian Gulf War, the administration of the first President

---

* According to the catechism (paragraph 1707), "Man is divided in himself. As a result, the whole life of men, both individual and social, shows itself to be a struggle, and a dramatic one, between good and evil, between light and darkness."

Bush expected Saddam Hussein to be driven from power by his own people. That did not happen. As a result, "temporary" economic sanctions were put in place and then were extended every six months for more than a decade. The sanctions did not apply to medicine or food, but the Iraqi economy still suffered and innocent civilians were harmed. Hussein milked the suffering for all the propaganda it was worth. Though shedding crocodile tears in public, he worked behind the scenes to delay and later to corrupt international efforts to help his people through a program that exchanged oil for food. If the sanctions had been lifted, Hussein would surely have rebuilt his military and become once again a genuine regional threat.

During my years in office, Iraq always involved a choice between two evils; we tried our best to mitigate the harm caused by the alternative we chose. Unfortunately, in the process of attempting to explain our policy, I said something that will cause many to wonder how I could possibly presume to write this book. A reporter had asked whether maintaining sanctions was important enough to justify the many deaths of Iraqi children that were alleged to have occurred as a result. I hesitated, then replied, "That is a very hard choice, but the price—we think the price is worth it." I should have said, "Of course not—that is precisely why we are doing everything we can to see that Iraq has the money it needs to buy medicine and food." Because my mouth worked faster than my mind, I came across as cold-blooded and cruel. I will leave it for others to judge whether, on the basis of my career as a whole, those adjectives fit. I plead guilty, however, to temporary brain-lock and a terrible choice of words.

A second moral dilemma involved genocide in Rwanda, a country torn by strife between two ethnic groups—the Hutus and Tutsis. In August 1993, the United Nations assigned a peacekeeping mission to monitor a cease-fire between the two sides. All such missions face problems; this was an extreme case. The end of the cold war had produced a rise in the number of UN peacekeepers from approximately 18,000 to almost 80,000 in less than two years, badly overextending the system. More than a dozen operations—including four others in Africa—were already under way. The UN commander for Rwanda was able to recruit only about half the desired number of troops, and many of those he did recruit had little enthusiasm for the job. Further, the mission's mandate was designed at precisely the time a UN mission in Somalia was ending in disaster. The lesson the UN drew from that calamity was to avoid ever again taking sides in a civil war. Thus the operation in Rwanda was ordered to remain strictly neutral. That meant its success would depend entirely on the willingness of the local parties to cooperate in fulfilling their obligations. In fact, the Hutu side was planning a war of annihilation.

When that war broke out, the European powers and the United States intervened immediately—to rescue their own citizens. Much too little was done until much too late to help innocent Rwandans, who were slaughtered in the course of two months of nonstop killing. In my memoir, I discuss in some detail why and how this occurred, but the outcome is both undeniable and indefensible. The major powers failed to act; the result was mass murder. The moral challenge, however, did not end there. As the killing wound down, the United States decided to lead a "humanitarian" effort to save refugees who had fled from Rwanda into neighboring countries. The plight of the refugees was depicted vividly on CNN. Onward they trudged, mile after mile, with fear in their faces, belongings on their backs, and children in their arms. The dramatic images tugged at the heartstrings and aroused sympathy; less well reported was the fact that among the refugees were many who had participated in the genocide—people fleeing the vengeance their own crimes had provoked. The office of the UN High Commissioner for Refugees did its job in caring for the transients. Many lives were saved. But the presence of killers in the camps later led to further violence, contributing to a disastrous war in the neighboring Democratic Republic of Congo. Not even refugee relief is morally pure.

That same year, closer to home, Democratic leaders in Congress criticized President Clinton for his policy of sending back to Haiti would-be migrants who had been apprehended at sea while trying to reach the United States. These well-meaning critics said it was immoral, even racist, to return such defenseless people to a country then governed by a ruthless and illegitimate military government. Reluctantly, the president yielded and the policy was changed. The result was an immediate upward spike in the number of Haitians trying to flee their island on leaky rafts and unseaworthy boats. Inevitably, some of the overcrowded vessels capsized; hundreds of people drowned.

As these cases illustrate, efforts to pursue an ethical course in foreign policy are frequently undermined by unintended consequences. To achieve moral results, a policy maker must both want to do what is right and be able to predict what that might be. Ideally, he or she would have the conscience of a saint, the wisdom of a philosopher, and the prescience of a prophet. In reality, we stumble along as best we can despite shortages in all three qualities.

By far the toughest policy decisions are those governing the use of force. While in office, I visited American troops serving at home and in more than a dozen foreign lands. On each of these visits, I tried to do more than just thank U.S. soldiers, sailors, and aviators. I sat down and ate with them, listened to their stories, tried to answer their questions, and studied their faces. I knew that any misjudgments on my part could lead to the destruction of their lives and, for their loved ones, to irreparable loss.

Back at the State Department, I could see through the window of my office the rows of white stone markers in Arlington National Cemetery and the crowds of visitors to the memorials of our wars in Korea and Vietnam. I could not help asking myself: when is it really necessary to go to war? Under what circumstances is there no other choice? How would I feel if I were a soldier? I believed that, if younger, I would have been prepared to serve, and also that I would have been terrified. It is a cliché, but true: ordering the military into combat is the hardest decision a president can make or a secretary of state can recommend. Fortunately, the use of force is not easily justified. Tragically, there are times it cannot be avoided.

Imagine the world's reaction if, on the evening of September 11, 2001, President George W. Bush had gone before the American people and said, "Resist not evil: but whosoever shall smite thee on thy right cheek, turn to him the other also." Yet what could have been more natural for a devout Christian president than to refer for guidance at a moment of crisis to the Sermon on the Mount? What would have been more logical than for America's chief executive to ask his fellow citizens to heed the advice of his favorite political philosopher—Jesus of Nazareth—and to suggest forgiving those who had trespassed against the United States? Instead, President Bush did the opposite, vowing to strike back hard and hold the terrorists accountable for their deeds. Was this hypocrisy? Does a government, in fighting back against evil, and in using military force that results in the death of innocents, commit a sin? Or are governments exempt from the injunctions of the Bible?

To summarize centuries of scholarship in a single sentence, most would agree that governments cannot realistically be held to the scriptural norm, but that does not mean there are no standards. Tian Rangju, ancient China's foremost military scholar, declared nearly 2,500 years ago, "If you attack a country out of love for the people of that country, your attack is justified; if you wage war to end a war, that war is also justified." In the fifth century, Saint Augustine pondered the question whether a Christian could justify going to war. Observing the horrors then being inflicted on Roman citizens by barbarian invaders, he answered "yes." War was justified to "defend the vulnerable other." Later scholars (most notably Saint Thomas Aquinas and Hugo Grotius, the founding architect of international law) developed over time a set of criteria commonly referred to as the doctrine of the "just war," much of which is now reflected in the Geneva Conventions and other secular international legal documents. The criteria seek to define what is morally necessary both before a war and while it is being waged.

Generally speaking, a "just war" is one carried out by a competent authority with moral intentions for a cause that is right. The effort must have a reasonable chance of success, with the expectation that it will result in no greater harm than the injury that produced it. Those who order military actions must discriminate between combatants and noncombatants and should seek to avoid unnecessary damage. Before going to war, a government should explore thoroughly and in good faith all other options.

Countries also have the right to defend themselves. The charter of the United Nations calls on every member state to attempt to settle disputes peacefully and, failing that, to refer matters to the Security Council for appropriate action. Article 51 provides that nothing in the charter "shall impair the inherent right of individual or collective self-defense if an armed attack occurs against a Member of the United Nations, until the Security Council has taken measures necessary to maintain international peace and security." In practice, countries have frequently taken military action outside these guidelines, sometimes provoking censure by the UN, sometimes not. Despite such violations, the standards in the charter remain relevant, just as laws against murder remain relevant even though murders are still committed.

Although most rules limiting the use of force have their origins in religious tradition, those rules are not sufficiently strict to satisfy all who profess religious faith. In the spring of 2004, I delivered a speech on religion and American foreign policy to an audience at Yale Divinity School. Editors of the school's journal invited experts to respond and received a letter from Stanley Hauerwas, who was once hailed by *Time* magazine as "America's best theologian."

Hauerwas wrote to protest not so much the substance of my speech as the notion—preposterous to him—that I might have something of interest to say to students of religion. He wrote that my record in government had been "anything but honorable," and that "being a Christian . . . made it difficult, difficult but not impossible, to be the American Secretary of State." To Hauerwas, pacifism is a fundamental part of being Christian. He suggests that Americans who fight or support military action have no rightful claim to be Christians at all. I understand his logic, but do not accept it. No story is more uplifting than Christ's example in dying while forgiving at the same time. But the whole point of the doctrine of "just war" is that military actions are sometimes necessary for moral reasons. Hauerwas rejects the doctrine because, he says, it has been used to justify too many wars, and he is right about that. However, a sound doctrine does not become discredited because it is, on occasion, misused. Hauerwas may feel it is irrelevant who wins battles here on Earth because, in the end, we are all in God's hands; but it is due to past American military actions that he is able to take his own freedom for granted.

Attending church while in office, every time I heard "Blessed are the peacemakers," I took the words deeply to heart. I cherish peace and admire Gandhi, the Quakers, and other proponents of nonviolent resistance; but when I consider Hitler and the many episodes of ethnic cleansing and genocide, I cannot agree that nonviolence is always the best moral course. In some circumstances, the results are unacceptable. Here again, my views are a reflection of my heritage. The pros and cons of armed resistance were intensely debated in the Czechoslovak republic between the two world wars. President Masaryk declared passionately that the meaning of Czechoslovakia's history and democracy could be found in the life of Jesus, not Caesar. He wrote also, however, that "war is not the greatest evil. To live dishonestly, to be a slave, to enslave, many other things are much worse." At age eighty, he told the novelist John Galsworthy, "Old as I am, if someone attacked me, I would seize a brick with these old hands and throw it at him." Sometimes the only way to achieve peace is to fight for it.

This is not to imply that a decision to initiate the use of force should ever be entered into without deep reflection. Violence wreaks damage on those who use it as well as those against whom it is used. It is also likely to result, sometimes disastrously, in consequences that were not foreseen. As Mark Twain's harrowing *War Prayer* reminds us, even to pray for victory in war is tantamount to asking that horrors be visited upon the innocent of the opposing side. The duty of leadership, however, is inescapable: to try to make moral choices despite the immense difficulty of doing so, and at the risk of being wrong.

In recent years, the United States has had to confront the

question of "just war" in Afghanistan and Iraq. As secretary of state, I faced a similar challenge in the Balkans. Early in the 1990s, the Serbian dictator Slobodan Milošević had initiated three unsuccessful wars: against Slovenia, Croatia, and Bosnia. In 1999, he directed his wrath toward the ethnic Albanian majority in Kosovo, a province of Serbia. For a year, I explored every possible avenue to secure a diplomatic settlement that would have respected the rights of both sides. The Albanians ultimately accepted our proposal; Milošević refused, instead unleashing his security forces against the civilian population. His intent was to drive the Albanians from Kosovo by killing their leaders, burning their villages, and spreading terror. His goal was to "solve" the problem of Kosovo once and for all.

Since the province was part of Serbia, Milošević's crimes could not be characterized as international aggression. No member of NATO was under attack, so the alliance could not claim the right of self-defense. Serbia had not threatened to invade another country, so there was no rationale for a preventive strike. We did, however, have a duty "to defend the vulnerable other." The UN Security Council approved a resolution demanding the withdrawal of the marauding Serb troops; but Russian diplomats, historically sympathetic to their fellow Slavs, promised to veto any measure authorizing force to stop them.

This left the Clinton administration and NATO with a difficult choice. We could allow Russia's threatened veto to stop us from acting, or we could use force to save the people of Kosovo even without the UN's explicit permission. I pushed hard and successfully for the second option. My reasons were partly strategic: Europe was never going to be fully at peace as long as the Balkans were unstable, and the Balkans were never going to be stable as long as Milošević was in power. My primary motive, however, was moral: I did not want to see innocent people murdered. NATO's presence in Europe gave us the means to stop ethnic cleansing on that continent, and I hoped that by doing so we could help prevent similar atrocities elsewhere. This was indeed one of those times when, to echo the words of Martin Luther King Jr., our position should be based not on what was safe, but on what was right.

Because we lacked a specific UN mandate for military action, we worked particularly hard to demonstrate the justness of our cause. First, the Clinton administration secured the unanimous support of NATO. Second, I remained in constant touch with UN Secretary General Kofi Annan, who agreed publicly with us that the Serbs' actions were morally unacceptable. Third, during the war itself, NATO targets were vetted by military lawyers who compared each with the standards spelled out in the Geneva Conventions. In every instance a judgment was made as to whether the value of the target outweighed the potential risks to civilians.

As the war progressed, we increased the military pressure on Belgrade, while still exercising care to minimize unnecessary casualties. Three civilian targets (the Chinese embassy, a passenger train, and a refugee convoy) were struck by mistake. Estimates of the number of civilians killed by the bombing range from 500 to 2,000. The Serbs, before they were stopped, killed an estimated 10,000 Albanians in Kosovo and drove hundreds of thousands more from their homes. Throughout the war, we continued our diplomatic efforts to bring peace. Ultimately, these efforts succeeded. Milošević capitulated; the Serbs withdrew their security forces from Kosovo; refugees were allowed to return; a peacekeeping force, led by NATO, was introduced; and the UN organized a reconstruction effort that has since produced several rounds of democratic elections.

The seeds of conflict in Kosovo, as in earlier wars that

stemmed from the dissolution of Yugoslavia, were planted in the religious history of the region. Pleading Serbia's cause, Milošević told me that his people had spent centuries defending "Christian Europe." Serbia's epic national story is a recounting of the battle of Kosovo, fought against the Ottoman Turks on the Field of Blackbirds in 1389. According to legend, the prophet Elijah appeared to Serbia's Prince Lazar on the fateful day. Elijah offered the prince a choice between victory in battle (and an earthly empire) and defeat (compensated by a place in heaven.) The prince chose the lasting victory of heaven. It is an inspiring story, one that played a role in Serbia's brave decision to resist the Nazis during World War II.* The problem is that some Serbs have remained intent on avenging the defeat in Kosovo for more than 600 years, motivated by a fierce sense of nationalism and a belief in their own special relationship with God.

While the war in Kosovo was under way, Václav Havel characterized it in these terms:

> If one can say that any war is ethical, or that it is being waged for ethical reasons, then it is true of this war. Kosovo [unlike Kuwait] has no oil fields to be coveted; no member nation in the alliance has any territorial demands; Milošević does not threaten the territorial integrity of any member of the alliance. And yet the alliance is

---

* When Serbia's civilian leaders chose collaboration, they were overthrown by their own military. In a radio broadcast, the Serbian Orthodox patriarch explained the decision to resist: "Before our nation in these days the question of our fate again presents itself. This morning at dawn the question received its answer. We chose the heavenly kingdom—the kingdom of truth, justice, national strength, and freedom. That eternal idea is carried in the hearts of all Serbs, preserved in the shrines of our churches, and written on our banners." In response to this brave choice, the Nazis invaded—but faced indomitable fighting from Serb partisans.

at war. It is fighting out of concern for the fate of others. It is fighting because no decent person can stand by and watch the systematic government-directed murder of other people.... This war places human rights above the rights of states.

Most of us would agree that morality, though often hard to define, is essential if we are to get along with one another. We would feel more secure in a world where the conscience served as the primary guide to the actions of both nations and individuals. But what about religion? Religion is perhaps the single largest influence in shaping the human conscience, and yet it is also a source of conflict and hate. After what we have witnessed in the Balkans and other regions ripped apart by faith-based strife, is religion also something we should want in greater abundance?

Five

Faith and Diplomacy

———— ∾ ————

"This would be the best of all possible worlds if there were no religion in it!!" So wrote John Adams to Thomas Jefferson. The quotation, well known to proselytizing atheists, appears differently when placed in context. The full passage reads:

> Twenty times in the course of my late reading have I been on the point of breaking out, "This would be the best of all possible worlds if there were no religion in it!!" But in this exclamation I would have been ... fanatical. ... Without religion this world would be something not fit to be mentioned in polite company, I mean hell.

In his song "Imagine," John Lennon urged us to dream of a world free of religious doctrines. For many nonbelievers, religion is not the solution to anything. For centuries, they argue, people have been making each other miserable in the name of God. Studies indicate that wars with a religious component last longer and are fought more savagely than other conflicts. As the acerbic liberal columnist I. F. Stone observed, "Too many throats have been cut in God's name through the ages, and God has enlisted in too many wars. War for sport or plunder has never been as bad as war waged because one man's belief was theoretically 'irreconcilable' with another."

The fault in such logic is that, although we know what a globe plagued by religious strife is like, we do not know what it would be like to live in a world where religious faith is absent. We have, however, had clues from Lenin, Stalin, Mao Zedong, and, I would also argue, the Nazis, who conjured up a soulless Christianity that denied and defamed the Jewish roots of that faith. It is easy to blame religion—or, more fairly, what some people do in the name of religion— for all our troubles, but that is too simple. Religion is a powerful force, but its impact depends entirely on what it inspires people to do. The challenge for policy makers is to harness the unifying potential of faith, while containing its capacity to divide. This requires, at a minimum, that we see spiritual matters as a subject worth studying. Too often, as the Catholic theologian Bryan Hehir notes, "there is an assumption that you do not have to understand religion in order to understand the world. You need to understand politics, strategy, economics and law, but you do not need to understand religion. If you look at standard textbooks of international relations or the way we organize our foreign ministry, there's no place where a sophisticated understanding of religion as a public force in the world is dealt with."

To anticipate events rather than merely respond to them, American diplomats will need to take Hehir's advice and think more expansively about the role of religion in foreign policy and about their own need for expertise. They should develop the ability to recognize where and how religious beliefs contribute to conflicts and when religious principles might be invoked to ease strife. They should also reorient U.S. foreign policy institutions to take fully into account the immense power of religion to influence how people think, feel, and act. The signs of such influence are all around us in the lives of people of many different faiths. By way of illustration, I offer three stories.

In 1981, I visited Poland; it was during the second year of the uprising by the Solidarity movement against the communist government. I had long studied central and eastern Europe, where, for decades, very little had changed. Now the entire region was awakening, as from a deep slumber. A large part of the reason was that Pope John Paul II had earlier returned for the first time to Poland, his native land. Formerly Karol Wojtyla, a teacher, priest, and bishop of Kraków, the pope exemplified the pervasive role that religion had played in the history of Poland. While communist leaders in Warsaw dictated what Poles could do, parish priests in every corner of the country still spoke to what Poles believed. The government, alarmed by the prospect of the pope's pilgrimage, sent a memorandum to schoolteachers identifying John Paul II as "our enemy" and warning of the dangers posed by "his uncommon skills and great sense of humor." The authorities nevertheless made a tactical mistake by allowing church officials to organize the visit, giving them a chance to schedule a series of direct contacts between the "people's pope" and the pope's people.

One of the titles of the bishop of Rome is pontifex maximus, or "greatest bridge-builder." In Poland, John Paul II helped construct a bridge that would ultimately restore the connection between Europe's East and West. For bricks, he used words carefully chosen to expose the void at the heart of the communist system, arguing that if people were to fulfill their responsibility to live according to moral principles, they must first have the right to do so. He made plain his conviction that the totalitarian regime could not survive if Poles had the courage to withhold their cooperation. Above all, he urged his countrymen not to be afraid—a simple request with enormous impact. Slowly at first, but with gathering momentum, the pope's listeners drew strength from one another. No longer were they separated into small, controllable groups; the communists' obsession with isolating dangerous ideas had met its match. Standing amid huge crowds, the listeners recognized in each other once again the qualities that made them proud to be Polish—faith in God and a willingness to run risks for freedom. The pope's visits—for he made more than one—sparked a revolution of the spirit that liberated Poland, brought down the Berlin Wall, reunited Europe, and transformed the face of the world.

The pope helped the people of Poland to overcome their fear. Bob Seiple, who served with me in the State Department as the first American ambassador-at-large for international religious freedom, tells a second story, this one about overcoming hate. It concerns Mary, a young Lebanese woman he encountered while working as the head of World Vision, a Christian relief and development agency. In the 1980s, Lebanon had been the scene of a destructive and multisided civil war. Mary lived in a mostly Christian village; and when a Muslim militia invaded it, everyone fled. Mary tripped on a root, plunging face-first to the ground. As she scrambled to her knees, a young man of no more than twenty pressed the barrel of a pistol into the side of her head and demanded, "Renounce the cross or die." Mary did not flinch. "I was born a Christian," she said. "I will die a Christian." The pistol fired, propelling a bullet through Mary's neck and spine. Remorselessly, the militiaman carved a cross on her chest with his bayonet, then left her to die.

The following day, the militia returned and prepared to occupy the village. As they carted off the dead, a few of them came across Mary, still alive but unable to move; she was paralyzed. Instead of finishing her off, the militiamen improvised a stretcher out of wood and cloth and took her to a hospital. Seiple continues:

> And I'm talking to Mary, sitting across from her, and I said, "Mary, this makes absolutely no sense. These are people who tried to kill you. Why in the world would they take you to the hospital the next day?"
>
> She says, "You know, sometimes bad people are taught to do good things."
>
> And I said, "Mary, how do you feel about the person who pulled the trigger? Here you are, an Arab woman in a land twice occupied at that time—the Israelis in the south, the Syrians every place else—strapped to a wheelchair, held hostage by your own body, a ward of the state for the rest of your life. How do you feel about the guy who pulled the trigger?"
>
> She said, "I have forgiven him."
>
> "Mary, how in the world could you forgive him?"
>
> "Well, I forgave him because my God forgave me. It's as simple as that."

In Seiple's view, there are two lessons in this story. The first is that there are people who are willing to die—and kill—for their faith. This was true thousands of years ago and is no less true today. The second lesson is that religion at its best teaches forgiveness and reconciliation, not only when those acts are relatively easy but also when they are almost unbelievably difficult. (Mary, I need hardly add, is a more forgiving person than most—including me.)

The third story involves a boy with haunted eyes whom I met on a blisteringly hot afternoon in December 1997 during my first trip to Africa as secretary of state. The youngster looked about five years old and spoke softly, in a voice drained of emotion. He told me that, two weeks earlier, the small village where his family lived had been attacked. His mother had thrown him to the ground, shielding him with her body. When it was quiet, he wriggled his way out from under her and looked. His mother was dead. The bodies of other women were nearby, more than a dozen, drenched in blood. The boy then heard an infant crying; it was his sister, lying among the corpses. He gathered the baby into his arms and started walking. For hours, as the youngster stumbled along over hills and rocks, the infant wailed. Eventually they came to a place where the boy knew from experience that they would be welcomed and kept safe.

That place was Gulu, a town in a remote part of northern Uganda. World Vision ran the camp and hospital there—a haven for local villagers, who were being terrorized by an outlaw militia group. During the previous decade, an estimated 8,000 children had been kidnapped; most were presumed dead. Boys who survived and did not escape were impressed into rebel units; girls were taken as servants or "wives."

Camp officials blamed rebel leaders who had twisted religion into something grotesque. The tragedy had begun in 1986, when a change in government threatened the privileges of a previously dominant tribe, the Acholi. Fear is a powerful motivator, and the Acholi feared retribution for the many abuses they had committed while in power. A potential savior arrived in the unlikely form of a thirty-year-old woman, Alice Auma, who said that she was able to commune with spirits—a rare but by no means unique claim in her culture. She told her companions that she had been possessed by a deceased Italian military officer who had instructed her to organize an army and retake Kampala, the Ugandan capital. Once victory was achieved, commanded the spirit, the Acholi should cleanse themselves by seeking forgiveness. Auma's sacred campaign was launched but lacked the military clout to match its supernatural inspiration. After some initial successes, the movement—armed only with sticks, stones, and voodoo dolls—was crushed. Auma, her mind no longer host to the Italian officer, found refuge across the border in Kenya.

That would have ended the story had not Joseph Kony, Auma's nephew, decided to take up the cause of holy war. Piecing together a small force from various rebel groups, he assembled what came to be known as the Lord's Resistance Army (LRA). From 1987 on, the LRA has attacked villagers throughout the region, also targeting local governments and aid workers. Because Kony finds adults hard to control and reluctant to enlist, he kidnaps children as a means of procuring troops. Once captured, the children are forced to obey or be put to death; and obedience demands a willingness to kill anyone, including one another. Discipline is administered in the form of beatings, lashings, and amputations predicated on their leader's reading of the Old Testament. The LRA's professed goal is to overthrow the Ugandan government and replace it with one based on the Ten Commandments—or actually ten plus one. The eleventh, added by Kony to restrict the movements of adversaries, is "Thou shalt not ride a bicycle."

Itself a product of fear, the LRA has survived twenty years by instilling fear in others. The Ugandan government has veered between efforts to make peace with the LRA and efforts to destroy it, but officials lack the resources to protect those living in the vicinity of the rebel force. That task has been left to World Vision and similar groups whose resources are also limited, as I saw during my tour of the camp in Gulu. The surroundings reminded me of pictures I had seen of the Crimean War. The camp hospital smelled of disinfectant and human waste. Ancient IVs dripped. Mosquitoes were buzzing everywhere. There were hundreds of patients, most of them children, many covered with welts and scars, some missing a limb. I met a group of teenage girls sitting on mattresses, braiding each other's hair. They looked as if they belonged in junior high school, yet several were already mothers, their babies sired by LRA rapists. "Even if you are a very young girl," said one, who was wearing a Mickey Mouse T-shirt, "you would be given to a man who was the age of my father."

As I started to leave, a young man came up to me holding an infant. "This is the girl that little boy brought to us, his little sister. Her name is Charity." As I cradled the tiny orphan, I was told that the girl had been named for one of the volunteers at the mission. There were many such volunteers. It was a place filled with terrible suffering but also a resilient joy. Patients and volunteers laughed, sang, played games, and cared for each other. The Italian doctor who ran the facility had been in Gulu for more than twenty years. What a contrast between the faith that manifests itself in such love and the twisted fantasies pursued by the LRA.*

One insight that is present in these stories and often in religious faith more generally is that we share a kinship with one

---

* In October 2005, the International Criminal Court issued arrest warrants for Joseph Kony and four other LRA leaders on the charge of crimes against humanity. The court does not, however, have any independent capacity to enforce those warrants.

another, however distant it may sometimes seem; we are all created in the image of God. This in turn places upon us a responsibility to our neighbors. That principle provides both a solid foundation for religion and a respectable basis for organizing the affairs of secular society. What complicates matters is that religion can be interpreted in ways that exclude large numbers of people from any claim to kinship. Those truly imbued with religious faith—such as Pope John Paul II, Bob Seiple's Mary, and the volunteers in Gulu—may affirm "We are all God's children"; but others may follow their convictions to a more argumentative conclusion—"I am right, you are wrong, go to hell!"

When I appeared on a panel with the Jewish writer and thinker Elie Wiesel, a survivor of the Holocaust, he recalled how a group of scholars had once been asked to name the unhappiest character in the Bible. Some said Job, because of the trials he endured. Some said Moses, because he was denied entry to the promised land. Some said the Virgin Mary, because she witnessed the death of her son. The best answer, Wiesel suggested, might in fact be God, because of the sorrow caused by people fighting, killing, and abusing each other in His name.

This is why so many practitioners of foreign policy—including me—have sought to separate religion from world politics, to liberate logic from beliefs that transcend logic. It is, after all, hard enough to divide land between two groups on the basis of legal or economic equity; it is far harder if one or both claim that the land in question was given to them by God. But religious motivations do not disappear simply because they are not mentioned; more often they lie dormant only to rise up again at the least convenient moment. As our experience in Iran reflected, the United States has not always understood this well enough. To lead internationally, American policy makers must learn as much as possible about religion, and then incorporate that knowledge in their strategies. Bryan Hehir has compared this challenge to brain surgery—a necessary task, but fatal if not done well.

In any conflict, reconciliation becomes possible when the antagonists cease dehumanizing each other and begin instead to see a bit of themselves in their enemy. That is why it is a standard negotiating technique to ask each side to stand in the shoes of the other. Often this is not as difficult as it might seem. The very fact that adversaries have been fighting over the same issue or prize can furnish a common ground. For centuries, Protestants and Catholics competed for religious ascendancy in Europe. That was a point of similarity: wanting to be number one. For even longer, Christians, Muslims, and Jews have pursued rival claims in Jerusalem; that, too, is a point of similarity—wanting to occupy the same space. In parts of Asia and Africa, Christians and Muslims are fighting, but they share a desire to worship freely and without fear. When people are pursuing the same goal, each side should be able to understand what motivates the other. To settle their differences, they need only find a formula for sharing what both want—a tricky task, but one that can at least be addressed through an appeal to reason.

Not all conflicts lend themselves to this sort of negotiation. During World War II, the Axis and the Allies were fighting for two entirely different visions of the future. Today, Al Qaeda's lust for a war of vengeance fought with the tools of terror cannot be accommodated. Some differences are too great to be reconciled. In most situations, however, reconciliation will be eminently preferable to continued stalemate or war. But how is reconciliation achieved?

When participants in a conflict claim to be people of faith, a negotiator who has the credentials and the credibility to do so might wish to call their bluff. If the combatants argue the morality of their cause, how is that morality reflected in their actions? Are they allowing their religion to guide them or using it as a debating point to advance their interests? Has their faith instilled in them a sense of responsibility toward others or a sense of entitlement causing them to disregard the rights and views of everyone else?

If I were secretary of state today, I would not seek to mediate disputes on the basis of religious principles any more than I would try to negotiate alone the more intricate details of a trade agreement or a pact on arms control. In each case, I would ask people more expert than I to begin the process of identifying key issues, exploring the possibilities, and suggesting a course of action. It might well be that my involvement, or the president's, would be necessary to close a deal, but the outlines would be drawn by those who know every nuance of the issues at hand. When I was secretary of state, I had an entire bureau of economic experts I could turn to, and a cadre of experts on nonproliferation and arms control whose mastery of technical jargon earned them a nickname, "the priesthood." With the notable exception of Ambassador Seiple, I did not have similar expertise available for integrating religious principles into our efforts at diplomacy. Given the nature of today's world, knowledge of this type is essential.

If diplomacy is the art of persuading others to act as we would wish, effective foreign policy requires that we comprehend why others act as they do. Fortunately, the constitutional requirement that separates state from church in the United States does not also insist that the state be ignorant of the church, mosque, synagogue, pagoda, and temple. In the future, no American ambassador should be assigned to a country where religious feelings are strong unless he or she has a deep understanding of the faiths commonly practiced there. Ambassadors and their representatives, wherever they are assigned, should establish relationships with local religious leaders. The State Department should hire or train a core of specialists in religion to be deployed both in Washington and in key embassies overseas.

In 1994, the Center for Strategic and International Studies published *Religion, the Missing Dimension of Statecraft.* The book makes a compelling case for recognizing the role of religion in affecting political behavior and for using spiritual tools to help resolve conflicts. Douglas Johnston, the book's coauthor, subsequently formed the International Center for Religion and Diplomacy (ICRD), which has continued to study what it calls "faith-based diplomacy" while also playing an important mediating role in Sudan and establishing useful relationships in Kashmir, Pakistan, and Iran. Johnston, a former naval officer and senior official in the Defense Department, believes that, ordinarily, everyone of influence in a given situation is not necessarily bad, and those who are bad aren't bad all the time. He argues that a faith-based mediator has means that a conventional diplomat lacks, including prayers, fasting, forgiveness, repentance, and the inspiration of scripture.

The ICRD is not alone in its efforts. After leaving the State Department, Bob Seiple founded the Institute for Global Engagement, which is working to improve the climate for religious liberty in such volatile nations as Uzbekistan and Laos. The institute's mantra is, "Know your faith at its deepest and richest best, and enough about your neighbor's faith to respect it."

While in office, I had occasion to work closely with the Community of Sant'Egidio, a lay movement that began in Rome in the 1960s, inspired by the Second Vatican Council of Pope John XXIII. Over a period of years, Sant'Egidio successfully brokered negotiations ending a long and bloody civil war in Mozambique. It has also played a constructive role in, among other places, Kosovo, Algeria, Burundi, and Congo. The community sees prayer, service to the poor, ecumenism, and dialogue as the building blocks of interreligious cooperation and problem solving.

Numerous other faith-based organizations, representing every major religion, are in operation. They are most effective when they function cooperatively, pooling their resources and finding areas in which to specialize. Some are most skilled at mediation; others are best at helping former combatants readjust to civilian life. Still others emphasize prevention, addressing a problem before it can explode into violence. Many are experts in economic development or building democracy, both insurance policies against war. Together, these activists have more resources, more skilled personnel, a longer attention span, more experience, more dedication, and more success in fostering reconciliation than any government.

The most famous example of faith-based peacemaking was orchestrated by President Jimmy Carter at Camp David in 1978. Most observers acknowledge that the peace agreement between Egypt and Israel would never have come about if not for Carter's ability to understand and appeal to the deep religious convictions of President Sadat and Prime Minister Begin. I recently asked the former president how policy makers should think about religion as part of the foreign policy puzzle. He told me that it is not possible to separate what people feel and believe in the spiritual realm from what they will do as a matter of public policy. "This is an opportunity," he argued, "because the basic elements of the major religious faiths are so similar—humility, justice, and peace." He said that in the unofficial diplomacy he is often asked to conduct through the Carter Center, one of the first aspects he investigates is whether the parties to a dispute represent the same faith. He said it is often simpler to deal with people of completely different faiths than with those who share a religion but disagree about how it should be interpreted. As a moderate Baptist, Carter said he found it less complicated to have a conversation with a Catholic than with a Baptist fundamentalist; with the Catholic it was easier simply to accept the differences and not feel obliged to argue about them.

When I broached this same subject with Bill Clinton, he stressed two points. First, religious leaders can help to validate a peace process before, during, and after negotiations; through dialogue and public statements, they can make peace easier to achieve and sustain. Second, persuading people of different faiths to work cooperatively requires separating what is debatable in scripture from what is not. "If you're dealing with people who profess faith, he said, "they must believe there is a Creator; if they believe that, they should agree that God created everyone. This takes them from the specific to the universal. Once they acknowledge their common humanity, it becomes harder to kill each other; then compromise becomes easier because they've admitted that they are dealing with people like themselves, not some kind of Satan or subhuman species."

Faith-based diplomacy can be a useful tool of foreign policy. I am not arguing, however, that it can replace traditional diplomacy. Often the protagonists in a political drama are immune to, or deeply suspicious of, appeals made on religious or moral grounds. But if we do not expect miracles, little is lost in making the attempt. The resurgence of religious feeling will continue to influence world events. American policy makers cannot afford to ignore this; on balance they should welcome it. Religion at its best can reinforce the core values necessary for people from different cultures to live in some degree of harmony; we should make the most of that possibility.

Six

The Devil and
Madeleine Albright

B etween 1981 and 1993, I was out of government, pursuing a career as a university professor and, when called on, advising Democratic presidential candidates—who, until Bill Clinton came along, were uniformly trounced. At the end of that period, I returned to government service to find a world transformed by the breakup of the Soviet Union, the reunification of Europe, and the victory of the coalition in Operation Desert Storm. It was an extraordinary moment. Events around the globe were in flux; the Berlin Wall was no more; millions of people were newly free. It appeared to me the right time to try to restore bipartisanship to American foreign policy. After all, conservatives and liberals had quarreled about how best to fight communism; with that threat gone, what cause did we have to disagree?

The answer, it turned out, was plenty. As I set to work in New York in my new post as U.S. ambassador to the United Nations, I found quickly that our policy toward that institution was at the heart of a new divide. On one side were the advocates of using the UN to attack global problems; on the other was a conservative Christian movement of growing power. I knew, of course, that there was an extensive network of right-wing Christian radio and television stations stretched across the country. What surprised me was the degree to which this movement had become politically organized in response to a perceived assault on traditional family values. During the preceding quarter century, the Supreme Court had interpreted the Constitution as protecting a woman's right to have an abortion; sex education had been introduced into classrooms; prayers in public schools had been prohibited; feminists had campaigned for an Equal Rights Amendment; gays and lesbians had become markedly more open about their lifestyles; and Hollywood had been producing "entertainment" containing ever larger doses of sex and gore. As for popular music, parents who had once been upset by Elvis's swaying hips and the Beatles' Liverpool haircuts now had to deal with androgynous creatures setting fire to guitars while screaming indecipherable lyrics to nonexistent melodies.

Some of these trends concerned individual rights, others the direction of popular culture; these are different categories, but the trends all appeared threatening to the Christian right. My own reaction was to embrace some of the changes while doing my best to ignore others. I oppose discrimination against gays and lesbians and am convinced that heterosexual adultery is a greater danger to the institution of marriage than homosexuality will ever be. I believe sex education prevents many more problems than it creates. I am a supporter of *Roe v. Wade* because I think women should have the right to choose and because illegal abortions too often put the life of the woman at risk. President Clinton's formulation seems on target to me: abortions should be safe, legal, and rare, and we should do everything possible to encourage adoption as an alternative to abortion and to reduce unwanted pregnancies through counseling and improved social conditions. As for television, movies, and radio, I oppose any kind of "thought police," but I am also appalled by vulgarity and violence. I am mortified that the image America presents to people overseas is influenced so heavily by dumbed-down television shows and garish action films. As a mother and grandmother, I am tempted to apply a bar of soap to the mouths of many performers; I am all for V-chips and rating systems and think no punishment is severe enough for offensive spammers. I don't mind being called a hopeless prude.

Despite all the mind-polluting background noise, my daughters turned out magnificently, and overall I have coped. If something disgusts me, I change the channel or look the other way. Members of the Christian right are evidently far more alarmed. Like the religious conservatives in pre-revolutionary Iran, they believe that their core values are under assault and that they are being compelled to raise their children in surroundings hostile to their deepest beliefs. Many are receptive to the argument that evil forces conspire against them and that they need to unite and fight back. One conservative Christian leader, James Dobson, describes such people as "just ordinary folks . . . trying to raise their kids . . . do a good job and . . . cope with the pressures that are on them. They're worried about what their kids are being taught in safe-sex classes. They're worried about the spiraling drug problem in this country. They're worried about the epidemic of sexually-transmitted diseases. They're especially worried about a culture that is at war with what they believe."

Senator Jesse Helms of North Carolina has addressed the same general issues but more bluntly. "Especially in the past twenty-five years," he wrote, "the federal government has not even tried to conceal its hostility to religion; now, with many of our churches in disarray, the attack is being waged against the family as the last bastion of those opposing the totalitarian state. Militant atheists and socialists have gone very far in imposing their view of life and man on almost every American institution." The result of all this, Helms declared, has been "atheistic schools, rampaging crime, God-forsaken homes, drugs, abortion, pornography, permissiveness and a sense of cynicism and spiritual desolation absolutely unprecedented in our country's history."

By the time I took up my duties at the UN, the Christian right was a rising political power. Senator Helms was the vice chairman of the Senate Committee on Foreign Relations. Reverend Pat Robertson's Christian Coalition had become a major force within the Republican Party. The country's largest women's organization was not the secular National Organization for Women but Concerned Women for America (CWA), made up of socially conservative Christians. This movement had developed a list of items to oppose internationally that mirrored its domestic concerns: abortion, threats to American sovereignty, and "betrayal" of family values. To the Christian right, within the United States "big government" was the enemy of all that was good; in the international arena, world government (in the form of the United Nations) played the villain's role.

In 1991, Pat Robertson had written a best-seller, *The New World Order*, in which he described a plot to place a "satanic dictator" in charge of us all.* Once in power, the dictator would control every aspect of our lives. All human activity

---

* According to Robertson, the conspiracy was hatched in Bavaria in 1776 and has been unfolding ever since. The list of conspirators, either as knowing participants or as unwitting dupes, includes the ancient order of Freemasons, the leaders of the French Revolution, Karl Marx, Margaret Sanger (the first president of Planned Parenthood), Adolf Hitler, the Rockefellers, Henry Kissinger, the

would be monitored by satellites. Every man, woman, and child would have to carry an international identity card. Freedom of religion would be abolished and the right to own guns terminated. Anyone uttering a politically incorrect statement could be prosecuted in a world court, possibly under Islamic law. Nothing could be bought or sold without the permission of global authorities. Children would be indoctrinated from birth to obey their wicked masters and the American military could be ordered by the UN Security Council to invade Israel. "For the past two hundred years," Robertson declared, "the term 'new world order' has been the code phrase of those who desired to destroy the Christian faith. . . . They wish to replace it with an occult-inspired world socialist dictatorship." Naturally, in Robertson's account, the headquarters of this global dictatorship would be the United Nations.

I had assumed, as ambassador to the UN, that I could best silence domestic critics by striving to make the organization more effective. I did not understand that a significant portion of those critics had no interest in a more efficient UN. To them, I was less a diplomat striving to protect American interests than I was—quite literally—the devil's advocate. Traveling around the country to explain my plans to reform the UN, I often found myself on the defensive, trying to dispel the misapprehensions of alarmed questioners. No, I said, the UN is not about to impose a global income tax; it does not have the authority to order us into war; it is not planning to confiscate our handguns; it is not conspiring to abolish the concept of private property; it does not operate a fleet of black helicopters that fly over American cities at night; it is not plotting to take over the world.

Trilateral Commission, the authors of New Age literature, the administrators of global financial institutions, the designers of the American dollar bill, Zbigniew Brzezinski, and members of the Council on Foreign Relations (on whose board of directors I serve.)

The notion that the UN has or ever will have the ability to dominate the United States is laughable. The authority of the UN flows entirely from its members; it is servant, not master. It has no armed forces of its own, no authority to arrest, no right to tax, no mandate to regulate, and no capacity to override treaties. Its General Assembly has little power. The Security Council, which at least theoretically has the authority to command action, cannot do so without the agreement of its five permanent members. So where is the danger?

Meanwhile, the UN's World Food Program feeds 90 million people each year; the UN High Commissioner for Refugees maintains a lifeline for the international homeless; the UN Children's Fund has launched a campaign to end forced childhood marriage; the UNAIDS initiative remains a focal point for global efforts to defeat HIV/AIDS; and the UN Population Fund helps families plan, mothers survive, and children grow up healthy in the most impoverished places on earth. All this, I used to say in my speeches, for a cost to the average American each year that was less than the price of a movie ticket.*

The UN does, however, occasionally provide its critics with damaging ammunition. Like most international institutions, it maintains a list of unofficial organizations that are allowed to send representatives to observe its meetings and conferences. One such group, I learned from the press, was the National Man/Boy Love Association (NAMBLA). The next thing I knew, I was sitting in my apartment watching a news broadcast about NAMBLA's link to the UN; the picture then

---

* Anti-UN sentiment within the political right has not receded. This is an excerpt from the official platform of Texas Republicans in 2004: "The Party believes it is in the best interest of the citizens of the United States that we immediately rescind our membership, as well as financial and military contributions to, the United Nations. . . . The Party urges Congress to evict the United Nations from U.S. soil."

changed to show me in the Security Council with my hand raised on some routine measure as if I were instead voting in favor of sex between men and boys. A skilled satirist could not have cooked up a more embarrassing juxtaposition. It took me months of painstaking effort, amid gloating from the right-wing press, to purge NAMBLA from the UN's list.

Most often, it was the excesses of the UN General Assembly that attracted criticism from conservatives, but if ever there was an occasion tailored to arouse the passions of the Christian right, it was the Fourth World Conference on Women, held in Beijing in 1995. Here was a UN conference, convened to advance the status of women, hosted by Communist China, and attended by First Lady Hillary Clinton and Ambassador Madeleine Albright.

In the weeks preceding the gathering, columnists and talk-show hosts claimed that the American delegation was intent on redefining motherhood, fatherhood, family, and gender; that we sought statistical parity between men and women in every office and on every work floor; and that the conference would demand that fathers and mothers record equal hours tending their children. A report by the conservative Independent Women's Forum alleged that our plan was to sell the world on the international legal equality of "five genders" (male and female heterosexuals, male and female homosexuals, and trans-bisexuals); we were also said to be contemplating support for a sixth gender, referred to ominously as "omnisexuality." The result, declared the report, is that "our understanding of marriage and the particular legitimacy accorded to children born in marriage is to be overturned by radical feminist moral dictat." James Dobson, whose radio ministry reaches millions of listeners in dozens of countries, called the conference "the biggest threat to the family that's ever occurred in the history of the world."

According to Concerned Women for America, "Hillary Rodham Clinton flew to the 'Women's Conference' with a planeload of lesbians and radical feminists." Actually I flew with her. Moreover, the priorities that mattered most to us and to the vast majority of delegates were not the ones that so excited the passions of our conservative critics—or, to be honest, the most liberal of our colleagues. We sought and obtained support for the rights of women and girls to have equal access to education and health care, to participate in the economic life of their societies, and to live free from the threat of violence. To establish a consensus behind these goals, we assured Catholic and Muslim representatives that we were not asking them to consent to policies contrary to their ethical or religious beliefs—such as claiming that abortion is an international legal right. The Beijing conference was just a conference, but it addressed the status and treatment of more than half of the world's people, many of whom face abuse and discrimination that remain all too real. I am proud to have led the United States' delegation. James Dobson was less enthusiastic, describing the Platform for Action as "Satan's trump card."

Before serving at the UN, I thought that morality in world affairs revolved around issues of war and peace, liberty and despotism, development and poverty. In the 1990s, matters that had once been considered primarily personal—abortion, contraception, gender roles, the rights of children, and sexual orientation—found a prominent place on the international stage. As if on cue, American activists from the left and the right began accusing each other of trying to impose their own moral values on everyone else and of tarnishing the country's international reputation in the process. As is generally the case in politics, the more extreme advocates from one side helped to validate the arguments of extremists on the other. Hence, the political right warned of secular socialist feminism run amok; the left warned of fundamentalist Christians making it impossible to deal with real world problems.

Both the right and the left have sought to recruit international allies. Conservatives have joined forces at times with Muslims and the Vatican, liberals with like-minded Europeans and activists in the developing world. For each group, there have been surprises. Conservatives eager to enlist Muslims in condemning abortion and homosexuality have had to work around their differences concerning arranged marriages and polygamy. Liberals eager to denounce such objectionable practices as female genital mutilation have sometimes found their expected allies from developing countries uninterested, preferring instead to concentrate on economic justice.

The debate between right and left has often been heated, with name-calling, exaggerations, and scare tactics. I personally disagree with much of the conservative position. When I was in government, I fought for more generous funding for comprehensive HIV/AIDS education, child and maternal health programs, and international family planning. I oppose the restrictions the Bush administration has since placed on those programs, and also efforts by religious conservatives—whether Catholic, Protestant, or Muslim— to discourage the distribution of condoms. I do not, however, fault members of the Christian right for expressing and fighting for a moral view, since many others engaged in public policy—including me—do the same. Articulating moral principles is what movements to establish international norms are in business to do. That is precisely how military aggression, slavery, piracy, torture, religious persecution, and racial discrimination have come to be outlawed.

It is also how abuses against women, including domestic violence, "dowry murders," "honor crimes," trafficking, and female infanticide may one day be further reduced. This is not a question of imposing our views on others, but of convincing enough people in enough places that we are right. That is persuasion, not imposition.

Both the political left and the Christian right agree that "moral values" should be near the center of U.S. foreign policy. Each is patriotic and has high aspirations for America; and both would probably agree, although for opposite reasons, with the conclusion of Oliver Wendell Holmes's whimsical rhyme:

> God's plan made a hopeful beginning;
> But man spoiled his chances by sinning;
> We trust that the story will end in God's glory;
> Though, at present, the other side's winning.

The right tends to see the United States, at least ideally, as distinct from and morally superior to the rest of the world. In the view of Richard Land, a thoughtful and widely quoted executive of the Southern Baptist Convention, "We are not, and never have been, a nation in the ordinary sense of the word. We are in many ways unique. This does not mean that the United States is God's chosen nation or the successor of Israel. It does not mean that God has a special relationship with the American people. It does mean, however, that our nation still has the heart and soul of our Puritan ancestors and still sees itself as 'a city on the hill.' "

To those on the right, America's shortcomings are primarily in the realm of personal behavior: pornography, homosexuality, and a falling away from traditional values and the church. They tend to see criticism of America's global role, especially under a favored president like George W. Bush, as providing aid to the enemy and comfort to the forces of evil. There is a parallel, I think, between religious fundamentalism and the unquestioning jingoism that views all of history through a narrowly American lens. Both traits are fed by a desire for certainty, a hunger for solid answers on which to build a comforting and coherent picture of the world.

A similar thirst for certainty may be found at the other end of the spectrum among people who focus primarily on the blemishes in American history. In their worldview, the cold war was less a morally essential struggle to defeat communism than an ethically ambiguous competition for power characterized on both sides by hypocrisy, militarism, and heavy-handed interventions in the affairs of others. Perhaps because I am from a country that was taken over by communists, I find the tendency to fault American policies during the cold war to be overdone. Mistakes were certainly made, but the moral superiority of the West compared with the Soviet Union cannot be seriously questioned. Similarly, I see much that is simplistic in the stance of the left on globalization and the use of force. I do, however, sympathize with the concern of the religious left about the huge gap between rich and poor. I think there is some truth in their perception of America less as a city on a hill than as a gated community that has tried to avert its eyes from those in need.

Especially since the bitterly contested national elections of 2000 and 2004, commentators have made much of the role of religion in widening political and cultural divisions within America. Conventional wisdom suggests that those divisions will continue to grow. If that happens, the America I grew up in and fell in love with will become harder to recognize. I am already angered by the facile discussion of a split between so-called "red" states and "blue" states, as if Americans did not all pledge allegiance to the same tricolor flag. I regret that we have fostered a political culture that rewards the extremes, a culture in which dogmatic belief is deemed a virtue and open-mindedness a weakness, and sarcasm and slanderous attacks frequently drown out intelligent discussion. Haven't we had enough of this? We need a dose of unity. Perhaps we should indeed begin by recalling John Winthrop's prediction that "the eyes of the world will be upon us," and by asking, "What kind of America do we want the world to see?"

Seven

"Because It Is Right"

Americans think of themselves as generous, and it is true that a host of international charitable organizations rely upon us for the donations they need to carry out their work. But the U.S. government is stingy, ranking next to last among the twenty-two most industrialized countries in the proportion of wealth devoted to international development. In 2002, at the summit on global poverty, President Bush endorsed the Monterrey Consensus, committing wealthy nations to allocate 0.7 percent of their income to helping others. Five European countries already give that much; half a dozen more have established a timetable for doing so.* Despite some recent increases, the percentage given by the United States remains stuck at 0.16, a shortfall of some $40 billion a year.

---

* The five countries that are over 0.7 percent are Sweden, Norway, Denmark, the Netherlands, and Luxembourg. Britain, France, Finland, Spain, Ireland, and Belgium are committed to reach that level on specific timetables. Economist Jeffrey Sachs points out, "Some have claimed that while the U.S. government budget provides relatively little assistance to the poorest countries, the private sector makes up the gap. In fact, the Organization for Economic Cooperation and

It wasn't always so. Following World War II, America changed history by helping war-torn Europe to rebuild. The Marshall Plan was a classic example of "doing well by doing good"; Europe was revitalized, and the United States benefited from a strong and prosperous West European partner. That was only a start. In 1949, President Truman created a program to assist needy countries everywhere. "Our aim," he said, "should be to help the free peoples of the world, through their own efforts, to produce more food, clothing, housing, and power. Only by helping the least fortunate of its members to help themselves can the human family achieve the decent, satisfying life that is the right of all people."

Truman's initiative was expanded by John Kennedy, who established the U.S. Agency for International Development, the Peace Corps, and the Alliance for Progress. In his inaugural address, Kennedy pledged America's commitment "to those peoples in the huts and villages across the globe struggling to break the bonds of mass misery . . . our best efforts to help them help themselves, for whatever period is required—not because the Communists may be doing it, not because we seek their votes, but because it is right."

Foreign aid was supported at first by leaders from both major political parties, but critics soon began to speak out. The concept of "giveaway" programs ran contrary to the American ethos of self-reliance. Charity, it was widely thought, should go only to the deserving poor, and not all the poor were deserving. In any case, charity rightly began at home. Why devote money to helping people overseas when those same dollars could be used to address America's own social needs? No politician cap-

---

Development has estimated that private foundations and nongovernmental organizations give roughly $6 billion a year in international assistance, or 0.05 percent of U.S. gross national product (GNP). In that case, total U.S. international aid is around 0.21 percent of GNP—still among the lowest ratios of all donor nations."

italized on these misgivings more creatively than Ronald Reagan. In 1964, in a speech that was to begin his career as a conservative icon, Reagan claimed that American aid had "bought a two-million-dollar yacht for [the Ethiopian leader] Haile Selassie...dress suits for Greek undertakers, extra wives for Kenyan government officials, [and]...a thousand TV sets for a place where they have no electricity." Reagan insisted that American assistance expanded foreign bureaucracies, and that "a government bureau is the nearest thing to eternal life we'll ever see on this earth." The "great communicator" did not always have a firm grip on the facts, but no one was better at turning half-truths into enduring myths. As president, he actually increased foreign aid but did nothing publicly to dispel the impressions he had popularized. By then the stereotype was well established: these programs accomplished nothing, encouraged dependence, and wasted the hard-earned dollars of American taxpayers.

It is true that some aid projects were badly designed, and that some others were aimed more at luring governments to the right side of the competition between East and West than at improving the lives of the disadvantaged. The actual record of assistance, however, was better than advertised. Between 1960 and the mid-1990s, the average person's life expectancy in poor countries increased by twenty years. The rate of infant mortality was cut in half. The introduction of low-cost vaccines saved tens of millions of lives. Smallpox was wiped out, and polio was brought to the edge of extinction. Foreign assistance helped many nations in Asia, Latin America, and Africa to become more prosperous, with hundreds of millions of people climbing out of poverty.

These accomplishments should have impressed, but did not. During my years in government, I found that foreign aid was about as popular as fleas. It didn't help that the term "foreign aid" sounded vaguely treasonous. I removed the phrase from my own vocabulary, referring instead to "national security support." This may have eased resistance a bit, but not much. With a lingering budget deficit and no further threat from the Soviet Union, members of Congress were reluctant to allocate money for projects overseas. The chairman of the congressional subcommittee responsible for funding the program informed me with relish that not once had he voted for a foreign aid bill, implying that he never would. Leading Republicans bragged that they had no interest in even visiting foreign countries. Many of their constituents were convinced that foreign "giveaways" already swallowed up 20 percent of the federal budget, instead of nibbling away at less than 1 percent. As secretary of state, I was frankly embarrassed at times when visiting clinics, refugee camps, and impoverished neighborhoods in distant lands, because I knew that, even though the American economy was booming, the only immediate help I could offer was in the form of coloring books and crayons.

By the late 1990s, the Republican arguments had become so predictable I never expected to hear anything different. Then suddenly I did. Among the usual questions I received at hearings, there were some with a fresh slant—accusing us not of trying to do too much to help people abroad, but of doing too little. I had grown accustomed to hearing liberals express horror about the devastation caused by HIV/AIDS, while conservatives implied that the victims had only themselves to blame. But during my final years in office, and ever since, much of the Christian right has come to agree that halting the pandemic is a moral imperative. A few years ago even Jesse Helms came around, admitting, "It had been my feeling that AIDS was a disease largely spread by reckless and voluntary sexual and drug-abusing behavior, and that it would probably be confined to those in high-risk populations. I was wrong."

What is going on? The answer is that religion is becoming entwined with U.S. foreign policy in a new way. When I was in office, partisan Republicans often delighted in calling me "naive" or a "do-gooder." One disgruntled academic even sneered that the Clinton administration was conducting "foreign policy as social work." Now, the Republican senator Sam Brownback of Kansas, as conservative a man as you will find, argues that the United States "must move humbly and wisely, not just for our own economic and strategic interests but for what is morally right."

The ideological right and left have long stood at opposite poles on almost every international issue; that is no longer true. Especially on humanitarian matters, in which religious conservatives have expressed a special interest, the two extremes overlap. Both sides recognize not only a practical interest but also a moral obligation to help those in direst need. Both believe that the story of the Good Samaritan, cited by President Bush in his first inaugural address, should find at least an echo in American foreign policy. This is not just interesting; it is a potentially historic opportunity.

We have heard much in recent years about the "axis of evil." Those searching for evil will find it in the suffering caused by poverty, ignorance, and disease, compass points on a circle of misery in which between two and three billion human beings are trapped. An estimated 30,000 children die each day from preventable disease and hunger: that is—for purposes of comparison—almost the equivalent of ten 9/11 attacks every twenty-four hours. Billions of people still live under governments that fail to recognize or protect basic human rights. The plight of the poor and repressed should be reason enough for Americans to close ranks, if not always in common cause then at least in separate causes that come together at key points. The list of potential cooperative projects is long, but let me suggest three to start.

The first is support for the principle and practice of religious liberty.

About a decade ago, a coalition of Christian and Jewish activists in the United States began a campaign against religious persecution overseas. In response, Congress approved legislation—the International Religious Freedom Act of 1998—that was signed into law by President Clinton. The statute created an independent United States Commission on International Religious Freedom and required the State Department to prepare an annual report on the status of religious liberty around the world. This landmark law has made identifying and condemning all forms of religious persecution an integral part of U.S. foreign policy and has caused American diplomats to become more comfortable and practiced at raising the issue.

It is natural for Americans to care about religious liberty. Not only is this principle at the center of our own democracy; it provides a reliable litmus test for judging other governments. If a government does not respect the dignity of its own citizens, it is unlikely to honor the rights of anybody else. The countries where religious persecution is widespread (such as North Korea, Burma, Iran, and Sudan) are also—and not coincidentally—a source of broader dangers, including terrorism and the proliferation of weapons of mass destruction. The decision by the Taliban in 2001 to destroy two ancient stone Buddhas in central Afghanistan displayed the same contempt for world opinion as its willingness to host Al Qaeda. China is another country whose government fails to observe religious freedom, but that nation, because of its size and influence, presents some unique complications for American policy makers.

Members of Congress frequently complained to me during my years in office that Chinese Christians could worship legally only in churches registered with the government. I promised to raise the issue with officials in Beijing, and I did so both in meetings and by making a point of attending church services in China myself.* My to-do list, however, did not end there. I also presented my concerns about the mistreatment of Tibetan Buddhists and members of the Falun Gong, a spiritual health organization. I urged China to allow its citizens to organize politically and to have independent labor unions; expressed my interest in the fate of political prisoners; asked for clarification of China's controversial population control policies; and explored a series of political and military issues with a moral dimension—North Korea's nuclear programs, peaceful relations with Taiwan, Burma's military dictatorship, the treaty on global climate change, and international peacekeeping. Years later, these issues and more remain on the agenda for the United States and China. With a list this long, there is always a chance that questions of religious liberty, whether affecting Christians or others, will get lost. They shouldn't. In fact, I would not be surprised if the growth of religion in China turns out to be among the most significant developments of the next quarter century and—for China's authoritarian leaders—the most difficult to manage.

Those eager to promote religious liberty must also recognize that there is a right and a wrong way to go about it. Lasting change is more likely to come through persuasion than by making blunt demands. In Laos, Bob Seiple's Institute for Global Engagement has adopted a step-by-step approach in a desperately poor country with a Soviet-style government, a Buddhist majority, and no democratic tradi-

---

* In February 1998, President Clinton sent a delegation of American religious leaders to China to emphasize the importance of religious liberty. The delegation consisted of Rabbi Arthur Schneier of New York; Roman Catholic Archbishop Theodore McCarrick; and Donald Argue, a minister of the Assemblies of God and president of the National Association of Evangelicals.

tion. Stressing the importance of religious freedom in a nation mired in economic and social troubles is a dicey proposition. Still, there is steady, visible progress. Prisoners of conscience have been released. Officials are being trained to respect freedom of worship. Study centers have opened to encourage interreligious cooperation. In one village, a government official who had forced more than a thousand Christians to renounce their faith later apologized; before his death, he received hospice care from a church he had previously tried to shut down.

A second area for cooperation across the American political spectrum should be the struggle to alleviate global poverty. In the late 1990s, many segments of the religious community joined with the Clinton administration in supporting a plan to write off much of the debt of the world's poorest countries. Although falling short of its most ambitious goals, the gains made were precedent-shattering—a watershed. Liberal organizations that had long campaigned for debt relief suddenly found themselves working in partnership with powerful politicians from the Christian right who, in turn, found themselves sharing a stage with Bono, the activist and rock star. Advocates of debt relief were clever enough to package their initiatives around a biblical reference to the semicentennial "jubilee year," during which the ancient Israelites were instructed by God to forgive debts and "return every man unto his possession." This initial step was followed by another, a decision in 2005 to write off the debts owed by the eighteen poorest countries to the International Monetary Fund and World Bank.

Notwithstanding the progress in reducing debt, the drive to defeat poverty still lacks momentum. One reason is that the old myths are hard to kill. Many self-described experts continue to argue that foreign assistance will be wasted; that "big government" solutions don't work; and that poverty is a permanent part of the human condition. To an extent, this line of thinking is understandable. Decades of aid have not eliminated poverty, and in sub-Saharan Africa the situation has worsened considerably in recent years. Why? Among the culprits cited are ethnic conflicts; flawed economic models; and demographic factors such as population growth, disease, and the exhaustion of natural resources. Some people point to the lack of truly democratic governments, Robert Mugabe's corrupt regime in Zimbabwe being one blatant example. Those on the left tend to blame economic and trade policies that stack the deck against poor countries (and against the poor within countries) in favor of large corporations and the rich. In my judgment, each factor plays a role and must be taken into account.

Fighting poverty is not, of course, just a matter of shoveling money in the direction of the poor. Historically, the left has put too much faith in aid administered through foreign governments while the right has preached discredited ideas of trickle-down economics. Both sides have grown more sophisticated. Specialists in the field have also learned more about how to make effective use of aid money by channeling the majority of funds through nongovernmental institutions, emphasizing opportunities for women, stressing low-tech solutions, heeding environmental considerations, and finding ways to let even the poorest participate economically. It is essential, as well, for developed countries to end the hypocrisy of advocating free markets while spending huge amounts in agricultural subsidies for their own farmers that make it impossible for those from poor countries to compete.

Another way to help the poor is to extend to them the protections of law. The High-Level Commission on Legal Empowerment of the Poor, which I cochair with the Peruvian economist Hernando de Soto, is looking at ways to do this. Many poor people who have property in the form of land, housing, and livestock are unable to make the most of it because they lack any legal title. In some countries, as much as 90 percent of property is owned outside the law. This means that people are vulnerable to exploitation and theft and are barred from using their assets to obtain credit, make investments, or start saving. This hurts them and their societies, for it leaves their governments without the tax base necessary to provide basic services. The result is a social fabric that remains unwoven, causing economic stagnation and civil strife. I like the approach of extending legal protections to the poor in part because it defies any particular ideological label. It is a hybrid—a blend of the "ownership society" and "power to the people."

President Bush has declared, "We fight against poverty because hope is an answer to terrorism." In July 2005, he joined the other G-8 leaders in pledging to double total assistance to Africa over the next five years from $25 billion to $50 billion annually. Two months later, the U.S. trumpet sounded a less certain note. America's ambassador to the UN, John Bolton, caused a commotion by distancing his government from the international goal of halving the rate of extreme poverty by 2015. After a week of confusion and mixed signals, President Bush said that the United States did indeed support the goal and would work to meet it. We should keep that pledge and more, not only because we hope it will make us safer, but because—as John Kennedy said—it is right.

A third item I would place near the top of any agenda for bipartisan cooperation is preventing the mass killing of human beings. Over time, the world has become reasonably adept at delivering food, water, and medicine to places that don't have them, provided that people with guns are not standing in the way. It has not, however, developed a reliable means for preventing genocide.

Ever since the massacres in Rwanda in 1994, there has been much talk about how we must never allow something similar to happen again. Meanwhile, something similar has happened again. Over the past decade, a sporadic, pointless, and inconclusive war in the Democratic Republic of Congo has led to the deaths of more than 3 million people. In the Darfur region of Sudan, as many as 300,000 people have died in genocidal violence. The outbreak of killing in these countries—unlike Rwanda—was gradual rather than volcanic, giving the international community ample time to respond. It has responded, however, only slowly and feebly. The problem is not a lack of moral indignation—the violence in Darfur was widely publicized—but a failure to use force effectively.

One possible solution in such cases is for the Security Council to deputize an appropriate major power to organize a coalition that can enforce the world's will. The intervention in Haiti, led by the United States in 1994; the rescue of East Timor, led by Australia in 1999; and the British action in Sierra Leone in 2000 were largely successful. The problem with relying on "coalitions of the willing," however, is that there are sure to be times when no one steps forward. This is less because world leaders are callous than because international peacemaking is an expensive, hard, dangerous, and often thankless task.

To deter people with guns, well-equipped and adequately trained forces are needed; but finding them is not easy. Expecting a soldier to risk everything in defense of his or her homeland is one thing; expecting that same soldier to travel thousands of miles to intervene in, and perhaps die because of, somebody else's quarrel is another. Most people are not that altruistic, especially when, as is typical, they see an international force more blamed for its failures than credited for what it has achieved. As a result, we are left with a system of responding to crises that will occasionally work well, usually not so well, and sometimes not at all.

In September 2005, the UN General Assembly for the first time acknowledged a collective international responsibility to protect populations from genocide, war crimes, ethnic cleansing, and crimes against humanity. Accepting the existence of this responsibility, however, will not help anyone unless there is also both a capacity to protect people and a willingness to do so. The UN was created sixty years ago with the expectation that it would develop its own army. The rivalry between the superpowers put a quick end to that idea, and there is little support for reviving it. The logical role of the UN in a crisis is to authorize an intervention by some combination of national military forces. The logical role for the United States is to take the lead in ensuring that such a combination of forces will be available when needed and successful when deployed. To do that, we must work hard to allay suspicions about our intentions. We must also be clear about what is required.

A force intended to prevent genocide must be a serious military enterprise; it cannot be cobbled together from the bits and pieces of underfunded armies, detailed for brief periods, and assembled at the last minute. Countries must be asked to identify capable personnel who will be dedicated to the job of humanitarian response and prepared over a period of years to excel in that function. Ideally, these forces would train together long enough to develop complementary skills and maintain their readiness for deployment at short notice. They would be equipped with the latest communications, transportation, and weapons and would be supported by real-time intelligence provided by countries with the necessary equipment and know-how. Their military and paramilitary components would be accompanied by civilian administrators and prosecutors affiliated with international legal authorities. When a force is dispatched, the job of the military would be to restore order; the job of the civilians to jump-start reconstruction; and the job of the prosecutors to give those responsible for war crimes their day in court.

Once again, this would *not* be a standing UN army. It would be the international equivalent of a cavalry that leaders could call on to ride to the rescue in emergencies. There are many details (including financing) that would have to be worked out,* but in concept it is a better way to prevent future Darfurs than anything we have now. Before the United States could design or even participate in such an effort, however, conservatives and liberals would have to shed some traditional prejudices. A reliable mechanism for preventing genocide could not be created without unprecedented levels of international military cooperation. The UN might not be in charge, but it would surely have to be involved. Is the Christian right ready to explore such concepts with an open mind, or does it remain shackled by its long-standing suspicion, even paranoia, regarding the UN? Meanwhile, the political left would have to agree to spend substantial amounts of money to improve international military capabilities, even at the expense of pressing social needs.

If the past is truly prologue, there is no hope. But if the past is past, perhaps it is worth a try. After all, people who once opposed foreign aid, nation-building, and combating HIV/AIDS now endorse all three. And Ronald Reagan, after retiring from the presidency, told the Oxford Union in 1992, "We should rely more on multilateral institutions. . . .

---

* One such detail would be a more favorable attitude by the United States toward the International Criminal Court. Even if we continue to refrain from participating in that tribunal, we should want it to succeed.

What I propose is nothing less than a humanitarian velvet glove backed by the mailed fist of military power."

Widespread cooperation between the Christian right and other American activists on international humanitarian issues is no pipe dream; Senator Brownback and I cohosted a well-attended conference devoted to the topic in November 2005. Cooperation matters not only because of what it can help us accomplish overseas, but also because of the extent to which it can help Americans understand each other. We are not, I am convinced, as divided as we sometimes seem. Most of us do not want our leaders confusing their own will with God's, but neither do we want them to ignore religious and moral principles. We support the separation of church and state but not the enforced separation of religion from the public life of our nation. Many of us pray regularly that God will guide our leaders. We hope that those who make decisions in our name will think hard about questions of right and wrong. We want them to protect us but also to make us proud.

Bipartisan cooperation on humanitarian issues can also help to influence for the better how America is perceived in the world. I suspect that most of us would like our country to be seen as confident, caring, principled, honest, and strong. We learned long ago, however, in Vietnam and Iran, that we are not always seen as we would like. Some may think that the views of others do not matter, that we are so powerful we need no longer exhibit, as our Declaration of Independence once urged, a "decent respect for the opinions of mankind." To indulge such arrogance would be a fatal mistake and a disappointment to America's true friends everywhere. The standing of the United States would be crucial at any point in history; it is especially vital now, as we seek the key to victory in two wars simultaneously. That search begins with the knowledge that we cannot succeed in the world unless we first understand those whom we most need to influence, including especially the followers of Islam.

Part Two

Cross, Crescent, Star

Eight

Learning about Islam

Christians and Muslims first met in battle in 636 near the Yarmūk River, a tributary of the Jordan; the fierce fighting ended with the massacre of 70,000 Christians and the inauguration of Islamic control in Jerusalem, previously a western outpost of the Byzantine Empire. In 1099, crusaders retook the holy city in the name of the cross; this time the result was the massacre of 70,000 Muslims and the killing of every Jew the triumphant Christians could track down. In 1187, Jerusalem was claimed once again for Islam under the generalship of Saladin the Great, a triumph followed by more crusades and tens of thousands of additional deaths. Through much of the world there echoed the call for holy war.

Civilization has since marched boldly into the twenty-first century; yet the same cry is heard again. Jews and Arabs are contesting the very lands and holy places fought over 1,000 years ago. A gang of terrorists, acting in the name of Islam, inflicted the deadliest single attack ever on American soil. The Bush administration's response has stirred intense anger among many Muslims. Anxiety is growing in Europe, where Muslim immigration has expanded and acts of terror and examples of bigotry are on the increase. In Africa, resurgent Islam is colliding with resurgent Christianity. In Asia, from Chechnya to the Philippines, the divide between the followers of Islam and those of other faiths is causing bloodshed. Like a family torn apart by a disputed will, the children of Abraham are too often inspired less by feelings of kinship than by jealousy, insecurity, and hate.

When I raised my hand to take the oath of office as secretary of state, I had in mind a list of priorities; prominent among them was a desire to strengthen America's ties with the Muslim world. This seemed essential. The United States had long-standing interests to protect in the Middle East and south Asia. The end of the cold war had created an opportunity to forge partnerships with the newly independent and strategically located countries of central Asia. The surprise election of a moderate to the presidency of Iran would soon offer the prospect of a warming in our long-frozen relationship with that country. Democratic openings beckoned in Indonesia and Nigeria, each a regional giant where the influence of Islam was widely felt. Throughout the 1990s, foreign policy journals featured articles about "Islamic extremists." In meeting after meeting, I found myself scrawling on a notepad, "Learn more about Islam."

I did, of course, already know something of the subject. When I was ten, my father had served as chairman of a UN commission on India and Pakistan charged with resolving the status of Kashmir. Even at that age, I understood the basic facts. Because of religion, the Indian subcontinent was splitting apart. The leaders of India wanted a secular, multi-ethnic state. The leaders of Pakistan wanted a country for

Muslims. Kashmir was caught between the two; it had a Muslim majority, but a large Hindu minority and a Hindu ruler. The job for diplomats was to find a solution that would leave all sides satisfied. That was almost sixty years ago; now my father is dead and I am old, both countries have nuclear weapons, and the problem is little nearer to being solved.

There were not many Muslims in Denver, where I spent my teenage years. My father had made contacts while at the UN, however, and some of his acquaintances came to visit. One I remember particularly was Sir Zafrullah Khan, a former foreign minister of Pakistan. I liked him because he was dignified, erudite, and charming. When he took me to breakfast one day, my envious classmates jokingly pointed out that he could choose a second wife while keeping his first. What impressed me in talking to him about Kashmir, however, was how complicated life could be when a dispute is fueled by both religion and nationalism and each side is convinced that it has sole possession of the truth.

Sitting in the State Department many years later, I thought of Sir Zafrullah and how out of place he had seemed in Denver. The truth is that he would have seemed almost as anomalous in the State Department in 1997: we had no Muslims serving in senior positions and just a few in midlevel jobs. I decided that we had to improve communications. To that end, we reviewed everything from personnel recruitment and training to the listing of Islamic holidays alongside Jewish and Christian ones on our official calendar. We began a series of discussions with representatives of American Muslims, inviting them during Ramadan to the first *iftaar** dinners hosted by a secretary of state. We also

---

* *Iftaar* refers to the daily breaking of the fast after sunset by Muslims during the holy month of Ramadan.

developed an introductory guide to Islam to be available to persons traveling on behalf of the United States to countries that had a Muslim majority. The publication contained information such as the following, which, though basic, is still novel to many Americans:

- Muslims worship the same God (in Arabic, Allah) as Christians and Jews.*

- "Islam" means submission to God. A person who surrenders to God and lives faithfully will find that life has harmony and purpose.

- Muslims believe in the day of judgment, in an afterlife, and in the ethical accountability of every individual. A Muslim's first responsibility is to care for the poor, the orphaned, the widowed, and the oppressed.

- The Muslim holy book, the Quran, contains the exact words believed to have been revealed by God and conveyed by the Archangel Gabriel to a Meccan merchant, Muhammad ibn Abdallah (the Prophet), over a twenty-two-year period beginning in 610.

- Sharia, or Islamic law, is based on the Quran, the deeds and words of the Prophet, and scholarly interpretations. The law governs virtually every aspect of personal, social, and civic life.

- The five pillars of Islam are: (1) profession of faith; (2) ritual prayer; (3) purification through charity; (4) fasting; and (5) pilgrimage to Mecca.

---

* *Ilah* in Arabic means "god"; Allah is a contraction of *al-ilah*, "the god." The same word for God is used by Arabic-speaking Christians and Jews. The term is similar in Aramaic, the language spoken by Jesus, who is said to have cried out on the cross, *Eili, Eili lama sabachtani?*—"My God, my God, why have you forsaken me?"

- Muhammad is considered by Muslims to have been the last in a series of prophets that began with Adam and Noah, continued through Abraham and Moses, and included King David and Jesus of Nazareth. The Quran stipulates that the revelation to Muhammad confirmed the teaching of earlier prophets. Muhammad (like Jesus) did not think of himself as the founder of a new religion; he considered himself, instead, a messenger calling his people back to the one true God.

- Arabs trace their lineage to Abraham through Ishmael, son of Hagar—just as Jews trace theirs through Isaac, son of Sarah. The issue matters because both Muslims and Jews (as well as Christians) believe God commanded Abraham to go into the Land of Canaan with the promise that his descendants would settle the land and become a great nation.

- Muslims believe that Jesus was a major prophet, but they do not accept the possibility that God could have a "son." They agree that Jesus was born of a virgin and that he ascended into heaven, but they do not believe that he was either crucified or resurrected.

- In Muslim tradition, the first altar to God was built in Mecca by Adam and later rebuilt by Abraham and Ishmael. The mosques in Mecca and Medina, two cities where the Prophet lived, are the two holiest sites in Islam. The third holiest is Al-Aqsa Mosque in Jerusalem, on a site the Prophet visited—whether in a dream or physically is debated—to pray with Jesus and earlier prophets and climb to the seventh heaven in the company of Gabriel.

- The Quran provides that Jews and Christians living in areas ruled by Muslims should have protected status— meaning that their property, laws, religious customs, and places of worship should be preserved. Through most of the second millennium, Islamic societies showed more flexibility toward other religions than did Christian Europe. Although free to practice their faith, Christians and Jews living in Muslim societies were ordinarily treated as political inferiors.

- The Islamic concept of jihad is often and somewhat simplistically equated—even by some Muslims—with holy war. *Jihad* is correctly translated as "effort" or "striving" for the sake of God. For most Muslims, "greater jihad" refers to the individual's attempts to remain virtuous (the personal struggle). "Lesser jihad" refers to the struggle for justice, including the defense of Islam against those who attack it.

- Muslims draw a distinction between wars that are justified and those that are not. A war fought in the cause of God—in self-defense or against tyranny—is just. A war fought for other motives, such as the conquest of territory belonging to another, is unacceptable. There are also rules concerning how wars are fought. Noncombatants are not to be attacked, nor prisoners mistreated. According to Khaled Abou el Fadl, a leading expert on Islamic law who now lives in the United States, jurists "insist that even if the enemy tortured or murdered Muslim hostages, Muslims are forbidden from doing the same."

- Suicide is prohibited by Islam, but dying while in genuine service to God is martyrdom, guaranteeing a place in heaven.

- Although Islam originated in the Arabian Peninsula, today only about one Muslim in five is Arab (and about one Arab in five is non-Muslim). The largest Muslim populations are in Asia.

- Muslims have a duty to help other Muslims, especially those who are suffering or oppressed.

Islamic tradition discourages the depiction of Muhammad in pictures or art, even in mosques. In his lifetime, however, he was described as being of moderate height, with black eyes, a pale complexion, long thick hair, and a profuse beard that fell to his chest. His home city, Mecca, was a commercial cross-roads, where pilgrims came to worship and offer sacrifices to hundreds of tribal gods. Local businessmen profited by cater-ing to the pilgrims and selling them objects, animate and inanimate, to use in their tributes. Muhammad's revelation, centering as it did on belief in a single all-powerful God, threatened to undermine this lucrative practice, causing local authorities to plot to kill him. Narrowly escaping death, he journeyed in secret to the nearby city of Medina, where he established himself as a political and spiritual leader. As soon as he had gathered sufficient support, he returned to Mecca in triumph, smashing the pagan idols, dedicating the holy shrine to Allah, and asserting authority over the entire Arabian Peninsula.

Shortly after he turned sixty years of age, Muhammad delivered a farewell sermon on the Mount of Mercy, located across the plain of Arafat, east of Mecca. He cautioned his people to "hurt no one so that no one may hurt you. Remember that you will indeed meet your Lord and that he will indeed reckon your deeds." He also spoke of racial equal-ity, a decision that would help smooth Islam's acceptance as a global religion. "An Arab has no superiority over a non-Arab," he said, "nor a non-Arab over an Arab; also a white [person] has no superiority over a black [person] nor a black over a white—except by piety and good action."

Like the other monotheistic faiths, Islam is a "big tent,"

interpreted and practiced in diverse ways. The richness of thought is due to ethnic and national influences, differences among leading scholars, and sectarian splits. As a result, almost every generalization about Islam is partly wrong. The requirement in some societies, for example, that women cover themselves completely while in public is more a reflection of Arab culture—Arab men also dress with extreme modesty—than a mandate of Islam. The majority of Muslim women do not wear the veil. The Quran does include passages that discriminate against women (for example, language on polygamy, divorce, and inheritance), but in each case the verses are less discriminatory than Arab customs prevailing at the time. Muhammad told his followers, "It is true that you have certain rights with regard to your women, but they also have rights over you."

Queen Noor of Jordan has pointed out, "Few Westerners realize that seventh-century Islam granted women political, legal, and social rights then unheard of in the West, rights, in fact, that women in the U.S. and elsewhere still struggled for in the twentieth century. Early Islam based these new rights, such as the equal right to education, to own and inherit property, to conduct business, and not to be coerced into marriage, on the equality of men and women before God—this when the rest of the world considered women chattels." Nor is there anything in the Quran that would prevent women from voting in an election, driving a car, associating with males in public, or working outside the home (the Prophet's wife, Khadija, was a successful businesswoman). The countries with the largest number of Muslims—Indonesia, India, Pakistan, Bangladesh, and Turkey—have each elected a female head of government; this is a distinction that neither any Arab state nor the United States can claim.

Muhammad's death in 632 ignited a series of battles over who should succeed him as ruler, eventually leaving Islam divided into two broad camps. The larger faction, which later became the Sunnis, initially supported the Prophet's father-in-law. A second group, the Shia, favored the descendants of Ali, the Prophet's son-in-law. Almost 1,400 years later, this schism continues to influence regional and world politics. The Sunnis are the majority in most regions, but the Shia predominate in Iran, Iraq, Bahrain, and Lebanon and are influential in Syria, Azerbaijan, and south Asia. The split is far more than a polite difference of opinion. Shiite minorities in Sunni-dominated countries frequently and justifiably complain of intolerance and discrimination. To Sunni extremists, the Shia are not Muslims at all.

A second division, between modernizers and conservatives, affects both Shia and Sunnis. Modernizers draw on a mainstream strand of Islam that seeks to reconcile "rationalim" and religious belief. They tend to be more comfortable coexisting with secular governments; more convinced of the value of education in science, mathematics, history, and foreign languages; more liberal in their treatment of women; and more likely to embrace democratic institutions. Conservatives insist on a high degree of control in family matters, separation of the sexes, and resistance to foreign customs.

Heavily influenced by the eighteenth-century Wahhabi (or Salafist) religious movement, Saudi Arabia has long served as the center of conservative Sunni Islam. The revolution of 1979 in Iran marked the high point for conservative Shias. As the fervor generated by that event faded, Iran gradually became what it is today: a battleground between conservatives and modernizers.

Muslims agree that the Quran is the literal word of God, but differ among themselves about how particular verses should be explained and implemented. For several centuries, a practice known as *ijtihad* was used by Muslim intellectuals to interpret and apply the principles of law in new contexts as

Islam spread through much of the Byzantine and Persian empires and outward to Spain, North Africa, Turkey, India, central Asia, and beyond. This expansion was helped by the accessible nature of Islam combined with the decadent condition of the Christian church and other religious institutions of the period. Islam did not require its followers to accept or understand a complex theology such as the Trinity. All it demanded was submission to God, whom every person could address as directly as any other. In the words of one historian, Islam "opened the door wide in a world of uncertainty, treachery and intolerable divisions to a great and increasing brotherhood of trustworthy men on earth, and to a paradise ... of equal fellowship and simple and understandable delights."

At the center of the Muslim world was Baghdad, which by the end of the first millennium had become an educational, scientific, and cultural capital. Here, Muslims worked alongside Christians and Jews to translate and study the finest works of ancient China, India, Egypt, Israel, Greece, and Rome. At a time when the practice of medicine was forbidden by the church in Christian lands, Arabs were using anesthetics and performing complex operations. Muslims developed the numerical system still in use today and invented the pendulum, algebra, and trigonometry. After learning from the Chinese how to make paper, they kept administrative records, wrote books on a wide range of subjects, and designed the world's first system of international banking. During this golden age, Islam was modern and forward-looking, eager to embrace learning of all kinds.

Why doesn't Islam enjoy the same reputation today? In the thirteenth century, Mongol horsemen brought a new and fearsome style of warfare from the east, conquering Baghdad and much of the Islamic empire. The invaders extended themselves too far, however, and were soon supplanted in the Near East by the Turks. Under the Ottoman sultans, the perceived need for innovative interpretations of Islamic law declined. The emperors were more concerned about ensuring obedience and preserving traditions. Today, the majority of Muslims would agree that the interpretation of Islam remains open, but how open is a matter of fierce debate. Some scholars are calling for a revival of *ijtihad*, especially as it applies to the role of women, participation in the global economy, relations with non-Muslims, and the definition of an Islamic state. These reformers are often critical of the West, but are nevertheless sometimes accused by conservatives of acting on behalf of the West to dilute or destroy the real spirit of Islam. Since the Sunnis lack a centralized clerical hierarchy, allegations of blasphemy are frequently made and rarely resolved.

Christian Europe, scarred from its battles with Muslims through much of the Middle Ages, bequeathed to the United States a suspicion of Islam. Most Americans saw it as an alien and somewhat mystical faith, outside the Judeo-Christian tradition with which they were comfortable. In the 1960s, the Nation of Islam acquired notoriety within the United States for its disputes over leadership and for its angry, separatist rhetoric. Many Americans were surprised when widely admired athletes such as Cassius Clay (Muhammad Ali) and Lew Alcindor (Kareem Abdul-Jabbar) converted to Islam and proudly replaced their "slave names" with African or Islamic ones. This puzzlement was acknowledged in the challenging words of Muhammad Ali: "I am America. I am the part you won't recognize. But get used to me. Black, confident, cocky; my name, not yours; my religion, not yours; my goals, my own, get used to me." Internationally, the sense of unease about Islam was periodically reinforced by Arab oil embargos, the hostile rants of Iranian ayatollahs, and incidents of terror.

These issues did not, however, prevent the United States

from having cordial diplomatic relations with most Muslim-majority states. From the beginning, American policy has been consistent in rejecting any thought of a cultural war. During his first term, President Clinton told the Jordanian parliament, "There are those who insist that between America and the Middle East there are impassable religious and other obstacles to harmony; that our beliefs and our cultures must somehow inevitably clash. But I believe they are wrong. America refuses to accept that our civilizations must collide."

The Clinton administration stressed this theme because we wanted Arabs and Muslims to look to the future with practical concerns rather than religious rivalries foremost in mind. We also hoped to show that we were ourselves free of prejudice against Islam. This was entirely sincere. We viewed terrorism as an aberration. Just as there is nothing Christian about the violent bigotry of the Ku Klux Klan, there is nothing Islamic about terrorism. One billion three hundred million people can hardly be characterized by the violence of a tiny fraction. The Quran is explicit that the taking of a single innocent life is prohibited, even equating it with the killing of all humanity.

This has not stopped some people from portraying Islam as "wicked and evil," or calling Muhammad a "terrorist."* Reading selectively, critics cite passages in the Quran that

---

* Reverend Jerry Falwell has called Muhammad a "terrorist." Reverend Franklin Graham has called Islam "wicked and evil." Graham later added, "I respect the people of the Islamic faith that have come to this country. I have Muslim friends. But that doesn't stop me from wanting to help them. I certainly don't believe the way they believe, and they don't believe the way I believe either. That doesn't make me dislike them, and I love them very much. I want to do all I can to help them.... I want them to know about God's son, Jesus Christ. I want them to know, but I certainly don't want to force it on them. I would like some day for Muslims to know what Christians do."

instruct believers to use force against enemies of the faith, instructions that violent extremists—who tend to have the loudest voices—can exploit to justify their actions. But incendiary language is also present in the Hebrew Bible, what Christians call the Old Testament. The books of Joshua and Judges provide a catalog of holy wars, and Deuteronomy includes a virtual endorsement of genocide in God's name.* In the New Testament, Jesus warns, "Think not that I am come to send peace on Earth: I came not to send peace, but a sword." As for the Book of Revelation, it can be interpreted in many ways, but peaceful it is not.

The Quran was compiled over a period of more than two decades, the Hebrew Bible over centuries. The New Testament was assembled in about 100 years, amid much squabbling about whose testimonies to include and whose to dismiss. Within each book there are inconsistencies and frequent shifts of subject and tone. To construct a dogma out of a few quotations is sophistry. A reader trolling the scriptures for language sanctifying intolerance and war will find it whether the texts are sacred to Christians, Muslims, or Jews. To be understood fairly, each of the holy books must be read and studied both comprehensively and in the context of its place and time. That is why generations of scholars have labored to highlight core passages, explain contradictions, clear away discrepancies, correct mistranslations, and detect the significance of obscure phrasings.

I know from experience that those responsible for managing U.S. foreign policy will want religious doctrines interpreted in ways that minimize the dangers of international

---

* E.g., Deuteronomy 20:16–17: "Of the cities of these people, which the LORD thy God doth give thee for an inheritance, thou shalt save alive nothing that breatheth: But thou shalt utterly destroy them; namely, the Hittites, and the Amorites, the Canaanites, and the Perizzites, the Hivites, and the Jebusites."

conflict—possibly a vain hope. Two ideas have proved particularly troublesome. The first is the claim made by some extreme Zionists (and backed by many Christians) that God's gift of land to Israel provides a license to ignore Palestinians' rights. Set against this are provisions of the Quran that exhort believers to fight to regain any lost lands. Khaled el Fadl writes, "Some jurists argue that any territory that has ever been ruled by Muslims remains forever a part of the abode of Islam."

Doctrines such as this, if followed blindly and without regard to other teachings, are written in blood. History has left little emotional padding between and among the major religions. It does not take much to lead groups of people with extreme views to believe that their faith is under attack and that their duty is to defend it by every available means.

Nine

Holy Land, but Whose?

———— ❧ ————

November 2, 1917, marked the beginning of a new era in
the Middle East; it was a day long-awaited and prayed
for by some; long-feared and prayed against by others. A letter signed by the British foreign secretary, Arthur J. Balfour,
conveyed the news:

> His Majesty's Government views with favour the estab-
> lishment in Palestine of a national home for the Jewish
> people, and will use their best endeavours to facilitate
> the achievement of this object. It being clearly under-
> stood that nothing shall be done which may prejudice
> the civil and religious rights of existing non-Jewish
> communities in Palestine.

When, after World War I, the League of Nations granted
the British a mandate to govern Palestine, political authority
over the Holy Land passed out of Muslim hands for the first
time since Saladin's victory in the twelfth century. The Balfour

Declaration became official policy, enlisting the strength of the West to encourage, legitimize, and protect Jewish immigration. This historic shift, the product of decades of lobbying by Zionists, had also been sought by influential Christians. In 1891, a petition—the Blackstone Memorial*—addressed to President Benjamin Harrison and other world leaders urged an international conference to establish a Jewish state. Hundreds of prominent Americans signed the appeal, including the chief justice of the United States, the Speaker of the House of Representatives, John D. Rockefeller, and J. P. Morgan. The petition pointed out that the major powers had already "wrested" Bulgaria, Serbia, Romania, Montenegro, and Greece "from the Turks" and returned them "to their rightful owners." Why not, it asked, give Palestine back to the Jews? "According to God's distribution of nations it is their home."

To the frustration of future generations of diplomats, neither the Blackstone Memorial nor the Balfour Declaration addressed a crucial question: how, exactly, could a Jewish state be created without prejudice to the "civil and religious rights of existing non-Jewish communities in Palestine"? Balfour, for one, did not consider the matter important. "Zionism," he said, "is rooted in age-long traditions, in present needs, in future hopes of far profounder import than the desires and prejudices of the 700,000 Arabs who now inhabit the ancient land." When a fellow diplomat cautioned, "Let us not, for heaven's sake, tell the Moslem what he ought to

---

* The memorial emerged from a conference of Christians and Jews held in Chicago and organized by William E. Blackstone, who was a businessman and lay evangelical minister. Blackstone, who referred to himself as "God's little errand boy," also wrote a best-selling pamphlet, *Jesus Is Coming*, that described the return by Jews to Israel as a prerequisite to the second coming of Christ.

think," Balfour replied tartly: "I am quite unable to see why heaven or any other power should object to our telling the Moslem what he ought to think."

A little less than three decades later, as World War II drew to a close, the United States was in the process of replacing Great Britain as the country whose influence mattered most. To promote stability in the postwar Middle East, Franklin Roosevelt met secretly with Ibn Saud, the king of Saudi Arabia, on a warship moored in the Suez Canal. The president tried to persuade Ibn Saud to support Jewish claims in Palestine. Although the king was impressed by Roosevelt's wheelchair, a device he had never before seen, he was little taken with the president's words. "Make the enemy and the oppressor pay," he reasoned. "Amends should be made by the criminal, not by the innocent bystander. What injury have Arabs done to the Jews of Europe? It is the Christian Germans who stole their homes and lives." Roosevelt, though disappointed by the rebuff, nevertheless assured the king, "I will take no action with respect to the Palestine Mandate without consulting the Arabs." He also gave Ibn Saud a wheelchair as a gift. Two months later, Roosevelt died. As I am reminded on every trip I take to the Middle East, Arab leaders have not forgotten his promise, which they insist was never honored. They are half right. The State Department did consult regularly about Jewish emigration from Europe to Palestine, but without arriving at a common position. The Arabs wanted to halt the emigration; President Truman felt a moral duty, in the aftermath of the Holocaust, to support it. In May 1948, when the British mandate officially expired, Israel declared independence, which the United States was the first to recognize. Arabs complained that they had not been consulted; Truman insisted that his decision should have been no surprise.

Israel's declaration of statehood did not pass quietly. Arab armies attacked the new nation. The fighting that ensued caused hundreds of thousands of Palestinians to leave their homes, many settling in refugee camps in present-day Jordan and Lebanon, where large numbers of their descendants still live. In 1967, a second war, lasting only six days, expanded the territory under Jewish control as Israeli troops routed Arab forces on all fronts. As word of the victory spread, Menachem Begin, chairman of Israel's conservative Herut Party, rushed to the site where the temple of Solomon had once stood. For the first time since the ancient era, the sacred soil was in Jewish hands. Accompanied by other party leaders, Begin gave thanks and prayed:

> There has arisen in our Homeland a new generation . . . of warriors and heroes. And when they went forth to engage the enemy there burst forth from their hearts the call which echoes throughout the generation, the call from the father of the Prophets, the redeemer of Israel from the bondage of Egypt: "Arise, O Lord, and let Thine enemies be scattered and let them that hate Thee be put to flight." And we scattered and defeated them and flee they did.

Begin's prayer reflects the deepest yearnings of a people who had spent nearly 2,000 years in suffering and exile, held together by their traditions, their faith, and their dreams of returning to their historic homeland. Like the Babylonian, Greek, Syrian, Roman, Muslim, and Christian conquerors who preceded him in Jerusalem, Begin spoke in triumph. But for one side to triumph, another must be defeated. The war of 1967 extended Jewish authority over lands long occupied by Arabs and led to Israel's annexation of Arab East

Jerusalem. In most places, but especially in the Middle East, the reaction of anyone who loses land is to start laying plans to recover it.

I first visited Jerusalem in the mid-1980s. Standing by the window of my hotel room, I could see one of the world's most dramatic vistas—the stately Dome of the Rock, surrounded by the walls of the Old City, the holiest place in a holy land. This was during a relatively quiet moment in Israel's history; the first Palestinian uprising, or intifada, had yet to begin. I was overwhelmed, nonetheless, by the intensity of noise, light, and emotion. I couldn't help but reflect that the history that mattered most had happened here, in the narrow streets, stately olive groves, and surrounding hills.

The Church of the Holy Sepulchre, rebuilt by crusaders almost 900 years earlier, marked the site where, according to tradition, Jesus' body had been taken from the cross. I placed my hand on the spot where I was told the base of the true cross had been laid. Though tempted to ask how anyone could be so sure of such a thing, I still trembled. The experience was sadly undermined, however, by the history of squabbling evident within the church itself, which was and remains literally a house divided. Christian groups have fought over the space since it was first dedicated; today, the building is split into areas controlled by six groups—Greeks, Franciscans, Armenians, Copts, Ethiopians, and Syrians. The main key is retained by Muslims, whom the various Christian sects trust more than they do one another.*

---

* Violence broke out at the Church of the Holy Sepulchre as recently as September 2004, when Greek Orthodox and Franciscan monks were captured on film dragging, kicking, and punching each other.

Not far from the church is the place where Solomon had built his temple and Begin had offered his prayer. That shrine was first restored after the Jewish exile in Babylonia, then restored again by King Herod. It was destroyed in the first century by Romans, who leveled the entire city except for its outer walls, leaving intact the western side of the temple. This structure, which still survives, is sacred to Judaism. I watched as bearded men with covered heads and prayer shawls chanted in front of it and left pieces of paper between its stones. Observant Jews pray daily for God "to restore worship to Thy Temple in Zion."* A significant portion of Jewish law is devoted to the sacrifices that for centuries were offered inside the temple. Among the treasures once housed there was a gold-covered chest containing the Ten Commandments and thought to embody God's promise to Israel: the Ark of the Covenant.†

From the base of the Western Wall, a path leads up to a thirty-five-acre area of fountains, gardens, and buildings that Jews call the Temple Mount and Muslims know as the Haram al-Sharif, or "noble sanctuary." After the noise of the city, I welcomed its tranquillity. The sound of the water was soothing, as those preparing to pray washed themselves. The inside of Al-Aqsa Mosque was cool, adorned with arches and pillars, and filled with light. The Haram had been built by Muslims in the late seventh century. Their shrines commemorate Muhammad's celebrated night journey from Mecca to Jerusalem (*al-aqsa* translates as "most distant.")

---

* This is from the Amidah, or standing prayer, a collection of blessings. People reciting a blessing face in the direction of Israel if they are outside Israel; in the direction of Jerusalem if they are in Israel but outside Jerusalem; or in the direction of the Temple Mount if they are in Jerusalem.

† The Ark was lost, stolen, or hidden when the Babylonians conquered Jerusalem c. 587 BCE. Notwithstanding the final scenes of the film *Raiders of the Lost Ark*, it has not been found.

According to Muslim tradition, Muhammad began his ascent to the heavens from the rock now encased beneath the golden dome. Various Jewish traditions hold that this rock was the foundation used by God to create the heavens and Earth, or the altar upon which Abraham offered to God the sacrifice of his son Isaac, or the resting place where Jacob lay dreaming of the ladder to heaven. Tragically, holy ground is also coveted ground. During the crusades, triumphant Christians placed a cross atop the dome, used the rock to support an altar, covered the Quranic inscriptions with Latin texts, and converted Al-Aqsa Mosque into a military headquarters. Today, the Palestinian grand mufti of Jerusalem claims that the Temple Mount and all its structures, including the Western Wall, are sacred places for Muslims only. Fervently committed Jewish groups seek support for rebuilding the temple and moving the Muslim shrines elsewhere.

Ordinarily, when diplomats sit down to negotiate a border, they come equipped with maps, and with suggestions for compromise. In the Middle East, this is not enough. Israelis and Palestinians care as deeply as anyone about economic and security issues. They argue vociferously about security arrangements, access to water, transportation routes, and control of airspace; but to a negotiator these are all matters that can—at least potentially—be resolved through a process of give-and-take. Productive conversation stops, however, when the parties argue for the rightness of their positions not on the basis of human laws and precedents, but on the basis of the promises and intentions of God.

As this is written, early in 2006, the dream of Middle East peace has rarely appeared more distant. The Palestinians are divided against themselves. The Israelis have concluded that they have no partner with whom to make peace. Many look back upon the high-profile negotiations of the 1990s as a mistake, the result of a naïve belief that Yasser Arafat and the Palestinian Liberation Organization (PLO) were sincere in pledging their willingness to accept Israel's existence. The truth, I believe, is more complex. To understand the possibilities for the future, it is worth reviewing how the present stalemate came to be.

Throughout 2000, our final year in office, President Clinton, special negotiator Dennis Ross, and I struggled along with Israeli and Palestinian representatives to find a way around the obstacles to a peace settlement. Of these obstacles, the most troublesome was Jerusalem. The Palestinians insisted that the city, known to them as Al Quds ("the holy"), should be the capital of their state. They also demanded full sovereignty over the "noble sanctuary." In our discussions, we explored a host of creative variations on the themes of jurisdiction and authority. We even asked the two sides whether they could accept what we thought was a novel idea: "divine sovereignty" for the holiest sites. Searching for inspiration, President Clinton took time in private to study sections of the Quran and the Torah. In the end, he proposed that "what is Arab in the city should be Palestinian and what is Jewish should be Israeli." This would have meant Palestinian sovereignty over the "noble sanctuary" and Arab neighborhoods— where the Palestinians could have their capital—and Israeli sovereignty over the rest of the city, including the Western Wall. The Israeli prime minister, Ehud Barak, accepted the president's ideas. In so doing, he agreed to redivide Jerusalem, something successive Israeli leaders, including Barak himself, had promised never to do. He consented, as well, to the establishment of a Palestinian state consisting of 97 percent of the West Bank, Gaza, and East Jerusalem.

We were not, of course, the first to search for a formula that would bring peace to Jerusalem. In 1192, Saladin and Richard Coeur de Lion (Lionheart), both commanding armies that were weary of hardship and death, sought to negotiate an end to the Third Crusade. The terms proposed by Richard were uncannily similar to those considered by us (though affecting Christians, not Jews). Under Richard's plan, Muslims would have control over the Dome of the Rock and Al-Aqsa Mosque; Christians would have their holy sites; the rest of Jerusalem and the surrounding areas would be divided. In their exchange of letters, both leaders stressed the centrality of the holy city. "Jerusalem is for us an object of worship that we could not give up even if there were only one of us left," wrote Richard. Saladin responded, "Jerusalem . . . is even more sacred to us than it is to you, for it is the place from which our Prophet accomplished his nocturnal journey and the place where our community will gather on the Day of Judgment. Do not imagine that we can renounce it or vacillate on this point." In the end, the negotiations broke down amid political intrigue, military misadventures, and allegations of bad faith. Richard retreated, and the Christians were left in Jerusalem with only the rights of pilgrims.

Eight hundred and eight years later, our negotiations, too, collapsed. In contrast to Barak's flexibility, Arafat showed stubbornness, flatly rejected the deal Clinton had put forward. In our last-ditch effort to persuade him, we solicited the support of Arab leaders in Egypt, Jordan, Morocco, and Saudi Arabia. We hoped that their backing would make it easier for Arafat to say yes. In retrospect, their support mattered little. The Egyptians and Saudis did not push Arafat hard, and in any case their governments did not have enough credibility among Arabs to persuade him to run the personal risks a settlement would entail. In explanation, Arafat did not hesitate to offer his built-in excuse: he lacked the authority, he said, to make concessions related to Islam's holy sites. He could not compromise or "vacillate" on issues sacred to Muslims everywhere without inviting his own funeral. Worse, he fed us the lie—popular among Arab propagandists—that Jews have no claim to Jerusalem, because the first and second temples had actually been built elsewhere. Arafat could have been the first president of an internationally recognized Palestine; he chose instead the applause of supporters who praised him for refusing to sign away even a slice of "Arab land" or acknowledge the sovereignty of Israel over the Western Wall. Returning to the West Bank, he was greeted by banners hailing him as the "Palestinian Saladin."

The question for the future is whether any Palestinian leader will accept what Arafat rejected—even if it were offered. The answer is complicated by a Quranic injunction to Muslims: "Fight in the cause of God those who fight you. . . . Slay them wherever you find them and expel them from the lands from which they expelled you." It is made harder, as well, by Israel's long-standing policy of building settlements on territory occupied during the war of 1967.

The first settlements, established in the mid-1970s, were justified by the government based on specific security concerns, such as control of high ground. Then conservative governments headed by Menachem Begin and Yitzhak Shamir came to office intent on the idea of a "greater Israel," reestablishing the country's claim to the entire West Bank (all of biblical Judea and Samaria) and essentially ignoring the aspirations of millions of Palestinians. Under their leadership, Israelis were given financial incentives to establish communities in places historically lived in by Arabs. Begin referred to the conquered territories as "liberated Israeli land."* Shamir called the construction of settlements "holy work." As one rabbi explained, "the Redemption of the whole world depends on the Redemption of Israel. From this derives our moral, spiritual and cultural influence over the entire world. The blessing will come to all humanity from the people of Israel living in the whole of its land."

The rabbi may believe that the settlements have enhanced Israel's influence, but the evidence is sparse. As many Israelis have pointed out, the aggressive program of construction on disputed territory tarnished their country's moral standing, deepened Arab anger and contributed to Palestinian misery. The settlements also imposed an unsustainable burden on Israel's security forces, who were required to protect the settlers from their hostile, impoverished Palestinian neighbors. Much to his credit, Israeli Prime Minister Ariel Sharon recognized the need for retrenchment, ordering the withdrawal, in August 2005, of Israeli troops and settlers from the dusty, overcrowded Gaza Strip. The controversy over the West Bank, however, is still to be thrashed out. Looking back over the long decades of stalemate, I find myself in sad agreement with Leon Wieseltier, the literary editor of the *New Republic:* "The idea of Greater Israel ... was always a foul idea, morally and strategically. It promoted the immediate ecstasy of the few above the eventual safety of the many; [and] introduced the toxins of messianism and mysticism into the politics of a great modern democracy."

The settlements imposed another cost as well. Yigal Amir,

---

* Between 1977, when Begin took office, and 1992, when Shamir left office, the number of Israeli settlers in the West Bank, the Gaza Strip, the Golan Heights, and east Jerusalem rose from about 57,000 (of which 50,000 were in East Jerusalem) to more than 240,000.

the nineteen-year-old Israeli who murdered Yitzhak Rabin in 1995, claimed religious sanction for his despicable crime. An ultra-radical rabbi had assured him that he had a duty under Jewish law to murder Rabin, because the prime minister's support for peace had compromised the rights of settlers. Asked if he had acted alone, Amir said no; he was sure that he had acted with God.

Although I have disagreed with some policies of the Israeli government, especially the more aggressive ones regarding settlements, I am fully committed to the preservation of Israel's existence and security. The majority of Americans feel the same way. Why? We know that Jewish communities have long been persecuted, from the days of bondage in Egypt to the pogroms of czarist Russia. We consider the Holocaust to be in its own category—a tragedy beyond comprehension, never to be forgotten or repeated. We saw in the creation of Israel not only the rehabilitation of a people, but also a gesture of decency by the entire human race. We accept the argument that it was not too much to ask of the Arabs, who have other holy cities and much land, to make room for tiny Israel in the only place it has ever truly had a home. We have also seen the kind of country—a thriving democracy—that the Israelis have built. Foreigners, especially Arabs, wonder why America is allied with Israel. Searching for an answer, some subscribe to conspiracy theories or else wildly overestimate the percentage of Jews in the United States—according to one study, guesses range from 10 percent to 85 percent, when the actual proportion is less than 2 percent. Another recent survey found that Arabs believe the "Zionist lobby" to be the single most influential determinant of U.S. foreign policy. It is more accurate to say that Americans from across the ideological spectrum support Israel because we see in that society qualities with which we identify and that we admire.

Of course, Americans also care about Israel because of shared religious traditions. The Holocaust may have been the tipping point in U.S. support for Israel's statehood, but American policy has its roots in the Balfour Declaration— that there is indeed a promised land and that Israelites were the recipients of the promise. For our diplomats, the challenge has been to reconcile this starting point with the legitimate rights of Palestinians. That would be a hard enough job under any circumstances. For some Americans, however, religious convictions transcend any consideration of fairness to the Palestinians. They are convinced, on the basis of numerous biblical passages, that Jesus will return to Earth only when Solomon's temple is rebuilt and the climactic war between good and evil, described in the Book of Revelation, is fought.

A best-selling series of novels imagines the story unfolding in this way. A general breakdown in civilization is followed by the "Rapture," during which faithful Christians are spirited to heaven, leaving everyone else behind.* There soon appears the Antichrist, masquerading as the secretary general of the United Nations. Lulled by his promises, Israel signs a peace treaty under which the temple in Jerusalem is rebuilt (though it is later defiled by the Antichrist). This sets

---

* This is Jerry Falwell's description of the Rapture: "You'll be riding along in an automobile. You'll be the driver perhaps. There'll be several people in the automobile with you, maybe someone who is not a Christian. When the trumpet sounds you and the other born-again believers in that automobile will be instantly caught away—you will disappear, leaving behind only your clothes and physical things that cannot inherit eternal life.... Other cars on the highway driven by believers will suddenly be out of control and stark pandemonium will occur ... on every highway in the world."

in motion the "tribulation," during which God, to encourage the wayward to find faith, pelts Earth with plagues. Distant armies gather to attack Israel—a force 200 million strong. The decisive battle takes place near the West Bank town of Megiddo, less than fifty miles from Jerusalem. It is there that Jesus reappears, descending from heaven to lead the Christian faithful and 144,000 Jewish converts (the only Jews who survive) to a bloody victory. This is followed by a thousand years of Christ's rule on Earth.

In 1999, a poll conducted by *Newsweek* found that 40 percent of Americans—more than 100 million people—"believe that the world will end, as the Bible predicts, in a battle between Jesus and the Antichrist." Nineteen percent of the respondents believed that the Antichrist is alive today. Thirteen percent believed in the "Rapture," including some who still display bumper stickers bearing the thoughtful warning: "Come the Rapture, this car will be without a driver."

Perhaps because I was raised in the Roman Catholic Church, which does not stress the Book of Revelation, I see the text less as an elaborately coded map to the millennium than as an apocalyptic vision shaped by the struggle of early Christians to survive the hostility of Rome. I am also wearied by sightings of the Antichrist. During the crusades, Richard the Lionheart was assured by his religious advisers that Saladin fit the description; not much good arose from that. Martin Luther, who began the Reformation, declared that the pope was the Antichrist; Europe was ripped apart by religious wars for the next hundred years. The Russian Orthodox Church pinned the label on Napoleon; further destruction and war ensued. The language of Revelation is so dramatic that it tempts one to cast friends and, particularly, enemies as specific characters. We are lured by the self-centered sense that if history is to have a climax it should occur during our lifetimes. Imagining a past without us is not difficult; imagining such a future is harder and less pleasant—so we look for reasons to imagine something else.

It may be that Armageddon will settle all our accounts. It would be inexcusable, however, if our leaders relied on that supposition to justify their own inaction, only to be proved wrong, leaving us with all the destruction and none of the paradise. Setting the stage for Armageddon is not a defensible foreign policy. Peace is. This has sometimes put policy makers and preachers at cross-purposes. In January 1998, Bill Clinton invited the Israeli prime minister, Benjamin Netanyahu, and Yasir Arafat to the White House. His goal was to persuade them to revive the peace process, which had been interrupted by terrorist incidents and by a spike in settlement activity. On the eve of the meeting, Netanyahu conferred with leaders of the Christian right, who saluted him as the "Ronald Reagan of Israel" and encouraged him—irresponsibly, in my view—not to compromise. Right-wing Christian activists and other critics of the Clinton administration argued that U.S. engagement in the peace process put undue pressure on Israel. To their way of thinking, any policy that resulted in Israel's returning more land to the Palestinians was either contrary to the Bible or dangerous to the security of Israel, or both.

When President Bush took office, he was determined not to repeat what he argued were President Clinton's mistakes. He refused to deal with Arafat, refrained from appointing a full-time negotiator for the region, and did not involve himself in efforts to stem the violence between Israelis and Palestinians that killed more than 4,000 people. Bush's approach may have had the advantage of conserving America's diplomatic resources for other purposes, but it also had the clear disadvantage of causing a sharp deterioration in America's standing among Arabs and Muslims.

Unfortunately, the issues that must be settled before a permanent peace becomes feasible grew more, rather than less, difficult during President Bush's first term. The years of fighting enabled the radical group Hamas—historically an opponent of peace—to become stronger compared to its secular rival, Fatah, the largest component of the PLO. The Palestinian economy stalled, but its production of bombs, grenades, and rockets increased. The defensive barrier being built by Israel through much of the West Bank created a de facto border that Palestinians refused to accept and that many Israelis have come to feel they cannot live securely without. Israeli leaders have consistently refused Palestinian demands to release Arabs from jail if, in Israel's judgment, the prisoners have "blood on their hands"; there are many more such prisoners now than there were in 2000.

Yasser Arafat's death in November 2004 did open the door to new leadership on the Palestinian side. Arafat's successor, Mahmoud Abbas, appeared to be a welcome change. During negotiations in the 1990s, he was the Palestinian we turned to most often for frank talk. He did not betray confidences, but neither did he grandstand. He insisted that the solution to Palestinian problems could be found through the give and take of negotiations. As president, Abbas challenged the old Palestinian consensus that violence was the most effective route to progress. Unlike Arafat, he does not promote fantasies about restoring Arab rule from the Jordan River all the way to the Mediterranean sea. His goal was to build a viable Palestinian state, which he said can only be done by peaceful means.

The problem is that Abbas—though democratically-elected—lacked a solid political base. Fatah, the organization he inherited from Arafat, had a well-earned reputation for corruption and was torn by generational, ideological and personal rivalries. Abbas' dilemma was compounded by a failure on the part of the United States or Israel to recognize the urgency of helping him to succeed. Instead, demands were made of the Palestinian president that he did not have the capacity to fulfill. This left Abbas with the worst of both worlds. He was pilloried by Palestinian opponents for being the preferred candidate of Israel and the West. Yet, he was not given the help required to meet the basic needs of the Palestinian people. To buy time, Abbas postponed parliamentary elections from July 2005 until January 2006. The tactic proved in vain as Fatah's popularity continued to plummet. When the elections finally did take place, Hamas found itself in the majority—to the amazement of Fatah, Israel, the United States and perhaps Hamas, itself.

The rise of Hamas has seemingly dragged the Middle East peace process back to the point where it began roughly fifteen years ago. Hamas, like the early PLO, does not accept the existence of Israel, nor is it willing to disarm or renounce violence. Until it does, a peace agreement will not be possible. The best that can be hoped for in the interim is a suspension of hostilities. This would enable each side to catch its breath. For Hamas, the challenge will be to deliver on its campaign promises of "change and reform." These pledges have little to do with Israel and much to do with improving Palestinian governance.

The Israelis, too, have much work to do. Before falling prey to a stroke in January, 2006, Ariel Sharon had embarked on a plan to make Israelis secure by taking unilateral steps to separate them from Palestinians. This plan, never fully spelled out, was designed to ensure the survival of a predominately Jewish state by leaving as many Jews and as few Palestinians as possible on Israeli-held territory. It specifically ruled out the possibility of dividing Jerusalem or of full Israeli withdrawal to the 1967 borders. The steps already taken toward implementation include the construction of the security fence, the redeployment from Gaza and the "thickening" of settlements in and around Jerusalem. The hardest measures, still to come, would require the closure of some Jewish settlements on the West Bank in order to safeguard the future of others.

Faced by opposition from conservatives in his own Likud party, Sharon created Kadima, a coalition that attracted support from a broad spectrum. It remains to be seen whether Sharon's successors will be able to pursue a consistent strategy. The prominence of Hamas, however, is sure to postpone indefinitely Israeli recognition of a Palestinian state, while Sharon's goal of separating Jews from Palestinians will likely remain the focus of Israeli policy.

The Middle East is a place where wounds rarely heal and grievances are not forgotten; time, thus, is not ordinarily a friend to peace. For the Palestinians, however, time will be essential for them to develop the institutions they need to govern themselves responsibly. Effective administration requires honesty, skill and a willingness to compromise. Neither Hamas nor Fatah seem richly endowed with these qualities. The Palestinian people, however, have made clear through their ballots that they expect more from their leaders than they have been getting. It is encouraging that the elections, themselves, were free, fair, and competitive. That is the first step toward the creation of responsive and accountable government. Many more such steps are needed. Outside countries and organizations should assist, but only if they are able to do so without smoothing the way for Hamas and other extreme elements to retain the option of violence.

The most hopeful commentators have suggested that participating in government will make Hamas more moderate. I have my doubts. I do think that the organization's new political status will aggravate the divisions that exist within it. Pragmatists will compete with ideologues for the upper hand. The United States should do all it can to help the more moderate Palestinian forces prevail, but the lack of American engagement these past five years has left us with less leverage and credibility than we have had in the past.

The changes in leadership in both Israel and the Palestinian Authority have created new political dynamics while further dimming the short-term prospects for peace. But what about the long-term? Is the possibility of peace truly dead? In the absence of fresh thinking, I fear the answer may be yes.

Many were the times I wanted to grab the Palestinian and Israeli negotiators by the ears and try to knock some sense into them. Ultimately, I placed my hopes in our ability to draft language smart and fair enough to enable leaders from both sides to defend a peace agreement to their constituencies. Despite the many setbacks, I would still like to think that devising such a formula remains a possibility. An arrangement along the lines suggested by Bill Clinton would give both parties as generous a set of terms as each could reasonably expect. The question is whether the logic of peace will ever be powerful enough to determine the future of the Middle East. Appeals to reason and self-interest may be the only practical way to proceed, but if designing a settlement were simply a real estate transaction, it would have been completed years ago. If negotiations do again become practical, traditional diplomacy will be indispensable, but something more may also be needed: a convergence in our appreciation of what God really wants.

Historically, the conventional wisdom among American negotiators for the Middle East has been that the less talk about God the better. That is understandable, given the volatility of the region; but it is not possible to isolate religion and the history that goes along with it from the peace process. Sharon referred to Jerusalem as "Israel's capital, united for all eternity." Divided as they are, the Palestinians are united in saying that they will not even consider a two-state solution without Jerusalem as their capital. The largest Israeli settlements on the West Bank are immovable; yet even the most forthcoming peace proposals by the Arabs include a demand for the return of all lands taken during the war of 1967. Sharon's relentlessness in fighting against the second intifada was intended to convince Palestinians that resistance was hopeless. During the withdrawal from Gaza, Palestinian T-shirts read "Today Gaza—Tomorrow the West Bank and Jerusalem." Beginning in the seventh century, Muslims controlled Jerusalem for most of 1,300 years; less than sixty years—a historical eyeblink—have elapsed since Israel became a state. What now do Palestinians want most—a long-shot chance (through an orgy of blood) to relive the victory of Saladin, or a real chance to raise their families in dignity and peace? Is their dream to be martyrs or builders?

Jimmy Carter was not afraid to talk about religion when he brought the Egyptian and Israeli leaders together at Camp David. Bill Clinton was able to make as much headway as he did because he understood the history of the situation and was comfortable talking about spiritual matters. Future negotiators will not achieve the breakthroughs required, however, unless they are truly able to confront and defuse the clashing senses of entitlement. Is this realistic? I do not know. I do like George Bernard Shaw's observation that "the reasonable man adapts himself to the world; the unreasonable one persists in trying to adapt the world to himself. Therefore, all progress depends on the unreasonable man."

If hard-liners can find in the Quran and the Bible justifications for endless conflict, I believe others can find overriding commandments to pursue the opposite. One encouraging initiative is the Alexandria process, launched in 2002, and sponsored by the Mosaica Association's Center for Inter-Religious Cooperation. The premise of this project is that peace between nations and peoples cannot be achieved without reconciliation between religions and cultures; accordingly, the power of religion must be transformed from a source of hostility to a source of tolerance and understanding. The principles of the Alexandria Declaration—support for peace, nonviolence, and respect for holy places—were used to resolve one standoff in 2003, when Palestinian fighters took over the Church of the Nativity; and another in 2004, when Islamic religious authorities met to discuss the problem of incitement of anti-Semitism within Arab societies. On a more routine basis, the principles are applied by "Adam" centers, located in Israel and the Palestinian Authority. The founder of and moving force behind this effort is Rabbi Michael Melchior, a brave and eloquent fighter for peace; he is receiving strong support from Sheikh Imad Falouji, a founder of Hamas who left the organization because its attacks on civilians were a violation of Islam.

Those who are so certain that God's intention for the Middle East is Armageddon might at least reflect on the passage in Isaiah foretelling the time when God will be worshipped not only by the Israelis but also by Arabs in Egypt and Syria. "In that day," declared the prophet, "shall Israel be the third with Egypt and with Assyria, even a blessing in the midst of the land, Whom the LORD of hosts shall bless, saying, Blessed be Egypt my people, and Assyria the work of my hands, and Israel mine inheritance." Since the time of Muhammad, most Arabs and Jews have worshipped the same God. However distant it may now appear, perhaps the moment will arrive when the spirit of the Alexandria Process is finally able to carry the day. Then, in the words of Yitzhak Rabin, Israelis and Palestinians will "draw on the springs of our great spiritual resources to forgive the anguish we caused to each other, to clear the minefield that divided us for so many years, and to supplant it with fields of plenty." Perhaps the time will come when both sides will heed the guidance of the Quran: "If the enemy inclines towards peace, do thou (also) incline towards peace and trust in Allah."

Until that day, the dilemma inherent in the Balfour Declaration will remain; the character of Middle Eastern leaders will be regularly tested; the proper approach for the United States will be debated; the peoples of the region will continue to live in fear; and the ever-present tension among Muslims, Jews, and Christians will exacerbate a confrontation that extends far beyond the Middle East and threatens truly to shake the globe.

Ten

"The Greatest Jihad"

———— ⚬⚬ ————

Driven by drought, the inhabitants of Israel gathered anxiously on the slopes of Mount Carmel to witness a contest. On one side were 450 priests of Baal, the Canaanite god of fertility. On the other stood Elijah, prophet of Jahweh, god of Abraham, Moses, and David. Among the onlookers was Ahab, Samaria's weak, wayward king. The question to be settled was whose god was the mightier. The proof demanded was a sign in the form of fire igniting an altar on which a bull had been sacrificed. The followers of Baal, going first, prayed, danced, chanted, and scourged themselves for hours, but their exertions were all in vain. Elijah taunted them: "Cry aloud: for he is a god; either he is talking, or he is pursuing, or he is in a journey, or peradventure he sleepeth and must be awaked." Then it was the prophet's turn. He constructed his altar, using twelve stones to symbolize the tribes of Israel; drenched his offering with water; appealed to the Lord; and stepped back. Within seconds, fire consumed the sacrifice. Those watching threw themselves to the ground and shouted, "The Lord is God; the Lord alone is God."

More than 2,800 years later, the relationship between humans and the divine has not changed much. We still look for signs and to events here on Earth for clues about God's nature and purpose.

On September 11, 2001, the twin towers of the World Trade Center were consumed by fire. Was this such a sign?

"God continues to lift the curtain and allow the enemies of America to give us probably what we deserve," said Jerry Falwell in a television broadcast two days after the tragedy. He continued, "I really believe that the pagans, and the abortionists, and the feminists, and the gays and the lesbians who are actively trying to make an alternative lifestyle, the ACLU, the People for the American Way—all of them who have tried to secularize America—I point the finger in their face and say, 'You've helped this happen.' "*

Falwell was not alone in seeing God's hand behind the terrorists' attacks. The leaders of Al Qaeda were certain that their success was evidence of God's blessing. A videotape shows Osama bin Laden and a Saudi sheikh celebrating in the aftermath of the strikes, crediting Allah with a "clear victory" and exchanging stories about the prophetic dreams of friends who had foreseen planes smashing into buildings. "It will be," exulted the sheikh, "the greatest jihad in the history of Islam."

In the tradition of the ancient Hebrews, triumphs and defeats are commonly attributed to God's will. "If thou shalt indeed obey," promises the Lord, "then I will be an enemy unto thine enemies and an adversary unto thine adversaries." Early Muslims credited Allah for the military triumphs that enabled the rapid expansion of their religion. Spanish

---

* Confronted by a storm of criticism, Falwell later apologized for these remarks.

Catholics were sure that their acquisition of an overseas empire in the fifteenth and sixteenth centuries was God's reward for persecuting Christian heretics, Muslims, and Jews. When the British and other European powers colonized Africa, they believed they were doing God's work. As we have seen, many Americans have associated their country's rise with God's favor. Julia Ward Howe's "Battle Hymn of the Republic," composed after a visit to an army encampment in the early days of the Civil War, stirringly equated God's cause with the Union's struggle against the Confederacy.

It is human nature to want to see God's work in our own doings, and God's purpose as our own purpose. As individuals, we can often indulge this impulse without causing harm; perhaps we may even do some good. As a practical matter, however, a nation (or group) that believes its success or failure is a direct consequence of the wishes of God is likely either to invite or create trouble. If victorious, the nation and its leaders may become self-righteous and filled with a sense of omnipotence. If defeated, they may descend into bitterness and division, with one faction blaming another for incurring divine displeasure. Either way, a nation that says to God, "It's all up to you," risks neglecting an obligation to act on its own behalf. As Emily Dickinson wrote in a far different context, "'Faith' is a fine invention / When gentlemen can see / But microscopes are prudent / In an emergency."

Not long after the attacks of 9/11, I was invited to speak at the spacious House of Hope Presbyterian Church in Saint Paul, Minnesota. The pews were packed and emotions ran high. As I climbed the stairs to the pulpit, I could see that handkerchiefs and tissues were already out. In my memory, the only comparable moment of national unity in the face of trauma had been the assassination of John Kennedy. I was not qualified to deliver a sermon, but I did want to capture as precisely as I could what 9/11 did and did not mean:

I see no sign of God's hand in these crimes, nor any trace of religious faith or social conscience in their motivation. The perpetrators could not be loyal to Islam, for, by their acts, they have betrayed the teachings of that benevolent faith. The perpetrators of these outrages do not care about the Palestinians, whose leaders have expressed anger and sorrow at the attacks. They do not care about the poor, for they use their resources not to teach skills but to instill hate. They are not crazy, for they acted with frozen-hearted calculation. These were crimes of purest evil, wholly unjustified by any reason of politics, culture, or faith.

We often ask in the wake of tragedy why a God who is both almighty and good would allow such events to occur. Part of the answer is that we have been given the liberty to think and act for ourselves. Some of us use that freedom to build, heal, teach, or compose great works of art; others blow up buildings. These are our actions, not God's (and, though it may be convenient to blame him, not Satan's). When illness or an accident takes the life of a child, we can only express anguish at the cruelty and unfairness of fate. As for hurricanes, earthquakes, and tsunamis, I blame Father Nature. The rest of the answer is beyond what any of us can know for sure. As preachers are at pains to remind us, we walk in faith, not in sight. However we walk, we have a responsibility to look after ourselves and to safeguard one another. The attacks of 9/11 added a new dimension to what that responsibility will require.

In the weeks following the attacks, President Bush proved to doubters that he has the capacity for true leadership. Addressing a joint session of Congress, he fulfilled the promise he had made before his election to be a uniter. He noted that people around the world had responded to the hijackings with prayers in English, Hebrew, and Arabic; and he called attention to the astonishing fact that the victims of 9/11 included people from no fewer than eighty nations. He expressed gratitude to international organizations and to friends in Europe, Africa, Latin America, and Asia. The president vowed to use every tool of foreign policy to oppose "terrorist organizations of global reach"; and he explained that Al Qaeda represented "a fringe form of Islam that has been rejected by Muslim scholars and the vast majority of Muslim clerics—a fringe movement that perverts the peaceful teachings of Islam." The president's words of healing seemed designed to bring the world together in opposition to Al Qaeda and its supporters. This was clearly the right strategy. To defeat terror, America would need help from friends and allies everywhere, and especially from those in predominantly Arab and Muslim societies.

The climactic line in the president's speech offered a stark choice: "Every nation, in every region, now has a decision to make. Either you are with us, or you are with the terrorists."* In subsequent weeks, most countries did not hesitate to make that choice.

America's allies in NATO invoked for the first time the mutual defense provisions of the North Atlantic Treaty, declaring the attacks an act of aggression against the entire alliance. Aside from Iraq, every government in the Muslim world, including Iran and the Palestinian Authority, condemned the strikes. When American troops were deployed to Afghanistan to oust the Taliban and round up Al Qaeda, allies such as Canada, Japan, and Australia rushed to assist them. Pakistan,

---

* In issuing his challenge, President Bush may well have been thinking of Jesus' warning, "He that is not with me is against me" (Luke 11:23). It is less likely that he was trying to remind the world of Lenin's statement during the Russian Revolution: "He who is not with us is against us."

despite close ties to the radical Afghan leaders, agreed to help. China and Russia, themselves challenged by Muslim separatists, pledged solidarity. Even those Muslims who initially protested the U.S. assault against the Taliban fell silent when it became clear that the Afghan majority welcomed the overthrow of the extremists. In the United States, a group of sixty academics—including Christians, Jews, Muslims, and atheists—signed a letter in support of the military operation in Afghanistan, calling it a defense of "universal human morality" and "a just war." For months after 9/11, it appeared that the administration would succeed in uniting most Americans and foreign governments in opposition to a common threat.

As a Democrat, I was proud of the way members of my party rallied to support the White House. Members of Congress and officials who had served in the Clinton administration led the applause. At every opportunity, I offered my own backing for the president's policies. When the Taliban were overthrown, I cheered. While I was in government, I had met with Afghan women and girls at a refugee camp in Pakistan near the Khyber Pass, listening to their accounts of deprivation and oppression. I promised those refugees that America would not forget them. I hoped now that they would be able to return to their homes, live safely, and have their rights respected. I also backed the Pentagon's decision to round up and detain suspected terrorists, taking for granted that the detainees would be questioned and investigated so that timely decisions could be made about whether to prosecute them or let them go.

I was, in short, pro-war, a hawk. So when the World Council of Churches opposed the military strikes in Afghanistan, I disagreed. When Gore Vidal argued that the invasion was all about oil, I thought he was delusional. And when Alice Walker suggested that, with respect to Osama bin Laden, "the only punishment that works is love," I was grateful that she was a prizewinning author, not our commander in chief.

In the weeks following the attacks, many commentators drew a comparison between what had happened on 9/11 and Japan's strikes on Pearl Harbor in 1941. Both took America by surprise, caused destruction on U.S. soil, and signaled the start of a larger struggle. Still, the differences were plain. In Hawaii, U.S. troops, ships, and aircraft were bombed by the clearly marked airplanes of an enemy state, a state that had uniformed armed forces and defined borders. The perpetrators of 9/11 wore no uniforms, raised no flag, commanded no air force, and bore allegiance to no nation or alliance of nations. Their attacks were designed not to destroy military targets, but rather to murder as many people as possible.

In February 1998, bin Laden had issued a fatwa in which he and other terrorist leaders called on Muslims to kill Americans everywhere. The reasons he cited included America's backing of sanctions against Iraq, its support for Israel, and the presence of American armed forces in Saudi Arabia. He accused the United States of having declared war on Allah, the Prophet, and all Muslims. To provide a facade of scholarship, he cited clerical rulings regarding the religious obligation to repel assaults on the faith. He then called on all Muslims to join in attacking "Satan's U.S. troops."

Bin Laden's pretensions aside, he is hardly qualified to instruct Muslims in the duties of their faith. Even his host and sponsor in Afghanistan, Mullah Muhammad Omar, admitted, "Bin Laden is not entitled to issue fatwas, as he did not complete the mandatory twelve years of Quranic studies to qualify for the position of mufti. Only muftis can issue fatwas. Bin Laden is not a mufti and therefore any fatwas he may have issued are illegal and null and void." The mullah's statement has not stopped bin Laden from being taken seriously. By its nature, Sunni Islam has no single uni-fying leader. There is no one person or institution that can speak authoritatively on behalf of all the religion's adher-ents to discredit bin Laden's message in a way that would be convincing to those most conditioned to accept that message.

During my years as secretary of state, bin Laden was on the run and being hunted in one of the most remote places on earth. To our knowledge, no government outside Afghanistan supported his activities. He was a terrorist, a murderer of Muslims, who had been disowned by his native land (Saudi Arabia) and expelled from his adopted country (Sudan). I knew he was trying to capture the sympathies of the Muslim world, but he seemed to have little to entice his followers except the opportunity to vent their anger and be blown to bits as "martyrs." A demagogue is always danger-ous when he is telling people what they want to hear, how-ever; and it takes only a small number of determined terrorists to create a large problem.

It was, of course, nonsense to say that America had declared war on Islam. Under President Clinton, the United States had been at the forefront in defending Muslims in Bosnia and Kosovo, aiding democracy in heavily Muslim Indonesia, denouncing the Russians' violations of human rights in Chechnya, and trying to broker peace in the Caucasus and Middle East. Under Carter and Reagan, America had helped the mujahideen expel the Soviet Union's troops from Afghanistan.

Proving a negative is never simple, though, especially to a deeply skeptical audience; many Muslims who had no use for bin Laden still shared his opposition to some U.S. poli-cies. They would at least listen when he talked about "puri-fying" the Holy Land of nonbelievers, restoring Muslim rule in Jerusalem, and reviving the warrior spirit that had existed in the early days of Islam. They might even nod their heads when told that Americans should be held collectively accountable for the objectionable policies of the U.S. government in the Middle East and the Persian Gulf. After the terrorist bombings at the U.S. embassies in Kenya and Tanzania in 1998, the State Department offered a $5 million reward for information leading to bin Laden's capture. This prompted a torrent of donations to bin Laden from wealthy Arabs. Although Muslim governments did not echo or embrace bin Laden's call for holy war, some of their citizens did.

Bin Laden seeks to generate support by appealing to a combination of resentment, envy, and guilt. He refers to events of long ago that few outside the Muslim world still think about, but that many Muslims cannot forget: the destruction of the Ottoman Empire, the parceling out of the Arab Middle East and North Africa among Christian powers, and even the ejection of Muslims (along with Jews) from Spain in the same year Columbus first set sail for the New World. The Muslims who claim that their faith is under attack may seem paranoid to westerners, but the boundaries of the Muslim world have been considerably reduced in recent centuries. When the French marched into Damascus in 1920, their commander, General Henri Gouraud, strode to the tomb of Islam's most revered warrior-hero. "Saladin," Gouraud declared, "we have returned. My presence here consecrates the victory of the Cross over the Crescent." In colonizing the Arab states, representatives of the western powers intentionally fostered the development of secular elites who usurped the authority of religious leaders. Meanwhile, the apparatchiks of the Soviet Union's politburo spent decades insisting to millions of Muslims that God did not exist. Pan-Arab nationalists such as Gamal Abdel Nasser of Egypt portrayed Islam as an enemy of progress. The Zionist dream was fulfilled with the help of western powers at the expense of Arabs.

Bin Laden's goal is to reap a harvest of bitterness by cultivating these and other, more recent grievances. He wants to create a great global divide with "right-thinking" Muslims on one side and the West on the other—precisely what we should seek to avoid. Bin Laden, and those who think like him, are focused on old injustices, not future opportunities. When they turn to the Quran, it is not to passages such as this: "It may be that God will grant love and friendship between you and those whom you now hold as enemies, for God has power over all things; and God is most forgiving, most merciful." Bin Laden and his followers prefer instead the more bloodcurdling Quranic commands about brandishing spears and slaying pagans. They do not offer ideas for improving or enriching the lives of people here on Earth; they are preoccupied with the glories they expect to encounter in the hereafter. For them, their own morality is taken for granted, and God's revelation is a mandate to kill.

The horrible events of 9/11 ended the lives of more than 3,000 human beings. That day also marked the full emergence of a new and complex challenge to the national security of the United States. Unlike the "godless" communists, this enemy claimed to be engaged in holy work. In responding, America would need to be inventive not only in devising the means by which further attacks might be prevented, but also in developing a message that would successfully erode the enemy's base of support.

Eleven

"God Wants Me
to Be President"

—————⋘⋙—————

When, after 9/11, President Bush presented his dramatic choice to the world, his message was clear: the
globe had changed and America would fight back. The military intervention that the United States led in Afghanistan
reinforced that message, scattering Al Qaeda and toppling
the Taliban. The next steps, it seemed to me, were obvious:
first, *military* action to prevent Al Qaeda from finding sanctuary across the Afghan border in Pakistan; second, *political*
action to build democratic institutions throughout
Afghanistan and ensure that radical elements would not
reestablish a foothold there; and third, *diplomatic* action
enlisting the help of Afghanistan's neighbors—including
Iran, Pakistan, and the Muslim countries of central Asia—to
forge the most powerful possible coalition against Al Qaeda.
The overriding goal would be to destroy as much of bin
Laden's network as possible, isolate the rest, and prevent it
from putting down new roots.

To these ends, I expected the president to continue high-
lighting the themes he had raised so effectively during the

first weeks after 9/11: global unity, defeating the terrorists, working with allies, and reaching out to Arabs and Muslims. These expectations were not met. At a moment when continuity of direction was both logical and essential, the president shifted course.

Instead of sticking to the job of smashing Al Qaeda, he adopted an approach with precisely the opposite effect. In 2002, in his State of the Union address, he focused not on the terrorists and the nation-building barely begun in Afghanistan, but on the so-called "axis of evil"—Iraq, Iran, and North Korea. In public remarks later that year, he emphasized not the urgent need for a multinational antiterror coalition, but America's unilateral intention to maintain "military strength beyond challenge." In publishing his national security strategy, the president asserted the right to attack foreign nations, even in the absence of an imminent threat, if he suspected that they might one day take hostile action against the United States. This was the controversial "preemption doctrine," which asserted for America a right we would never recognize as legitimate if claimed by any other government. He also asked Congress to authorize a new generation of nuclear weapons to add to the already daunting arsenal of the United States.

These bursts of muscular rhetoric evoked cheers from the president's admirers, but did nothing to make America safer. On the contrary, they complicated what should have been a simple choice. The president had asked every country to oppose Al Qaeda. Now he was asking them to oppose Al Qaeda while also endorsing an unrestricted view of U.S. power. Faced with this choice, many who loathed terrorism were nevertheless reluctant to be "with" the United States. By failing to heed Theodore Roosevelt's advice to talk softly, the administration began inadvertently to shift the world's attention away from what the terrorists had done to what America might do.

In September 2002, President Bush again commanded a vast audience when he traveled to Manhattan for his annual appearance before the UN General Assembly. If I had been in a position to advise him, I would have urged him to rally nations against Al Qaeda; thank governments that had helped to track down terrorist suspects; and appeal to clerics, scholars, and educators to confirm that there are no circumstances under which terrorism could be justified. The president chose instead to demand support for fighting Saddam Hussein. Throughout that autumn, when the president did discuss Al Qaeda, he portrayed the challenge less as a multinational struggle against a global threat than as a campaign to bring terrorists to "American justice," as if "justice" alone were not enough.

In January 2003, the president had another opportunity to make known his priorities through his State of the Union address. This time, he devoted four times as much attention to Iraq as to Al Qaeda—citing Saddam Hussein by name eighteen times, and bin Laden not at all. To support the decision he had already made to invade Iraq, the president simply lumped Al Qaeda and the government in Baghdad together, describing them as two aspects of the same threat. This tactic led many Americans to conclude, wrongly, that Hussein had been behind the attacks of 9/11—why else would we be going to war with him? It also enabled the administration to accuse those who raised questions about invading Iraq as being soft on fighting terror. Thus countries such as Germany and France were castigated by the secretary of defense, Donald Rumsfeld, and scorned as virtual traitors by some members of Congress. This was unfair. French soldiers have served continuously alongside Americans in Afghanistan, where Al Qaeda had been based, and Germany had led the international security forces there.

At times during the months preceding the war with Iraq, a triumphal tone crept into the rhetoric of the Bush administration. Those planning the war boasted about the "shock and awe" that American military power would produce. Vice President Richard Cheney predicted that our troops would be welcomed as "liberators." Condoleezza Rice spoke of America's plan to transform the entire Middle East. The president responded to his failure to assemble a more impressive multinational coalition with the retort, "At some point, we may be the only ones left. That's OK with me. We are America."

During these months, the administration did succeed in mobilizing the support of many Americans, while persuading Tony Blair in Great Britain and a few other foreign leaders to contribute troops to the invasion force. But what did any of this have to do with winning the war on terror? That question was paramount because if America's proper goal was to isolate the terrorists, Al Qaeda had an aim, too. Its strategy was to lure to its side, or at least into a state of confused neutrality, every Muslim opposed to U.S. policies. Bin Laden sought to associate himself, in his words, with the Palestinians' quest to recover sacred land and the Arabs' struggle to resist the invasion and occupation of Iraq by Christian imperialists. This link between attacks on Islam and foreign occupation is critical because, research indicates, those behind suicide bombings are rarely motivated by religious beliefs alone. Organized terror campaigns are almost always designed to force a withdrawal from some disputed territory. American saber-rattling made Al Qaeda's job far easier than it should have been.

In the weeks after 9/11, public opinion was overwhelmingly sympathetic to the United States. Within two years, a far different picture had emerged. In Indonesia, the most populous Muslim-majority state, the attitude toward America plunged from 75 percent favorable in 2000 to 83 percent negative by 2003. Majorities in many Muslim countries feared that the United States was planning to attack them. In pivotal Pakistan, backing for the U.S.-led war on terror fell to 16 percent. Levels of support in 2005 remained disturbingly low: 12 percent in Jordan, 17 percent in Turkey, 31 percent in Lebanon.

Further, the motives of the United States in fighting terror are not considered sincere. Many people, and not only in Muslim societies, believe that America's real aims are to control oil, defeat Muslims, advance the interests of Israel, and dominate the world—just as Al Qaeda has alleged. An advisory panel of the State Department reported that in many countries the United States is viewed as "less a beacon of hope than a dangerous force to be countered," and that large majorities in Egypt, Morocco, and Saudi Arabia see "George W. Bush as a greater threat to the world order than Osama bin Laden." Historians may someday scratch their heads at the ability of stateless, on-the-run terrorists to compete credibly with the world's most powerful leader in framing public perceptions and debate.

Like Bill Clinton before him, President Bush has said many times and with the utmost sincerity that the United States is not engaged in a clash of religions. He knows that it is bad diplomacy, especially in this tempestuous time, to imply that America has a unique relationship with God. He has a way of speaking, however, that sometimes undercuts his intentions. The president's rhetoric, though of a type used by some earlier chief executives, is nevertheless an extreme example, steeped in a sense of mission and full of religious imagery. It is no accident that Al Qaeda is listened to when it excoriates him as a modern-day crusader.

For instance, the president has said repeatedly that America's duty is to "rid the world of evil"—for mortals, an impossible job. He has declared that "America's purpose is more than to follow a process. It is to achieve a result: the end of terrible threats to the civilized world." During his famous "mission accomplished" speech in May 2003, after the invasion of Iraq, the president quoted Isaiah, "To the captives, come out; and to those in darkness, be free." This was just a rhetorical flourish, perhaps, but it was a telling one. The president was talking about the fruits of U.S. military action; Isaiah was speaking of God's gift of eternal salvation. When Saddam Hussein was captured, the president argued that America was doing God's work in restoring liberty to the Iraqi people. On being asked by an interviewer whether his father would approve of the war against Iraq, he said, "You know, he is the wrong father to appeal to in terms of strength. There is a higher father I appeal to." Even before he announced his candidacy for the White House, he confided to evangelicals, "I believe God wants me to be president."*

The difficulty, of course, is not that the Bush administration has sought to exercise leadership on moral grounds; virtually every administration has tried to do that. The problem is that its rhetoric has come close to justifying U.S.

---

* Interviewed on NBC's *Meet the Press*, March 27, 2005, Richard Land of the Southern Baptist Convention was asked whether the quotation was accurate. He replied, "It is, but it's incomplete. And the media keeps insisting on making it incomplete, which changes the entire context. He said, and it was right after he had been to a worship service the morning he was inaugurated for his second term as governor, and the Methodist minister had made a very stirring sermon about 'God has a purpose for your life and a plan for your life,' and his mother reached over and said, 'George, he's talking about you.' And he came back to the governor's mansion and he met with several of us and he said, 'I believe God wants me to be president, but if that doesn't happen, that's OK.' "

policy in explicitly religious terms—and that this is like waving a red flag in front of a bull. These are precisely the grounds upon which Al Qaeda would prefer to fight. With strong leadership, the United States can bring the world together in opposition to the murder of innocent people. But we will never unite anyone around the proposition that to disagree with the president of the United States is to pick a quarrel with God.

While it may be second nature for President Bush to refer to the fight against terror as a battle between evil and good, is the contrast truly that stark? If Al Qaeda is not evil, nothing is. But who is completely good? As a proud American, even I must admit that in any strict sense the honest answer must be—not us. Our leaders may have the best of hearts; but whether we are battling terror or pursuing some other objective, often our motives are impure, our planning is imperfect, our information is incomplete, and our actions are marred by errors of omission and commission. This has been true at every stage in American history and to a greater or lesser extent in the experience of every other nation. Even Jesus of Nazareth, when addressed by a stranger as "good master;" replied, "Why callest thou me good? There is none good but one, that is, God." In battling terror, we might more accurately refer to a confrontation between evil and "pretty good," or between evil and "not bad," or between evil and "doing the best we can." Or perhaps we should adopt Abraham Lincoln's formulation—a fight between evil and "right as God gives us to see the right."

I made this point in a speech in the spring of 2004, adding, "I say this not to criticize the president, because I think he has generally tried to be careful with his words and because I am as prone to making prideful statements as anyone else. We all yearn to believe what we want to believe and what it makes us feel good to believe. But faith does not always lead to wisdom. And in today's tinderbox of a world, we had better find a way to start putting old fires out instead of lighting new ones."

My disclaimer failed to dissuade the president's media guardians from rushing to his rescue. The very next day, the talk show host Sean Hannity of Fox News labeled me "a shrill left-wing leader" and asked rhetorically, "Is it that liberals are so in love with getting their power back that they'll say anything at this point?" One of Hannity's colleagues suggested with a derisory smile that my plan for fighting terror would be to "sing *Kumbaya* in Arabic."

As we have seen, President Bush is hardly the first American leader to associate his agenda with God's. Supporters of the abolition of slavery, of the civil rights movement, and of efforts to fight poverty and disease have done the same. Especially in the present circumstances, however, it is a tactic to be used with caution, a quality not in much evidence at the Republican Convention in 2004. That is when the cochair of the Iowa state Republican Party declared that "GOP stands for 'God's official party.' " The Texas Republicans' platform affirmed that "the United States of America is a Christian nation." The College Republican National Committee solicited contributions to give the president "the shield of God." Vice President Cheney cited a historian who had written, "When America was created, the stars must have danced in the sky." And President Bush declared in his speech accepting the nomination that, "Like governments before us, we have a calling from beyond the stars to stand for freedom."

President Bush is proud of the faith he puts in his own judgments about right and wrong, and in his perceptions about what God does and does not want. He sees this level of certainty as an essential quality in a president. "You better know what you believe or you risk being tossed to and fro by the flattery of friends or the chorus of the critics," he told an audience in the fall of 2004. "It is crucial for America's president to be consistent," he continued, "America's president must base decisions on principle, core convictions from which you will not waver."

Who could quarrel with that? Without question, leaders need to have confidence in themselves, but there is a fine line between confidence and self-righteousness. Confidence comes from the effort to learn all one can about a problem; self-righteousness comes from a tendency to believe that one has learned all there is to know. A confident leader will make firm judgments about what is best, but also accept the need to revisit issues should new information surface; a self-righteous leader will resist any information that is at odds with what he already thinks.

It is a responsibility of leadership to draw moral distinctions, and it is a part of human nature to think in terms of absolutes; but discretion is advised. Few, if any, of us have moral vision that is 20-20. If we are sure we are right, we may be less likely to explore alternatives or to develop a plan B should plan A go astray. We may be so convinced of the merits of our cause that we neglect the effort to convince others. We may be so insistent about achieving the right goals that we fail to select the right means. History is filled with enterprises that have failed despite the firm beliefs of those who launched them. President Bush's core convictions led America from 9/11 to the invasion and prolonged occupation of a country that had nothing to do with the 9/11 attacks. This move has widened the split between Muslims and the United States, given new life to Al Qaeda, and made far more difficult the challenge fo defeating international terror.

Twelve

Iraq: Unintended Consequences

———— ⌇ ————

It makes a great difference," wrote Saint Augustine, "by which causes and under what authorities men undertake the wars that must be waged."

Roughly 1,600 years later, in March 2003, Cardinal Pio Laghi tried to persuade President Bush not to act on his plan to invade Iraq. The cardinal, a special envoy of the Vatican, warned of civilian casualties and damage to relations between Christians and Muslims; he insisted that it would be neither moral nor legal to attack a country even to oust a regime as repulsive as Saddam Hussein's. President Bush was unmoved. The war, he said, "will make things better."

In a speech that same week, I argued that "even if there were an adequate rationale for invading Iraq, it might not be wise for America to start a war under these circumstances and at this time." I worried that a conflagration would detract from efforts to capture Osama bin Laden and would be exploited by Al Qaeda to recruit more terrorists. I cautioned that internal divisions in Iraq would surely complicate the aftermath of the conflict. I was concerned, as well, by the lack of international support, saying that although the United States could win the war without much help, it would need a great deal of aid to establish a stable democracy. Though I suspect that some people in government, especially in the State Department and among our uniformed military, held similar views, my warnings and those of many others were in vain.

My doubts about the wisdom of war were not grounded in any illusions about Saddam Hussein. While in office, I had myself insisted that calibrated military strikes were justified to penalize Iraq's many failures, including its unwillingness to cooperate with the United Nations' weapons inspections. Now on the outside, I thought—on the basis of the intelligence data I had studied previously—that Iraq might possess chemical and biological arms, but not the means to deploy them effectively beyond its borders. There were no indications that the country had resumed trying to build nuclear weapons. Admittedly, there was also no reason to think that Hussein would not try to do so if given the chance. He was, however, effectively caged—a fox with no way to get into the chicken coop. Iraq's military was barred from purchasing heavy weapons and was surrounded by superior forces; even the greater part of its airspace was outside its control. Hussein had been warned, moreover, that he would be obliterated if he ever again tried to invade a country. As a rule, people who build statues to themselves are not suicidal. After more than a decade of containment, Iraq was not in a position to attack anyone.

In 2001, Colin Powell, who was then secretary of state, summarized the situation accurately. Referring to the sanctions, he said, "Frankly, they have worked." Powell noted that Hussein "has not developed any significant capability with respect to weapons of mass destruction. He is unable to project power against his neighbors. So, in effect, our policies have strengthened the security of the neighbors of Iraq, and these are the policies we are going to keep in place." Powell did not predict, however, how long those policies would continue. By early 2002, President Bush had decided to abandon them and instead prepared to invade.

The tradition of "just war" sets out a series of hurdles that must be cleared before a decision to initiate conflict may be judged legitimate. These include (1) just cause; (2) right intention; (3) right authority; (4) reasonable hope of success; and (5) a favorable balance between good achieved compared to harm caused. As the administration's intentions became clear, a chorus of religious authorities joined the Vatican in arguing that the prospective invasion fell short of these standards. The Methodist bishop of Chicago argued, "There is no way to read the criteria of the 'just war theory' that could justify this foolhardy adventure. This is not an act of self-defense. All other options have not been exhausted. The devastation envisioned is in no way proportional to the perceived original aggression of Saddam Hussein. Innocent civilians—particularly women and children—will not be protected."

Petros VII of Alexandria, the second-ranking patriarch of the Orthodox Christian Church, warned that invading Iraq "would be seen as an attack on Islam" and would have "unjust, far-reaching and long-lasting consequences." The executive committee of the World Conference on Religion and Peace called on Baghdad to comply with the resolutions of the UN Security Council, but expressed fear that "military action against Iraq has the potential to create a long-term humanitarian disaster, to further destabilize the region, and to fuel dangerous extremist tendencies." A Protestant network, Call to Renewal, proposed a six-point alternative to war, including Hussein's indictment by an international tribunal, coercive inspections, humanitarian relief, and a more intense focus on the threat posed by suicide bombers.

Supporters of the administration brushed such alternatives aside, countering that the attacks of 9/11 had made the conventional criteria for just war obsolete. They argued that the United States was vulnerable to surprise attack by an enemy that welcomed death and so could not be deterred. They raised the possibility that Saddam Hussein and Al Qaeda would team up (or perhaps already had teamed up), and that Hussein was in a position to supply the terrorists with formidable weapons. Even if the United States could not prove that Iraq was helping Al Qaeda, this did not mean that Iraq was not helping Al Qaeda. "Absence of evidence," said Donald Rumsfeld, "is not evidence of absence." These arguments were sufficient to win the support of conservative and some moderate Christian and Jewish groups.*

In making their case, administration officials referred to the "gathering danger" posed by the Iraqi regime. Condoleezza Rice even conjured up the image of a mushroom cloud, as a warning that a failure on our part to attack might lead to nuclear annihilation. I was impressed myself, in February 2003, by Secretary Powell's dramatic show-and-tell presentation before the UN Security Council. With the director of the CIA, George Tenet, at his side, Powell offered a litany of allegations, including the assertion—startling to me—that Iraq possessed a fleet of mobile biological weapons laboratories. It was powerful testimony; but, unbeknownst to Powell, the juicier tidbits—including the mobile labs—

---

* The National Association of Evangelicals, for example, called the proposed invasion an act of self-defense. The Union for Reform Judaism agreed to support military action, but only if all other options for resolving the problem of Iraq's "possession of nonconventional weapons" were explored first.

were lies. Iraqi exiles, most notably an informant with the code name Curveball, had manufactured the fictions for the express purpose of prodding America into war.* As we soon found out, the weapons of mass destruction (WMD) did not exist.

It is clear in retrospect that the Iraqi government was a diminishing danger to everyone except the Iraqi people. It certainly posed no imminent threat to America or to America's allies. There is no evidence that it was in league with Al Qaeda. There was no justification for the Bush administration, which had won a diplomatic victory by pressing successfully for the return of weapons inspectors to Iraq, to undo that victory by forcing a premature end to those inspections. The United States lacked the "right authority" to go to war in Iraq. It could hardly claim to have acted to enforce the will of the UN Security Council when a majority of the council opposed the president's plan. According to an official British account of conversations with American officials in the summer of 2002, "Bush wanted to remove Saddam through military action, justified by the conjunction of terrorism and WMD. But the intelligence and the facts were being fixed around the policy."

Early on, the war achieved one valuable purpose—the removal from power of Saddam Hussein. It rapidly became clear, however, that the price of this "mission accomplished" had been grossly underestimated. Administration officials expected the war and the subsequent transition to be easy,

---

* It appears, from all accounts, that Secretary Powell had made a diligent effort to ensure that the information he conveyed at the UN was accurate. He had asked the right questions; the problems arose from the answers he received. In September 2005, in an interview with Barbara Walters of ABC, Powell said, "There were some people in the intelligence community who knew at the time that some of these sources were not good, and shouldn't be relied upon, and they didn't speak up. That devastated me."

inexpensive, and risk-free. Failing to anticipate trouble, they neglected to plan for it. At a briefing shortly before the invasion, I sat patiently while the civilian leaders of the Defense Department pointed to their charts and outlined their expectations. Raising my hand, I asked, "All this is fine, but where is your postwar plan?" Instead of answering, the officials told me not to worry; everything had been thought of and would turn out right. They were all supremely confident. Given Hussein's record, I could at least accept that there were reasons to consider going to war. I could not understand the decision to do so at that particular time, without enough troops, without the right equipment, without a realistic strategy for restoring order, and without a serious analysis of the environment in which America's fighting men and women would be asked to risk their lives.

The American military has performed in Iraq with its characteristic skill and courage. The Pentagon's management of the occupation, however, has been a tragedy of errors. The security situation fell apart at the outset; economic reconstruction was stillborn; the contracting process reeked of cronyism; the administration's unilateral approach drove allies away; and the human and financial costs have skyrocketed. As this is being written, more than 2,400 coalition troops have been killed and another 16,000 wounded. Many of the latter have been permanently disabled. Tens of thousands of innocent Iraqi civilians have also died. In addition, more than $250 billion, which could have been used to fight Al Qaeda, to rebuild after natural disasters, or for other necessary purposes, has instead been swallowed up by Iraq. Meanwhile, America's military, including our National Guard and Reserve units, has been dangerously overextended.

One criterion for a just war is "right intention"; on this the administration is entitled to a passing grade. The president was undoubtedly sincere in telling the papal ambassador that he thought the war would "make things better." In fact, he had so much faith in the rightness of his opinions that he ignored the counsel of friends both at home and overseas. The chain of his logic, as evidenced by his statements, is as follows: (1) good and evil exist in the world; (2) Saddam Hussein is evil; (3) removing him will therefore be good; (4) the newly democratic Iraq will become a model for other Arabs. The main difficulty with this thinking is what it left out—the complexities created by history and religion.

The mandate establishing British authority in the Middle East after World War I was not limited to Palestine; it extended as well to three provinces of the newly dismantled Ottoman Empire: one consisting primarily of ethnic Kurds, the second of Sunni Arabs, and the third of Shia Arabs. The territories were situated along the Tigris and Euphrates rivers, whose valley formed the cradle of ancient Mesopotamia. For purposes of administration, the British combined the disparate provinces into a single country: Iraq.

Like American leaders eighty-some years later, the British expected to be greeted warmly by their new subjects; after all, Britain had just freed the people of the region from those who had long oppressed them. The British commander, Lieutenant General Sir Frederick Maude, met local officials with reassuring words: "Our armies do not come into your cities and lands as conquerors or enemies, but as liberators. . . . [It is our wish] that you should prosper even as in the past, when your lands were fertile, when your ancestors gave to the world literature, science and art, and when Baghdad was one of the wonders of the world."

The general's flowery words failed to soothe. The Iraqis had no interest in substituting a Christian master for a Muslim one; they wanted to govern themselves. By the summer of 1920, rebellion was raging through much of the country. Insurgents cut railway lines, attacked towns, and killed British officers. The English responded harshly, with bombs and poison gas, slaughtering rebels and civilians alike. Iraq's Shia authorities, who had led the uprising, refused to submit. When the British were finally able to restore order, they installed a constitutional monarchy that favored the Sunni minority, leaving the Shiites marginalized and embittered. As for Iraq's oil, it was divided among British, French, Dutch, and American interests.

Although the British mandate officially expired in 1932, Iraq remained under the crown's protection until 1958, when a renegade group of military officers overthrew the monarchy. A subsequent coup brought Saddam Hussein, in 1979, to the presidency. Hussein—a secular Sunni who patterned his leadership style after Joseph Stalin—brutalized all who opposed or questioned him and was especially vicious toward the Shia and the Kurds.

This history meant that in the spring of 2003—when Baghdad fell—American troops would encounter a sharply divided population that was profoundly suspicious of the West and instinctively hostile to the sight of a largely Christian military force occupying a city that had served for centuries as the capital of Islam during its golden age. Little wonder that, once again, good intentions and flowery words would fail to soothe.

Although we must fervently hope otherwise, the invasion of Iraq—and its aftermath—may eventually rank among the worst foreign policy disasters in U.S. history. The decision to attack has already become a case study in unintended consequences. It is extraordinary, for example, that the success of the Bush administration's biggest gamble in world affairs depends on the continued forbearance of a seventy-five-year-old Iranian-born ayatollah with a heart condition.

When the removal of Saddam Hussein turned Iraqi politics upside down, the long-dominant Sunni minority was supplanted by the long-repressed Shia majority, whose most influential leader is Grand Ayatollah Sistani.

Unlike the Shiite clerics in Iran, who insist on exercising political power, Sistani is a "quietist," part of a mainstream Shiite tradition in which the clergy remain aloof from the routine of public life, though reserving the right to assert themselves at critical moments. Since the fall of Baghdad, Sistani has fulfilled this role creatively. Rather than repeat the mistake of openly rebelling against a powerful western military force, Sistani has found a way to make the occupiers work for him. In 2003, when the United States unveiled a multistage plan for Iraq to select an assembly and draft a constitution, Sistani blocked it—not because it was democratic but because it wasn't democratic enough. The Americans wanted a carefully controlled process that would establish the rules before elections were held. Sistani said that a constitution drafted by unelected representatives would be illegitimate; elections, he insisted, must come at the beginning. After trying at first to ignore this demand, and then failing to broker a compromise, U.S. officials had no choice—given all their talk about democracy—but to yield. The ayatollah's subsequent support for the balloting ensured its success despite terrorists' threats; he even ruled that women were duty-bound to vote whether their husbands wanted them to or not. Sistani's preferred candidates easily defeated those more closely associated with the United States.

Ayatollah Sistani operates as his predecessors might have done centuries ago, except that he uses far more elaborate communications. He is ascetic, lives in a small house in the Shia holy city of An Najaf, and refrains from speaking or preaching in public. He also refuses to meet directly with officials of the United States. His image is nurtured by a circle of skilled advisers; his clout is magnified by the network of social and charitable organizations that he controls. Sistani is not strong enough to dictate Iraq's national agenda; but no other faction can achieve its goals without his acquiescence. He will use this power to ensure that Islam plays a prominent role in shaping Iraq's society and law. Sistani's wisdom will be tested repeatedly as conservative Muslims, long suppressed, vie with moderates and advocates of women's rights to determine how tolerant and diverse the new Iraq will be.

Among the most controversial Shiite leaders, and a rival of sorts to Sistani, is Moqtada al-Sadr, a young cleric with an impressive family tree. Al-Sadr's great-grandfather earned renown leading the Shiites against the British in the 1920s. His father, assassinated by government thugs in 1999, was also a major religious figure. Al-Sadr is determined to uphold the family tradition of rebellion but is apparently undecided about how best to do so. He has pursued an erratic strategy, sometimes calling on his loosely organized Al Mahdi militia to attack coalition troops, at other times assuming a defensive stance, at still others promising to renounce violence and go into politics. His role is critical because his demagogic style makes him more popular than any other figure among Baghdad's dispossessed, Shia or Sunni. This standing puts Al-Sadr in a position to cast the "swing vote": choosing either to help bring the country together or to rip it apart. He is, therefore, a litmus test of Iraqi progress. If his name is linked to efforts at promoting national unity, there is reason for encouragement. If his name is connected to new outbreaks of fighting, the chances are that dangers are multiplying.

While the Shiites and Kurds gained power when Saddam Hussein was ousted, the Arab Sunnis lost power. After dominating the country's governing institutions for more than eight decades, the Sunnis were suddenly on the outside. In

2003, American officials disbanded the Iraqi military and barred members of the old governing party from holding public jobs. These ill-advised steps deprived the country of a security structure and put tens of thousands of Sunnis out of work at a time when few replacement jobs were available. Many Arab Sunnis were stunned by their reduced standing. Some genuinely believe, even now, that they constitute a majority of Iraq's population, though experts agree that the proportion is closer to 20 percent.

The Sunnis lack a leader of prestige comparable to Sistani. Some of their more prominent spokesmen have been assassinated; others are tarred by past association with Saddam Hussein; still others are former exiles with little public following. The most influential have called for resistance to the occupation although there are disagreements about how much violence can be justified. Meanwhile, an indeterminate number of terrorists recruited from Sunni Arab states have been drawn to Iraq by the prospect of waging war against the American (i.e., Christian or atheist), Iranian (i.e., Shia), and Jewish agents they allege are intent on plundering their country and attacking their faith. The best-known of these foreigners has been a Jordanian-born terrorist, Abu Musab al-Zarqawi, who acquired notoriety from kidnappings and gory executions broadcast over the Internet. Although Zarqawi is thought to have planned some of the more spectacular attacks in Iraq, dozens of gangs have claimed responsibility for suicide bombings, assaults on security forces, murders, and sabotage. Taken together, these groups constitute a hydra-headed insurgency whose estimated size keeps increasing while it drains the country's resources and threatens to plunge Iraq into ever-widening sectarian strife. In part because it is so decentralized, the insurgency has shown an alarming capacity to absorb losses without losing the ability to carry out its crimes. The rebels have no chance of reestablishing Sunni control over Iraq, but neither does it appear that they can be defeated militarily, unless they fall to quarreling among themselves and begin to fight each other. Their agenda seems to consist entirely of trying to drive the coalition out and kill everyone who has cooperated with it. As one Sunni suicide bomber in training told *Time* magazine, "The first step is to remove the Americans from Iraq. After we have achieved that, we can work out the other details."

American leaders describe the confrontation in Iraq as a battle between the forces of freedom and those of tyranny, seeking without much success to downplay the religious dimension. Not everyone in the country is religious, of course, and millions are so focused on day-to-day survival that they have little time for other concerns, but faith is central to the identity of most Iraqis. Since the fall of Baghdad, religious leaders have repeatedly shown their ability to bring large numbers of people into the streets on behalf of a favored cause. The American military presence was tolerated by the majority of Iraqis at the outset because toleration was what Sistani instructed. It has been resisted by many Arab Sunnis, in part because the Association of Muslim Scholars, a leading Sunni group, claims that opposition is a religious duty. Though most religious Iraqis are not fanatics, some are. It is possible to pick up a newspaper almost any day and find stories about people who say they are willing to die (or kill) if so commanded by their imam. Mustafa Jabbar, for example, is a twenty-three-year-old with a baby son, his first child. He and his wife told an interviewer that they would readily "put mines in the baby and blow him up" if asked to do so by Moqtada al-Sadr.

One of the many ironies of U.S. policy is that the Bush administration, for all its faith-based initiatives, is far more comfortable working with secular leaders than with those

Iraqis (and Iraqi political parties) for whom religion is central. This is true even when the religious leaders are moderate in orientation and generally accepting of U.S. goals.

Evidence for this surfaced during preparations for the first round of elections in January 2005. The National Democratic Institute (NDI), which I chair, worked directly with Iraqi political parties as they prepared for the historic event. Our programs were designed to help the parties to understand the mechanics of the electoral process, organize and publicize their ideas, compile lists of voters, and ensure opportunities for the participation of women. NDI's ability to function in a place as riddled with strife as Iraq depended (then and now) on its neutrality. It cannot be seen as supporting one faction over another.

For this reason, I was stunned when I learned of a controversy within the State Department about whether to funnel tens of millions of dollars in material assistance to favored secular parties. As soon as we found out about this dangerous idea, Ken Wollack (NDI's president) and Les Campbell (its director for the Middle East) lodged a protest. Along with representatives of other organizations promoting democracy, they reminded the administration that the fundamental goal of U.S. policy was to help the Iraqi people elect and put in place a legitimate government. If we played favorites, we would confirm every suspicion about our intentions, make our rhetoric about democracy look foolish, and raise new questions about our attitude toward Islam. NDI warned that if the administration went forward with such a scheme, the institute would have to consider suspending its own programs, because its credibility would be destroyed and the security situation— already tense—would become intolerable.

The proposal to aid particular candidates was debated seriously for months before the top officials at the State Department finally turned thumbs down. Similar ideas, however, have been raised in connection with subsequent elections. To my knowledge, no such plan has been carried out by the State Department or by any other federal agency. Given all that America has invested in Iraq, there is a temptation to try to arrange outcomes that are pleasing to us. But either we have faith in democracy or we do not. Sending Americans to fight and die in Iraq was a questionable idea under any circumstances. Asking them to make such a sacrifice while sabotaging democracy ourselves would be shameful.

The invasion of Iraq was intended as a demonstration of America's power; it has instead shown the limits of that power. President Bush went to war because he believed that doing so was necessary to keep Americans safe. He surely did not intend, in the process, to cause what is taking place: a historic shift in the relative power of Sunni and Shiite Muslims not only in Iraq but throughout the region. The installation of a permanent government in Iraq marks the first time in history that Shiites have governed a leading Arab state. Officials in the major Sunni capitals of Saudi Arabia, Jordan, and Egypt worry about the emergence of a Shia "crescent" running from Bahrain to Iran, Iraq, Syria, and Lebanon. In a meeting in Washington during the spring of 2005, King Abdullah of Jordan expressed to me his concern about the possibility that the clash between the Sunnis and Shiites could supplant the conflict between the Arabs and Israelis as the core problem in the Middle East. For a millennium, Sunnis have been preeminent within Islam. The balance in the future will be more even; and no one can be sure what that will mean. King Abdullah warned, however, against allowing Shiite radicals in Iran and Iraq to represent themselves as legitimate descendants of Muhammad. Although moderates on both sides will seek to restrain the extremes, we should be aware of the potential for conflict—from verbal jousting to assassinations to the instigation, eventually, of a nuclear arms race between Sunnis and Shiites.

A related consequence of the war, also unintended, is the rising regional influence of Iran, thousands of whose citizens live in the Iraqi holy cities of An Najaf and Karbala. Many leaders of the new Iraq earlier spent years in exile in Iran, establishing close ties. In contrast to relations between Iraq and Sunni Arab capitals, which have been frosty, friendly high-level visits have been exchanged between Tehran and Baghdad; promises of cooperation, even on defense and security, have been made. The Shiite militia forces, which control security throughout southern Iraq, are virtual allies of Iran, whose intelligence and security agencies enjoy free rein. The war has already removed Iran's bitterest enemy, Saddam Hussein. Now two more of its adversaries, the United States and Sunni extremists, are engaged in a bloody confrontation. Within Iran itself, a religious conservative with fiercely anti-Israeli views scored a surprising triumph in the presidential election of 2005. From the perspective of the mullahs in Tehran, it is hard to imagine a more favorable sequence of events.

If American planners had had their way, the Shiite militias—and the Kurdish militias in the north—would long ago have disbanded or become integrated into a national army. This does not appear likely to happen soon, if ever. Instead of coming together, Iraq is in danger of falling completely apart. Although the Kurds will settle, for the time being, for a clearly marked-out autonomy, their preference—and ultimate goal—is an independent Kurdistan. The southern Shiites waited two years to declare officially their own interest in establishing an autonomous region complete with oil fields, a port (Basra) on the Persian Gulf, and a government with powers and privileges separate from

Baghdad. Although religious and ethnic politics play a big role in this sectarianism, so does money. By exercising control over borders, the various militias have ample opportunity for smuggling. By gaining jurisdiction over oil, regional leaders hope to land lucrative deals with foreign investors. If the middle of the country is left weak and poor, that is a payback for the decades during which the capital exploited the regions. For American policy makers, however, an Iraq split into three unequal parts would be unacceptable because it would also divide the region, deepening tension between Sunni Arabs and Shiites and complicating relations between Turkey and the Kurds. A divided Iraq would almost certainly lack the qualities of stability and democracy that would enable U.S. troops to depart at an early date, confident that their mission had been accomplished. American advisers have been urging Shia and Kurdish leaders to stop talking about separation and concentrate on working with the Arab Sunnis to build a single, unified country. That project will succeed only if enough Iraqis believe it is both desirable and possible, given past divisions and present crimes.

Adding to the mix is the situation faced by Iraq's Christian minority, which is nearly a million strong and includes Assyrians, Chaldean Catholics, Armenians, and Syrians. Because the Christians are associated in the minds of Muslim militants with the United States, many of their churches have been bombed. Most Iraqi Christians are determined not to be intimidated, but thousands of others have fled. The problem faced by Christian communities has been aggravated by the missionaries who eagerly followed American soldiers into Iraq.

After the battle of Baghdad, the executive administrator of the National Association of Evangelicals predicted that "Iraq will become the center for spreading the gospel of Jesus Christ to Iran, Libya, [and] throughout the Middle East. President

Bush said democracy will spread from Iraq to nearby countries. A free Iraq also allows us to spread Jesus Christ's teachings even in nations where the laws keep us out."

The Christian communities in Iraq are almost as old as Christianity itself, and they have survived by *not* trying to convert Muslims. According to the Roman Catholic bishop of Baghdad, "The way the preachers arrived here ... with soldiers ... was not a good thing. I think they had the intention that they could convert Muslims, though Christians didn't do it here for 2,000 years." No one has better intentions, and few have more courage, than missionaries willing to venture into potentially hostile areas. Given the current circumstances in Iraq, however, even the perception of Christian proselytizing is no help to U.S. policy, and proselytizing is no way to reduce the dangers faced by U.S. troops.

Despite the many unintended consequences of the U.S. invasion, the Bush administration insists it can nevertheless fulfill the president's promise to "make things better." To probe this, I attended a meeting at the White House on January 5, 2006, for all living former secretaries of state and defense. It was a distinguished group, and experienced enough to make me feel almost young. We assembled in the Roosevelt Room, where we received a determined talk from the president followed by a report via video from our ambassador in Baghdad. When the video proved partly inaudible, I was reminded of all the technical glitches that had interrupted meetings while I was in office. Even at the White House in the twenty-first century, we sometimes expect more of technology than it is able to deliver.

While we were sitting there, the president's staff distributed a brochure featuring an upbeat quotation on Iraq from Vice President Cheney and a collection of talking points about the political and military gains that were being made. After another briefing, this one from the U.S. military commander in Iraq, we were accorded the chance for a conversation with the president. The former secretaries of defense—and there are a lot of them, extending back to Robert McNamara—debated military tactics with the chief executive and expressed concern about the impact on our armed forces of their prolonged deployment overseas. When it was my turn, I thanked the president for the meeting and joined others in voicing the hope that our troops would be successful. I also shared with him my worry about the decline in America's global standing and about the extent to which Iraq is making it harder to deal with dangers elsewhere around the world. The president thanked me for my thoughts but also challenged my criticisms. We were then ushered into the Oval Office for a group photo. It had been a polite meeting but not, I fear, a productive one.

Although U.S. policy has suffered numerous setbacks in Iraq, the administration still talks of "victory." In truth, the chance for the kind of clear-cut triumph achieved during the first Gulf War probably never existed. More than three years after the invasion, Iraq's future remains murky. Both in that country and in America, there is a sense that the coalition military—by its very presence—may be doing as much to unite and sustain the insurgency as to defeat it. Even training the Iraqi military and police could backfire if those forces do not give their loyalty to leaders who represent the whole country. There is a fine line, but a significant one, between creating a true national army and just teaching a lot of people who don't like each other how to use guns.

By invading, the United States assumed a moral responsibility to help Iraq become peaceful and reasonably democratic. An Iraq that is in one piece, has legitimate leadership, and is able on its own to provide security to its people would be considered—at this point—quite an accomplishment.

That outcome is still feasible if the insurgency begins to break apart, torn by differences over tactics and targets. There is promise, as well, in the fact that many Iraqis, from all parts of the nation, are for the first time openly engaged in political activity, organizing, and debating what kind of society they want their country to be. Democracy is a powerful means for mobilizing hope. Respecting the rights of political opponents, however, can be viewed as too risky by those whose lives are dominated by fear. For decades, the people of Iraq have lived in fear—of Saddam Hussein and now the disruptions and uncertainty that have followed him. What remains of an American strategy is to reinforce hope through the workings of a representative government and the promise—eventually—of a prosperous economy. The question still to be answered is whether that strategy can succeed in the face of so many political and security challenges, and in light of the dread that many Iraqis feel both toward outsiders and each other.

Ignoring the advice of experts, President Bush gambled that invading Iraq would succeed despite the complications created by religion and history, the absence of a convincing "just war" rationale, and the consequent lack of international support. To justify the wager, he exaggerated both the dangers that Iraq's government posed and the benefits that ousting Saddam Hussein would bring. Most seriously, he promised U.S. troops that "the terrorist threat to America and the world will be diminished the moment that Saddam Hussein is disarmed." In fact, the invasion and occupation have heightened that danger.

Thirteen

Confronting Al Qaeda

I spent much of the first half of my adult life studying communist governments. During their heyday between the 1950s and early 1980s, they ruled half the world. The ideas behind communism, when cleverly packaged, held a powerful appeal. To the many people who were poor, they promised relief from the insecurities of daily life: the right to a job, education, decent health care, a place to live, and basic nutrition, all financed by efficient economies based on centralized planning.

To secure converts, communist propagandists needed a villain against which to set their own vision; they created one by holding up a fun-house mirror to the West—portraying a civilization notable not for its relative prosperity and freedom but for its racism, crime, drugs, unemployment, and exploitation. In world affairs, the West was denounced as imperialistic and aggressive, preying on less developed countries to reap profits for multinational corporations. To many in distant parts of the globe, these distortions were readily accepted. After all, most of Africa, Asia, and the

Middle East had long been subject to colonial domination; the natural resources of these regions had been pumped, mined, and harvested with little benefit to local populations. Communism failed, nevertheless, because its ideas, when put into practice, did not work. By the late 1980s, not even communist leaders could claim to be fashioning egalitarian societies or creating economic powerhouses that would "bury" the West. When the system started to collapse, it did so rapidly.

Unlike the Marxists, the leaders of Al Qaeda and its allies do not pretend to articulate a coherent economic philosophy; nor do they promise their followers better jobs, health care, or homes—though some terrorist operatives have quarreled about such items. Al Qaeda doesn't purport to be all things to all people; its goal is to seize control of a religion. Unlike communism after the Russian Revolution of 1917, Al Qaeda administers no government or defined territory; but like communism, it has been able to attract support for a reason: it explains suffering and directs anger at targets that, at least to some people, seem to deserve it.

Al Qaeda's most potent argument is that Muslims everywhere are under assault and that good Muslims are duty-bound to fight back. The terrorists compare U.S. troops in Afghanistan and Iraq to the Mongol hordes who stormed through those regions in the thirteenth century, wreaking havoc among the population, looting Muslim treasures, and destroying mosques. This thesis—that Islam is under attack—is believed not by extremists alone; on the contrary, it has become something close to conventional wisdom in Arab and Muslim-majority states. Muslims are threatened, it is thought, not only by American troops but by Zionists armed by the United States in the Middle East and by complicit regimes in the Caucasus, central Asia, Kashmir, China, the Balkans, Indonesia, the Philippines, Thailand, and parts of Africa. More humiliating still, it is alleged that much of the Arab world is ruled by apostate governments that have sold their souls to America or that have embraced atheist ideologies such as the Baathists of Syria or secularists in Turkey—ideologies at odds with the Islamic version of the "city on the hill" or "one nation under God." Islamic cultural values are also seen as endangered by the pervasive influence of the West, which is viewed as materialistic, pornographic, and superficial. This picture of the world is especially prevalent among the restless, unemployed, embittered young.

President Bush is fond of saying that Al Qaeda commits terrorist acts because it "hates freedom." Osama bin Laden has disputed this, asking why, if that were so, it has not attacked "Sweden, for example." Like President Bush, he portrays a clash between the good defender and the evil aggressor, but with the roles reversed. In 2004, one of the Defense Department's own advisory boards concluded that "Muslims do not 'hate our freedom,' but rather they hate our policies." "American actions and the flow of events," reported the panel, "have elevated the authority of the jihadi insurgents and tended to ratify their legitimacy among Muslims. What was a marginal network is now a community-wide movement." Just as communism once appealed to the world's poor as a means of defying the West, so Al Qaeda is being judged by many people based less on what it is than against whom it fights.

To lend emotional intensity to their cause, terrorist leaders hark back to the time of Muhammad, when Islamic warriors first proclaimed their faith, sweeping aside heretics and nonbelievers. The events of 9/11 were a psychological breakthrough, celebrated as "the holy attack that demolished the foolish infidel Americans and caused many young men to awaken from their deep sleep." In the time that has passed since that day, the frequency of suicide bombings has greatly increased; and the number of groups engaged in that loathsome practice has risen from half a dozen to more than thirty.

Now, say the terrorists, is the moment for true Muslims to define themselves through their actions and to secure their place in paradise by taking part in a sacred struggle. The prospective warriors are lured by the promise of fleshly delights and the expectation that they will be allowed to choose seventy friends and family members to join them in heaven. This highly credulous mind-set is made far more dangerous by twenty-first-century technology. Thousands of websites glorify the exploits of "martyrs," bewail the victimization of Muslims, and solicit new recruits. "Oh Mujahid brother, in order to join the great training camps, you don't have to travel to other lands," declares one online magazine. "Alone, in your home or with a group of your brothers, you too can begin to execute the training program." Like football fans, coin collectors, and quilters, jihadists congregate in multinational virtual communities to share the enthusiasms they have in common. For some, curiosity will grow into a commitment to act. Connections may be made to the shadowy network of terrorist recruiters who operate in parts of the Middle East, south and central Asia, North Africa, Europe, and, almost certainly, America.

Since 9/11, counterterrorism efforts led by the United States have seriously damaged Al Qaeda's network. Dozens of leaders have been killed or arrested, training camps have been dismantled, cells have been closed down, and planned attacks have been foiled. Communications are now more difficult; ringleaders must operate with extreme caution. As President Bush has said, "When terrorists spend their days and nights struggling to avoid death or capture, they are less capable of arming and training and planning new attacks." It is alarmingly apparent, however, that volunteers are stepping up to take the place of those who have been taken down or forced to lie low. In November 2005, for example, insurgents for the first time left Iraq to carry out a strike, this one in Jordan, where they killed fifty-seven people gathered at a hotel for a wedding celebration. According to an assessment by the CIA, Iraq may prove to be a more effective training ground for terrorists than Afghanistan was in the 1980s, because Iraq is serving as a real-world laboratory for urban combat. Experts fear that cadres of terrorists drawn from a score of countries are being trained in assassination, kidnapping, making bombs, and attacking fortified targets. "What we are now awaiting," says Claude Moniquet, director general of the European Strategic Intelligence and Security Center, "is the emergence of a new generation of terrorists; kids who were 12–15 years old on September 11, 2001, and who have taken a year to two to make the same ideological progress that leads to violence, and which took their elders around ten years or more."

If Al Qaeda and its allies are to be defeated, then plainly this assembly line must be shut down. That will require a political victory as decisive as the victory achieved by democracy over communism.

It should be an advantage that no government on Earth openly embraces Al Qaeda. One reason is that Al Qaeda would like to replace the current system of national states with a single religious government—a caliphate—that would command the loyalty of all Muslims. It is a rare regime that supports its own dissolution. This advantage, however, is offset by Al Qaeda's elusiveness and resilience. During the cold war, we could measure our progress on a map showing which countries belonged to the Soviet bloc, which were part of the free world, and which were aligned with neither. Gauging progress today is not as simple as making a list of bad guys and checking them off as each is captured or killed. The new recruits are joining a network that is becoming larger and more diffuse, as groups form that are inspired by Al Qaeda but not dependent on it for direction or resources. As Donald Rumsfeld complained, "We lack metrics to know if we are winning or losing the global war on terror. Are we capturing, killing or deterring and dissuading more terrorists every day than the *madrassas* and the radical clerics are recruiting, training and deploying against us?" Rumsfeld's question reminds me of "snakes and ladders," a game I played as a child and now play with my grandchildren; just when you think you're ahead, you land on a snake, slide back down, and have to begin climbing all over again.*

During the past decade, the United States has invested billions of dollars to restructure intelligence agencies, train security forces, improve surveillance capabilities overseas, and bolster homeland defense. All this is necessary; in fact, much more should be done. The truth, however, is that we have not yet figured out the best way to counter the terrorist threat. Conventional law-enforcement is insufficient while military theories about low-intensity conflict and asymmetrical fighting do not fit. Spokesmen for the administration have sought to reassure us by noting how many of Al Qaeda's leaders have been killed or captured. But as Rumsfeld's memo asks, how meaningful is this? Al Qaeda is not a criminal gang that can be rounded up on the streets or an army that can be crushed on the field of battle. It is like a virus that spreads from one infected person to

---

* Snakes and ladders originated centuries ago in India. In this Hindu game, each of the snakes was associated with a vice (such as theft or lying) and each ladder with a virtue (patience, sobriety). Reaching the end symbolized the quest for paradise, or nirvana. The newer, renamed version, "chutes and ladders," lacks this moral dimension.

another, becoming more virulent with every "sin"—real or alleged—committed by the United States.

It follows from this that America's leaders should minimize actions which terrorists can exploit to gain converts, but we have a hard time doing this. The attacks of 9/11 got our collective blood up; the spectacle of atrocities committed against U.S. servicemen and Iraqi civilians add to the emotions we feel. The terrorists want to provoke us, and they are succeeding. Consider the sentiments expressed by a retired colonel of the U.S. Army, who was speaking at the Forum on Religion and Security in Washington in the fall of 2004:

> On one front, we need to . . . capture and kill as many of the enemy as possible, show them we're the biggest, baddest, most fearsome force in the world who will stop at nothing to accomplish our mission. . . . On the other front, we need to target leaders indirectly. We need to . . . separate them from the people that follow them, and cause their internal support base to collapse. [And] we must take this two-front war on the offensive . . . all around the world. We must fight militant, radical Islam . . . from Africa to Southeast Asia, Central and South America, and Eastern Europe.

I expect that many Americans would agree with these words. I have participated in dozens of meetings about terrorism since 9/11 and have yet to hear anyone say that we should be anything other than tough in our response; and surely, the twin goals identified by the colonel—military success and isolating the bad guys—are exactly right. Separating hard-core terrorists from their base of support is essential. But how to do this? By fighting "militant radical Islam" wherever it exists? That is a recipe for exhausting our military, further alienating world opinion, and reviving the allegation that we want to refight the crusades. Surely this is too broad a target.

There are millions of politically active Muslims who believe in a narrow interpretation of Islam. Though otherwise diverse, most of these people may be antiwestern, undemocratic in their thinking, horrified by the American presence in Iraq, hostile to Israel, and eager to impose their own moral views on others; but they are terrorists only if they commit or facilitate terrorist acts. We should want to debate ideological adversaries with all the arguments at our command; but our government has no call, based simply on people's beliefs, to attack them militarily. Just as we did not shoot communists simply for being communist, we will never know peace if we fall into the trap of considering every Muslim with unwelcome political opinions a mortal foe. Our enemy isn't Islam or any variation of Islam; the enemy is Al Qaeda and its variations. As for the macho mantra that the U.S. military is big, bad, and fearsome and will "stop at nothing," that is hardly the way to persuade the Islamic silent majority to take a stand against terrorism. On the contrary, such boasting may lend support to the terrorists' assertion that they, too, are entitled to "stop at nothing."

Al Qaeda's style of terrorism will be defeated when its central arguments are understood to be lies by those most inclined to believe they are true. We cannot expect those who see themselves as defenders of Islam to abandon that self-image. We can, however, hope to persuade more of them that attacking the innocent on buses, trains, and planes is not the way to defend Islam. This message should not be hard to put across. Killing civilians, children, and fellow Muslims in the name of Islam is as rich a blend of hypocrisy and heresy as one could imagine. Communications across the cultural divide, however, are wretched. According to a study sponsored by the Defense Department, "The critical problem in American public diplomacy directed toward the Muslim world is not one of 'dissemination of information' or even one of crafting and delivering the 'right' message. Rather it is a fundamental problem of credibility. Simply, there is none—the United States today is without a working channel of communication to the world of Muslims and of Islam."

What has caused this breakdown? When the colonel talked about attacking "militant, radical Islam," he had in mind the human monsters in Iraq and elsewhere who are beheading or blowing up the innocent. His rage is understandable; we all share it. Responsible Muslim leaders around the world have condemned the killing of civilians in this or any other manner. But many Muslims are focused, as well, on the faces of noncombatants, including women and children, accidentally killed in the course of American military operations. The estimated number of civilians killed by coalition forces in Iraq ranges from 30,000 to as high as 100,000. If we also take into account the thousands more who have been wounded, whose houses have been destroyed or whose lives have been disrupted by U.S. military operations, we should not marvel at the bitter attitudes that have come to exist.

Muslims also have in mind the mistreatment of prisoners in Iraq, Afghanistan, and Guantánamo. The abuses at Abu Ghraib and other American detention facilities are inexcusable. Some will argue that they do not register heavily on the scale of human atrocities committed through the ages, nor compare to the many outrages committed by Al Qaeda and by Iraqi insurgents. There is, however, a reason why the Vatican's foreign minister called the prison scandal "an offense to God," and "a more serious blow to the U.S. than 9/11."

The issue of torture is simpler to think about in principle than in practice. Those of us who remember Vietnam also remember the demands by American authorities that North Vietnam be made to adhere to the Geneva Conventions regarding the treatment of prisoners of war. Ever since Jimmy Carter made human rights a priority for the United States, the State Department has regularly chastised foreign governments for holding prisoners in secret, denying them due process, or refusing to let them have access to humanitarian organizations. According to President Bush, mistreating prisoners is not the way we do things in America. But the reality is more complex. Especially after 9/11, U.S. officials were in no mood to observe legal niceties, and the American public did little to hold them accountable. Our anger at seeing the twin towers crumble produced an implicit question: why shouldn't we inflict pain on enemies who are out to destroy us, especially if by so doing we might obtain information that could save innocent lives? After all, a decade ago authorities in the Philippines reportedly used torture to make suspects talk, thereby foiling a plot to hijack airplanes. American popular culture, moreover, has long worshipped the kind of character typically portrayed by John Wayne or Clint Eastwood: the tough guy who makes villains pay regardless of the rules.

In 2005, the hero of the popular television drama *24* used torture repeatedly to obtain information in order to protect America from terror attacks. In this drama, when the president refused to authorize torture, he was portrayed as weak. When a human rights lawyer protested, he was shown to be a dupe of the evildoers. The deck was stacked in favor of torture: the person being abused was obviously a villain; the information being withheld was vital; time was of the essence; and the torturer, handsome and manly, was "only doing his job." The manipulations of television aside, many of us—if we are honest with ourselves—can at least imagine real-life circumstances in which the use of coercive measures to extract information would seem justified.

Since 9/11, this question has attracted much attention from experts on ethics and law. Professor Alan Dershowitz of Harvard caused a ruckus by calling for a system in which torture, like a wiretap, could be authorized by a judge when presented with due cause.* Such an idea is not likely to go far. America, like most countries, is on record as denouncing torture. In 2003 and 2004, memos of the Justice Department surfaced that seemed to legitimize torture; but the Bush administration quickly distanced itself from that interpretation. As a matter of principle, we will remain firmly opposed to torture. As a matter of fact, we may still have mixed feelings.

This is not good enough. We need to think the issue through. First of all, real life is not like *24.* It is an illusion to believe that torture is a generally effective means of obtaining accurate information. Torture may work sometimes but usually it does not. Napoleon, no bleeding heart, observed more than two centuries ago, "The barbarous custom of having men beaten who are suspected of having important secrets to reveal must be abolished. It has always been recognized that this way of interrogating men, by putting them to torture, produces nothing worthwhile."

Second, as John McCain has argued, this debate is not about what our enemies are like; it is about us. If we rationalize torture or make exceptions for special circumstances,

---

* Dershowitz does not advocate torture. He argues instead that authorities are likely to engage in the practice in extreme cases and that it is better for them to do so within the legal system than outside it. "If we are to have torture," he wrote in the *Los Angeles Times* on November 8, 2001, "it should be authorized by the law."

so will everybody else. Governments that routinely abuse prisoners will point to the United States for justification. Our standing to insist on the humane treatment of Americans in foreign prisons will be diminished. America will be known as the kind of country that tortures people or that arranges for others to do so. For what purpose? To defeat the terrorists? The effect will be just the opposite. Guantánamo has presumably kept some members of the terrorist class of 2002 out of action, but at the cost of significantly enlarging the class of 2006. The detention center there should have been shut down long ago. As for Abu Ghraib, it was the biggest gift Al Qaeda's propagandists could have received.

What has been singularly appalling is that so many of those who were abused appear to have been either innocent or not in a position to know much. There is profound ugliness in the spectacle of American guards doing their best to humiliate and hurt Arab men simply because they have the power to do so and were in need of entertainment. While most U.S. soldiers were seeking to build bridges of understanding and friendship to Muslims, the guards and interrogators—and those who gave them their instructions—were showing contempt for Arab culture and basic human rights. Their actions seemed designed to aggravate the feeling of many Muslims that they are victims who are under attack.

It is hard for those of us who believe in America's goodness to admit mistakes, but these abuses were serious and cannot be ameliorated by a few light punishments for those near the bottom of the chain of command. There must be accountability at the top. Otherwise, it will be virtually impossible for us to soften the harshly negative perception of the United States that so many Muslims have developed. In the time since the first photos from Abu Ghraib appeared, pamphlets have circulated in Arab communities showing those shameful images along with pictures of dead Palestinian and Iraqi children. "Where Are the Men?" reads the headline above the pictures, "Who Will Avenge Our Dignity?" In a region of long memories, I fear these images will be fueling anti-American violence for generations to come.

I know from experience that our military goes to extraordinary lengths to avoid civilian casualties. At the same time, political leaders can put our armed forces into situations where significant civilian casualties are virtually inevitable. The result can turn military success into political defeat. As in Vietnam, the battles may be won, but the war is not. Without an effective political strategy, the United States cannot defeat Al Qaeda.

That strategy should begin with confidence. Bin Laden and his cohort have nothing real to offer anybody. The attacks of 9/11 gave them a visibility and a following that they do not deserve and that they will not be able to maintain in the absence of further mistakes on our part. Our job is to keep the spotlight on their nihilism, cruelty, and lies. If we do that, we will ultimately attract the support we need. Being confident, however, does not excuse complacency. We must argue our case before even the toughest audiences.

The U.S. National Commission on the 9/11 attacks concluded:

> Bin Laden and Islamist terrorists mean exactly what they say: to them America is the font of all evil, the "head of the snake," and it must be converted or destroyed. It is not a position with which Americans can bargain or negotiate. With it there is no common

ground—not even respect for life—on which to begin a dialogue. It can only be destroyed or utterly isolated.

The commission is unquestionably right to identify bin Laden and his ilk as irredeemable, and yet the commission also tells us that the decision to launch the attacks of 9/11 was far from unanimous. Mullah Omar, the Taliban leader, was reported to have opposed striking the United States, fearing retaliation. Al Qaeda's chief financial manager sided with Omar. Al Qaeda's leading theologian said that the attacks were contrary to the Quran. The longtime spiritual mentor of Abu Musab al-Zarqawi, the leader of the foreign insurgents in Iraq, has broken with him over the issue of suicide bombings against civilians. These differences of opinion do not mean that the West should seek to "negotiate" with Al Qaeda; it does mean that within the terrorist networks there is a diversity of views, which we should do our utmost to exploit.

Many, perhaps most, of the people who are recruited as terrorists are beyond the reach of logical argument or appeals to conscience, but some may still be what I learned in college to describe as "rational actors." It may be possible to convince them that killing noncombatants offends, rather than defends, Islam; or they may find it harder than others to leave family and friends behind; or they may be motivated primarily by local goals and have little interest in taking on the United States or the entire West. Some may even be susceptible to offers of jobs or other material benefits. It helps us not at all to treat terror networks as a monolith. Like other groups, they comprise individuals who should not be abandoned without a fight. In Yemen since 2002, Islamic scholars have challenged imprisoned members of Al Qaeda to debate their tactics in light of the Quran, convincing more than 350 to renounce violence and cooperate with the authorities. Judge Hamoud al-Hitar, who conceived this effort, explains, "If you study terrorism in the world, you will see that it has an intellectual theory behind it, and any kind of intellectual idea can be defeated by intellect." In other words, the best way to defeat a bad idea is with a good idea.

It matters that Islam places such an enormous emphasis on law. In Amman in 2005, 180 Muslim scholars from forty-five countries (including the United States) representing eight schools of Islamic thought convened a conference on "True Islam." Their purpose was to discredit self-promoting zealots who issue fatwas without being qualified to do so, and who seek to justify violence against other Muslims by dismissing the victims as apostates. The scholars sought to turn the excesses committed by terrorists against them and to apply Islamic law in a manner that exposes the yawning gap between the terrorists' holy pretensions and their unholy actions. Ultimately, this is how terrorism will be defeated, by real Muslims uniting to protect Islam from the murderers who are trying to steal it.

Confronting Al Qaeda will require the full range of our foreign policy tools, including our intelligence assets and our military. There are certain to be times when terrorist targets of opportunity are exposed and deadly force should be used. It would be a mistake, however, to believe that terrorism is primarily a military threat. If it were, it would have been defeated long ago. It is primarily a political and psychological challenge and must be opposed in political and psychological terms. Nothing the United States does will alleviate the hatred that some Arabs and Muslims feel, but it is not necessary to change the thinking of everyone.

According to Václav Havel, "Communism was not defeated by military force, but by life, by the human spirit, by conscience, by the resistance of Being and man to manipulation." It was defeated, in other words, because those who opposed it were able to summon the better aspects of human nature to expose its lies and wear it down. Terrorists may still succeed on occasion in penetrating barriers designed to keep them out. But they can never succeed, unless we let them, in separating us from the values that, over the long term, hold the key to their downfall and our success.

The ending of the cold war was televised. Sitting in my study, I saw students dancing on the glorious wreck of the Berlin Wall and raucous crowds celebrating in the newly free capital cities of central and east Europe. I recall especially my joy at the spectacle in Wenceslas Square in Prague, where Václav Havel and other heroes of the "velvet revolution" accepted the call to lead Czechoslovakia into a time of independence and liberty. "This is it," I said to myself at the time. "Thank God."

How will our confrontation with terror end? Quite differently, one presumes. There may be spectacular events. Perhaps in the time it takes for this book to be published, we will have finally seen bin Laden's capture or demise. In Iraq, al-Zarqawi may already be yesterday's news. Certainly there will continue to be attacks, arrests, and takedowns. It seems unlikely, however, that we will ever see the equivalent of the celebration in Wenceslas Square. I doubt that we will be able to turn on our televisions one day and say, "This is it." In the worst case, we will see a constant drumbeat of attacks (some possibly involving biological or even nuclear weapons) against an expanding list of targets. We may see more areas, conceivably entire countries, become havens for violent extremism. We could see Islam further divided between the followers of a peaceful faith and those whose minds have been poisoned by hate.

In the best case, we will see the opposite: a reduction in the number of attacks, a shrinkage of areas where terrorists have support, a closing of the ranks within Islam. If that should happen, our confrontation will end with a nonevent: bin Laden, or his successor, will videotape a threat to incinerate us, and nobody will broadcast it, because the terrorists lack even a smidgen of public backing. Will we ever get to this point? The answer to that question will become clear only gradually and will be based on events in a broad area, extending from the Malay Archipelago to the mountains of the Caucasus to the coast of North Africa. Most important will be the Arab world, where Islam was born; and within that world, the country whose direction will likely matter most is the kingdom of Saudi Arabia.

Fourteen

The Saudi Dilemma

———— ⌁ ————

I am scared," said one Saudi Arabian during the summer of
2004. "There is no clear vision to where my country is
heading. We want to progress, but we also want to live like
good Muslims did 1,400 years ago. We want to change, but
we believe that change is the road to hell. We want the people to have a role in leading the country, but we don't want
democracy. We want to have dialogue with the West, but our
preachers are preaching every Friday that all Westerners or
non-Muslims go to hell."

The founder and uniter of modern Saudi Arabia, King Ibn
Saud, declared early in the twentieth century: "My kingdom
will survive only insofar as it remains a country difficult of
access, where the foreigner will have no other aim, with his
task fulfilled, but to get out." A statement issued by the
Saudi royal family early in the twenty-first century asserted
the contrary: "We are part of this world and cannot be dis-
connected from it. We cannot be mere spectators while the
rest of the world is progressing toward a new global system."

Since the attacks of 9/11, a small library's worth of books

and articles have appeared in the West suggesting that Saudi Arabia is, essentially, evil—the birthplace, breeder, and banker of terror committed in the name of Islam. As the quotations above suggest, a more apt term than "evil" might be "confused."

No country has tried to leap more suddenly into the modern age than Saudi Arabia. Few countries have been less well-equipped psychologically to make that leap. Saudi culture has been heavily influenced by Wahhabism, a puritanical Sunni movement that originated in the eighteenth century and became firmly established when the house of Saud conquered the Arabian Peninsula in the 1920s. Proponents of Wahhabi doctrine sought to return to what they considered pure, authentic Islam.* They imposed a sort of national uniform—white for men and black for women—banned music, and drained the country of much of its regional and cultural diversity. The result is a rigidly controlled society whose public places are monitored by religious police and where public displays of affection (even familial affection) between the sexes are forbidden, dancing is outlawed, and women in urban areas are not allowed to drive. The kingdom's very identity is centered on its status as custodian of the holy mosques in Mecca, where the Prophet Muhammad was born; and Medina, where he is entombed. This status inspires pride but also an emphasis on conformity. Worship is restricted for Shiite Muslims and prohibited for non-Muslims. Non-Muslim adults cannot even be buried in Saudi soil. Ninety percent of the books published in the kingdom deal with religious topics, and

---

* Because the term "Wahhabi" has developed negative connotations, many practitioners prefer to be known as "Salafists," followers who seek to model themselves after the first three generations of Muslims.

most university graduates receive their degrees in Islamic studies. The country has no written constitution other than the Quran.* Its ideal is to be an island of purity, separate from and untainted by the vulgarity of the West.

And yet Saudi Arabia also sits atop a quarter of the world's petroleum reserves, a mixed blessing that has brought the Saudis into intimate and highly materialistic contact with industrial nations. The oil has long provided a measure of wealth, and the price shocks of the 1970s multiplied those riches many times. Western entrepreneurs, eager to cash in, signed billions of dollars in construction, technology, and service contracts with the Saudis. As the petrodollars piled up, Saudi princes became familiar figures at international nightspots, dressed in the most stylish clothes, their wives in designer fashions. Two decades earlier, a prince might have lived in a modest mud house, with space set aside for receiving petitions from the public. In the new era, that same prince built palatial estates, filled them with expensive furniture and electronic gadgets, and surrounded them with high walls.

The Iranian revolution of 1979 threatened to spoil the party. Almost as soon as he took power, Ayatollah Khomeini called for an uprising against the Saudi government, which he described as "un-Islamic." The threat became real in November of that year, when militants staged a dramatic protest and took hostages at the Grand Mosque in Mecca. The rebels denounced the royal family as corrupt and demanded its overthrow. Following a three-week siege, Saudi security forces made a concentrated attack, killing some of the insurgents and capturing the rest, who were

---

* In 1992, the Saudis did, however, establish a "basic law of government" that is in some ways analogous to a constitution.

later beheaded. The government then sought to regain the loyalty of the religious establishment by giving it full control over education and granting it authority to police the behavior of citizens and visitors. The Saudi social code became more restrictive, further empowering the most conservative elements of society. These trends were reinforced by extremist scholars from Syria and Egypt, who, fleeing the hostility of their secular governments, brought with them a commitment to pan-Islamic radicalism that was more activist and political than the traditional agenda of the Wahhabis.

Meanwhile, the boom in oil prices transformed Saudi Arabia into the ultimate welfare state. By the late 1980s, every Saudi was entitled to free medical care and higher education. Any college graduate, male or female, was eligible for a $50,000 grant to start a small business. Upon reaching adulthood, each young man received a plot of land plus a construction loan of $80,000. Electricity and water were provided without charge. The Saudis and their advisers expected the good times to last. They did not. The country was brought low by its failure to plan ahead, its spendthrift ways—and a baby boom.

Between 1981 and 2001, the Saudi population more than doubled. If Saudi women continue to bear children at the present average rate (seven each), the population will double again by 2020. When all these young people go looking for jobs, many will be disappointed. Unemployment has risen to 20 percent while per capita production is lower than it was forty years ago. The country's oil revenues, equal to $22,000 per Saudi in 1980, dropped to $4,000 in 2004 despite record high prices. Once glistening Saudi cities have taken on the look of cities elsewhere, marred by dirty neighborhoods and overcrowded slums.

While the social pressures have mounted, the contrast

between western and Islamic lifestyles has been apparent to all. The newly widespread phenomenon of satellite television, combined with images of Arabs' and Muslims' suffering, have nurtured anti-western sentiments. Through the 1990s, American military forces were stationed in the kingdom to deter Saddam Hussein from once again invading Kuwait. This perceived desecration of the Holy Land created a casus belli for Osama bin Laden and Al Qaeda.

The convergence of these factors acquired new meaning after 9/11. Suddenly, Saudi Arabia—where fifteen of the nineteen hijackers had been born—no longer fit the stereotype of a rich and orderly society. In the time since, the house of Saud has come under siege from all sides. While some in the West accuse the royal family of supporting terror, Al Qaeda condemns it for colluding with the West. Al Qaeda says that the monarchy is illegitimate; President Bush's rhetoric about transforming and democratizing the Middle East, if taken to its logical conclusion, raises the same question. Domestically, the regime is facing pressure for wider political openness from un-enfranchised women, reform-minded intellectuals, the Shia minority, and the frustrated young. Conservative religious elements are fighting against any change that would reduce their influence. Almost everyone seems to want a more prominent voice in how and for whose benefit the country is run.

The Saudi government has found itself in the middle of a minefield. To navigate its way out, it will have to isolate and discredit those among its clerics who provide a rationale for terrorism. It will have to modernize its economy, create hundreds of thousands of new jobs, and reassess its attitude toward women. It must provide effective answers to critics in the West without seeming to validate Al Qaeda's allegation that it is too close to the West. All this is a tall order for a society whose most powerful leaders are in their seventies and eighties and who were brought up to expect a life of relative isolation based on old customs and simple truths.

Was the Saudi government responsible for 9/11? No. Is it in league with Al Qaeda? Of course not. Is it sinister that groups of Saudi nationals departed the United States on charter flights a few days after 9/11? Not according to the independent 9/11 commission, which found that every passenger was screened by the FBI and that "no one with known links to terrorism departed on these flights." The Saudi leaders are preservationists, not radicals; above all else, they prize stability. The connection between Saudi culture and the rise of Al Qaeda, however, goes beyond the question whether the government itself is implicated in terrorism. One cause for alarm is the extent to which private Saudi money has helped to finance terrorist operations. A second is whether Saudi leaders have inadvertently assumed the role of Dr. Frankenstein, creating a monster they are unable to control.

In 1986, King Fahd of Saudi Arabia formally changed his title from "His Majesty" to "Custodian of the Two Holy Mosques." Fahd (who died in August 2005) was proud of precisely what makes me nervous—the support his government has given to Islamic institutions overseas, including some 210 Islamic centers, more than 1,500 mosques, 200 colleges, and almost 2,000 schools. The Saudis are confident that their faith is the true one and thus see no inconsistency in subsidizing their own religion abroad and at the same time prohibiting the practice of other religions at home. In our discussions, Saudi officials made much of the kingdom's status as the protector and defender of Islam. This reflects their own sense of exceptionalism and a duty, as they see it, to propagate their faith. Whether this is a proper reason for pride, however, will depend on how and by whom that faith is being interpreted. During my meetings before 9/11, the Saudis reacted indignantly to any suggestion that Muslim terror networks were gaining strength. They viewed such allegations as an attempt to discredit Islam.

In light of what has happened since, the Saudis have to look at their responsibilities from a different perspective. It is true that some writers in America, Europe, and Israel have distorted Islamic beliefs and Saudi policies while pontificating with scarcely concealed bigotry about Arab culture. The real damage to Islam, however, is coming from the murderers who masquerade as pious Muslims, creating an ugly distortion of the faith. If Saudi Arabia is to lead in defending Islam, these are the enemies it must first defeat.

In Riyadh, the capital of Saudi Arabia, the initial reaction to the attacks of 9/11 was denial. Despite Osama bin Laden's role and the nationality of the majority of hijackers, Saudi officials did not want to admit that Al Qaeda had a significant presence in their kingdom. They saw this as a matter of public relations, not security. Then, on May 12, 2003, three terrorist bombings killed thirty-five people in Riyadh. In November, terrorist explosions rocked a housing complex there. In May 2004, gunmen murdered twenty-two people in a residential compound for oil industry workers in Khobar. The following month, again in Riyadh, kidnappers seized and executed Paul Johnson, an American contractor. In December that same year, gunmen attacked the U.S. consulate in Jeddah, killing five employees.

Even the Saudi authorities could not ignore such acts of violence; the government arrested hundreds of suspected terrorists; engaged in bloody shoot-outs with cells linked to Al Qaeda; and seized caches of illicit travel documents, grenades, and guns. Saudi officials also finally recognized— at least implicitly—the connection between what was happening in their streets and what was being taught in their mosques. More than 3,500 imams were required to attend programs of reeducation designed to promote tolerance within Islam. Clerics were encouraged to preach about the danger of exaggeration in religion. Passages promoting violence against non-Muslims were removed from school textbooks. Under pressure from the United States, the Saudis enacted laws to curb money laundering and track the flow of Saudi funds to suspect charities.

The Saudi press is far from free, but within limits it is host to an increasingly vigorous debate. Diatribes against Israel are mixed with introspective discussions about the meaning and obligations of Islam. The managing editor of one daily paper, a childhood friend of bin Laden, has written a denunciation of those who use the Quran to condemn all Christians and Jews. Numerous columnists have lambasted Al Qaeda for trying to portray Islam as a religion of war. Abdel Rahman al-Rashad, general manager of the satellite news channel Al Arabiya, has declared:

> It is a certain fact that not all Muslims are terrorists, but it is equally certain, and exceptionally painful, that almost all terrorists are Muslims. . . . We cannot tolerate in our midst those who abduct journalists, murder civilians, explode buses; we cannot accept them as related to us, whatever the sufferings they claim to justify their criminal deeds. These are the people who have smeared Islam and stained its image.

On the official level, Saudi leaders have been vehement in denouncing terrorism as "a global crime perpetrated by evil minds filled with hatred toward humanity." The kingdom's clerics appear regularly on television to denounce terror as contrary to Islam. These declarations are welcome, but the rest of us will not relax until we are satisfied that neither Saudi funds nor Saudi doctrines are being used to foster a future generation of Al Qaeda recruits. It is discouraging that Saudi officials insist on denying that violent extremists have much backing in their country; a poll conducted privately by the kingdom found 49 percent support for bin Laden's ideas. Equally disturbing, more than two dozen prominent Saudi clerics, most of whom lecture at state-supported universities, issued a fatwa in November 2004 calling on Iraq "to defend itself, its honor, its land, its oil, its present, and its future against the imperialist coalition, just as it resisted British colonialism in the past." The signatories argued that "jihad against the occupier is the obligation of any able person."* It should be no surprise that many of the foreign suicide bombers in Iraq come from Saudi Arabia.

In February 2005, I took part in the Jeddah Economic Forum. The event was held in an enormous hotel ballroom; the audience was a sea of men in white robes. Along one side of the room was a wall of mirrors, adding to the impression of size. In my remarks, I congratulated the Saudis on their decision to hold competitive municipal elections (which were under way at the time) and said that I hoped women would be given the right to vote in Saudi Arabia more rapidly than they had been in the United States.

To my surprise, these words elicited a vigorous round of applause. When I looked at the audience in front of me,

---

* The communiqué, issued on November 5, 2004, was denounced by the Saudi ambassadors to the United States and Great Britain. Numerous Saudi columnists condemned the fatwa for seeming to encourage their country's youth to go to Iraq to fight. Supporters of the communiqué praised it for urging unity between the Sunnis and Shiites in Iraq and for discouraging violence against noncombatants, including foreigners such as journalists and aid workers.

however, nobody was clapping. The sea of men was not generating any waves. Instead, the applause was coming from behind the mirrors; that's where the Saudi women were congregated. Separated as always from the men, they were invisible—but, having access to microphones, far from inaudible. When the Saudi labor minister claimed that women like the policy of gender separation in the workplace and had no interest in being allowed to drive, the women asked why he thought that; when he referred to all the e-mail he had received, they asked for his e-mail address. Women make up half of the Saudis' university population, but less than a tenth of the country's workforce. Sooner or later, these educated women—potentially an enormous national asset—will find broader expression outside the home.

During the discussion in Jeddah, one Saudi man rose to assure me that his country's policies toward women were based on a desire not to repress but rather to respect. "We believe women sit at the feet of the gates of heaven," he said, "Our only goals are to honor our women and to protect them." I said that I understood this and did not think the West had all the answers. I added, "I do, however, believe in the right of people to make basic choices. If women had alternatives, perhaps many would decide to live the way they do now. But women, as much as men, should have the chance to decide for themselves. They are adults, not children, and should be treated accordingly. What are you men afraid of anyway? No one is interested in starting a war of the sexes."

As a teenager, when I went on my first dates with boys who had automobiles, my father insisted on following along in our family's car. The Saudi system is similarly overprotective, except that the father is actually in the vehicle sitting next to the boy, with the girl in the back, behind a curtain.

I had a chance during my visit to renew acquaintances with Crown Prince Abdullah; this was about six months before he succeeded King Fahd, who had been ill for a long time. Although Abdullah is in his early eighties, he remains physically strong and full of life. He has a thick mustache and a goatee, both still black; and a quiet, dignified way of speaking. When I told him I was writing this book, he smiled approvingly and pointed to the green-covered copy of the Quran that sits beside him in his office.

During our discussion, he made plain his horror at the distorted picture some people have created of Islam, which he characterized as a religion of peace and compassion. He said that Christianity, Judaism, and Islam all attract their share of extreme elements, and that there are some Christian conservatives who feel they need to create a crisis in order to bring about Armageddon. I wondered if the Quran prohibited Muslims from ceding land they had once ruled. He said that there was nothing so rigid, except for special areas and holy sites. I asked him, "In this highly religious society, what role do you think God plays in the administration of the kingdom?" He replied, "Faith is a constant, but you do not go to God before you consult with friends, advisers, the public, and foreign countries. Then you rely on God to help you make the right decisions, and pray that everything turns out well." When I questioned him about Iraq, he grimaced slightly and said, "Perhaps we should change the subject."

Throughout this latest visit to Saudi Arabia, I found a startling difference from earlier trips. The prevailing attitude had been that every important question was already decided. Now, everything is in flux; the political atmosphere, long stagnant, is alive with speculation and argument; Saudi politics have acquired the attributes of drama.

During the past several years, the house of Saud has responded to calls for reform without yielding to them, parceling out progress in the thinnest of slices. That pace may accelerate because of Abdullah's new role. While still crown prince, he sponsored a series of national meetings on the rights of religious minorities and women, created a federal center for dialogue, and authorized competitive municipal elections. As king, he ordered the Jeddah Trade and Industry Chamber to allow female candidates for election to its board, and two were chosen. He has allocated $3.3 billion to modernize the Saudi education system and curriculum. On the economic side, he has brought Saudi Arabia into the World Trade Organization, an accomplishment he can use to justify anticorruption measures, reorganization of the country's sleepy bureaucracy, and educational improvements in such secular subjects as engineering, science, and mathematics.

More dramatically, within days of becoming king, Abdullah pardoned three activists who had been jailed for eighteen months for advocating a new constitution. This was an obvious rebuff to the official who had ordered the arrests, Prince Nayef, the interior minister. Nayef has long made it his business to promote the agenda of religious conservatives. Abdullah is a cautious reformer in a country where any kind of reform can seem radical. He is restrained by powerful rivals and bound by his family's tradition of making decisions by consensus. His policies are likely to produce not a series of bold steps but rather a sideways shuffle, inching ahead in some areas—elections, more options for women, economic change—before pausing to see if lightning strikes.

The Saudi dilemma and the associated challenge for the West may well prove intractable, but it must be confronted nonetheless. The country's economic position as a source of oil and an arbiter of oil prices will continue long after the reserves of most other suppliers have been exhausted. The kingdom's religious leaders still have much to say about how young Sunni Muslims are taught to view the world.

American leaders will be pushed by Congress, the public, and the press to take a tough stance with the Saudis on issues related to terrorism. However, America has less leverage than it once had. The Saudis no longer depend on the United States for technological expertise; and the importance of America as a customer for oil is diminishing as other countries buy more. Unless present security concerns ease, fewer Saudis will want to experience the indignities required to gain entry to the United States, and fewer Americans will travel to Saudi Arabia. Military-to-military contacts will become less frequent. If the negative perceptions on both sides persist, U.S. and Saudi leaders will gain little politically from helping each other.

The Saudis do not, however, feel comfortable in the role in which some have cast them: "a sort of oily heart of darkness," suggested one writer, "the wellspring of a bleak, hostile value system." They would surely be pleased with a return to a more relaxed time, when our two countries were on the same side in the biggest battles and were able to work around our differences regarding the Middle East. We should encourage the Saudis to restore that kind of relationship by persevering in their efforts to purge Al Qaeda, by denying funds to terrorists, and by seizing every chance to remind their citizens and coreligionists abroad that killing unarmed people is contrary to Arab values and no way to earn a place in paradise.

The philosophical battle in Saudi Arabia revolves around the fundamental question of what kind of country its people wish it to be: an isolated bastion ruled by conservative traditions or a modern country (albeit a deeply religious one) that is open to, and part of, the world. While some Saudis are eager to explore the boundaries of what Islam permits, others are determined to enforce as many limits as possible. Not surprisingly, many Saudis find themselves unable to line up unambiguously on one side or the other. The need for modernization is widely acknowledged, but so is the fear of losing control. This debate and the accompanying hopes and fears are echoed throughout much of the Arab world and many other Muslim societies. The resulting turbulence is the product of a momentous and inherently complex encounter between two profound ideas: that all power comes from God, and that legitimate authority on Earth comes from the people.

Fifteen

Arab Democracy

———— ᴗᵔᴗ ————

In July 1957, John F. Kennedy, at the time the junior U.S. senator from Massachusetts, declared that "the most powerful force in the world today is neither communism nor capitalism, nor the guided missile—it is man's eternal desire to be free and independent.

"The great enemy of that tremendous force for freedom," he continued, "is called, for want of a more precise term, imperialism. Thus the single most important test of American foreign policy today is how we meet the challenge of imperialism, what we do to further man's desire to be free."

In the depths of the cold war, Kennedy—remarkably—identified not communism but imperialism as America's premier foreign policy test. He did so at a moment when Algerian freedom fighters were engaged in a life-and-death struggle for independence from France, causing French leaders to decry his "rash intervention" in their affairs. The elder statesman of the Democratic Party, Adlai Stevenson, agreed, calling Kennedy's speech "terrible," an "invitation to chaos," and a threat to NATO. But independence was an idea whose time had come; Algeria achieved it in 1962. By then Kennedy was president, intent on putting the United States firmly on the side of liberty for colonized peoples throughout the developing world, a significant part of which was Muslim. When Kennedy spoke of man's desire to be free, he meant the yearning of nations to escape foreign domination. But independence provides no guarantee that people will also be free from repression by their own governments; establishing that kind of freedom is a separate and sometimes an even harder challenge.

In November 2003, President Bush announced that the United States would pursue "a forward strategy for freedom in the Middle East." Speaking before an audience gathered to celebrate the twentieth anniversary of the National Endowment for Democracy, Bush argued that "stability cannot be purchased at the expense of liberty. As long as the Middle East remains a place where freedom does not flourish, it will remain a place of stagnation, resentment, and violence ready for export. And with the spread of weapons that can bring catastrophic harm to our country and to our friends, it would be reckless to accept the status quo."

Having championed democracy for as long as I can remember, I welcomed the president's speech and agreed with its premise. Many of the countries that gained their independence from colonial rule simply exchanged foreign despotism for the homegrown kind. The Middle East is the only region where heads of government (as opposed to heads of state) still derive authority from their bloodlines. If President Bush is serious about challenging that tradition, he could alter relations between the United States and Arab governments and peoples for decades to come.

Supporting democracy in the Middle East is, however, much simpler in word than in deed. The State Department's original plan for the democratization of the Arab world was disclosed to the press before governments in the region had even been consulted, a diplomatic faux pas that elicited protests and allegations of arrogance. In Morocco in December 2004, Arab and western governments convened a "Forum for the Future" to discuss the need for democratic change, but while U.S. officials talked about opening the political process, Arab leaders stressed the need to end the U.S. occupation of Iraq and resolve the Israeli-Palestinian dispute. The view taken by the United States, then and now, is that extremism results from political frustration and that people become terrorists because they are unable to achieve change by other means. Arab officials insist that terrorism is a product of anger at U.S. actions, not a result of the Arabs' own undemocratic practices—and that the way to achieve stability is to alter American policies. This opinion is not restricted to Arab princes and kings. In Dubai in December 2005, I met with a group of young Muslim women, most of whom were dressed head to toe in black and expressed views that were decidedly feminist. When I made the point that the status quo in the Middle East is dangerous, one woman stood and made a point of her own. "It wasn't dangerous until the United States made it so."

In a region where conspiracy theories flourish, there is widespread suspicion about the intentions of the Bush administration. The proposition that America would back democracy because it has the best interests of Arabs at heart is not widely believed. Each side accuses the other, justly, of trying to change the subject: American officials would rather talk about the need for Arab governments to reform than the plight of the Palestinians; Arab leaders would rather talk about almost anything except democracy.

The president is right to try to correct the impression that America stands for freedom everywhere except in Arab countries, not least because there has been some truth to it. For decades, Republican and Democratic administrations alike have had good reason to seek smooth relations with autocratic Arab leaders. The governments of strategically vital countries such as Saudi Arabia and Egypt valued stability; so did the United States. The Arabs produced oil; American consumers demanded it. The Arabs wanted advanced technology; U.S. companies were eager to sell it. During the cold war, America needed Arab support against the Soviet Union. In the 1990s, the Clinton administration sought the backing of Arab governments for the Middle East peace process. These Arab governments, imperfect though they were, seemed preferable to likely alternatives. After all, we had our hands full with Saddam Hussein in Iraq, Muammar Qaddafi in Libya, and a theocratic regime in Iran. Although many of these practical considerations remain, the time is ripe for a new approach. One of Al Qaeda's major arguments is that the United States is propping up governments that are corrupt, illegitimate, repressive, and heretical. One way to rebut that is by honoring our ideals and supporting democratic reforms in every country that lacks freedom.

This is not a matter of trying to impose our system on people who don't want it. Islam teaches its followers to take the best from other civilizations; democracy is a big part of what is best about the West. Surveys have found that Arab and Muslim populations generally favor such concepts as freedom of expression, multiparty systems, and equal treatment under the law. Most say it is more important for a leader to be democratic than strong. Perhaps that is why democracy is already making inroads. The tiny emirate of Qatar has a new constitution that provides for a consultative assembly and protects religious liberty, freedom of the press, and women's rights. Kuwait's parliament, after years of rejecting the proposal, has finally granted women the right to vote. In 2003, Jordan and Yemen conducted legislative elections that were, if flawed, still partly competitive and reasonably free. The Palestinian Authority has held elections both for president and parliament. Most Arab countries now have some kind of representative legislative or advisory body, though its powers are often modest. Throughout the region, there is a sense that the old ways are changing, to be replaced by something not yet fully defined, but new.

The Bush administration had hoped that Iraq would emerge as a democratic model that other Arabs would be eager to emulate. Perhaps one day they will. However, given the daily spectacle of political infighting and violence in the streets, it may be some time before most Arabs look at Iraq and think, "I wish my country could be like that." So as yet there is no fully satisfactory Arab model of democracy.* In 1992, King Fahd of Saudi Arabia explained that "the election system has no place in the Islamic creed, which calls for a government of advice and consultation and for the shepherd's openness to his flock." This argument—that democracy is un-Islamic—may be convenient for Arab monarchs, but it carries little weight. The Arab tradition of consultation, referred to by Fahd, can readily be stretched to encompass democratic principles provided the will exists to do so. Certainly, outside the Arabian Peninsula Islam has been no barrier to political freedom; half the world's Muslims live under elected governments—in places such as Indonesia, India, Bangladesh, Malaysia, and Turkey.

Islam is no barrier to liberty, but neither is it irrelevant to the prospects for actually achieving democratic change. In countries where Islam is interpreted conservatively, there is a risk that democracy—especially when promoted in a triumphal way by the United States—will not be welcomed as

---

* Egypt between the two world wars developed a functioning multiparty system, but this vanished when the military seized power in 1952.

a companion to Islam but feared as a proposed replacement. Confusion about the intent behind certain words adds to the problem. Some Muslims, like some Christians and Jews, tend to equate the term "secular" with "godless," not accepting that one can be religious and still approach many matters of state without specific reference to religion. "To be a secularist," one expert writes, "has meant to . . . reject altogether not only religious faith but also its attendant morality and the traditions and rules that operate within Muslim societies." This perception has undoubtedly been strengthened by the experience of Muslims under such heavy-handed secular leaders as Nasser in Egypt and the shah in Iran.

These and other issues create an opening for some Muslims to argue that democracy is being advanced for the express purpose of weakening Islam. In rebuttal, advocates of reform should make clear that backing democracy does not mean choosing the rule of humans over that of God. On the contrary; it means denying to despots the right to play God. Democracy gives a voice to every citizen, not just the privileged few. I heard one Muslim leader, a Nigerian, argue that Islam is the most democratic of faiths for just this reason. Everyone is considered equal before God.

Some commentators suggest that the importance of religion is overstated and that the only truly relevant issues are economic—that once Arabs are convinced democracy will allow them to live more prosperously, nothing else will matter. This reminds me of the moment in the movie *The Graduate* when Dustin Hoffman's character is assured that the key to his future happiness is a career in plastics. There is a certain mind-set in the West that assumes everyone wants to live like a westerner. According to this line of thinking, if Arabs and other Muslims are resentful, it can only be because they envy the material wealth and comfortable lifestyle of the West. The opposing possibility is not considered: that at least some Arabs believe the West is trying to lure them into superficial, decadent lives and thereby leave them forever damned. Material interests matter, but history tells us that strongly held ideas, whether enlightened or misguided, matter more. "If one were to ask if Muslims want freedom," wrote one leading Islamic scholar, "the answer would definitely be yes. But the vast majority of Muslims would add that, first of all, for them freedom does not mean freedom *from* God and religion; they would embrace other freedoms, provided they do not destroy their faith and what gives meaning to their lives."

Another school of thought suggests that the two halves of democratic reform—economic and political—can come only in sequence. According to this theory, Arabs are not ready for democracy. They must first become better educated, more broadly prosperous, more middle-class: in other words, more western. This is condescending; it also ignores the fact that economic and political reforms reinforce one another. Authoritarianism is a roadblock to development whereas democracy helps smooth the way. Some Arab leaders are nevertheless strongly attracted to the idea of putting economic reforms first, hoping that this will enable them to delay real political change indefinitely. President Hosni Mubarak of Egypt is a prime example.

Since he came to power in 1981, Mubarak has been a responsible international figure who has endorsed moderate positions in world affairs and has lent vital backing to the peace process in the Middle East. He is also a skillful politician who has implemented some necessary economic changes. He is not, however, a democrat. For almost a quarter century, he has kept a lid on political dissent by maintaining a permanent state of emergency. Any Egyptian who opposes him on any major matter risks arrest and detention, even torture. Mubarak claims that his policies are harsh out of necessity and that they have largely worked; in recent years, there have been few incidents of domestic terrorism. President Bush argues that "liberty is the solution to terror," and that the rise of Al Qaeda should push Arab regimes in the direction of democracy. Not long after 9/11, the prime minister of Egypt asserted just the opposite—that terrorism should push the United States in the direction of Egypt. "The U.S. and U.K., including human rights groups, have, in the past, been calling on us to give these terrorists their 'human rights,' " he said. "You can give them all the human rights they deserve until they kill you. After these horrible crimes committed in New York and Virginia, maybe Western countries should begin to think of Egypt's own fight against terror as their new model."

President Bush has called on Egypt to "lead the way" toward Arab democracy. Mubarak responded by agreeing to allow opposing candidates when he ran for reelection in September 2005. This produced the kind of spectacle we have seen all too often in marginally democratic countries: presidential balloting with all the trappings of democracy but little of the substance. The campaign was absurdly short, only nineteen days. The governing party controlled most of the media and campaign cash. Candidates had to meet a set of criteria that squeezed out any serious opposition to Mubarak, who, predictably, won by an overwhelming margin. As unsatisfactory as the whole charade was, there were encouraging aspects. For the first time in the country's long history, Egyptians were treated to the sight of their leader appearing at campaign rallies to ask for support. Voters were given the experience of marking ballots with more than one option. Crowds found themselves able to chant antigovernment slogans without getting clubbed, or at least not every time.

The population of Egypt is sophisticated and educated enough to support political parties across the ideological spectrum. If truly open elections were held, however, the most potent opposition to the governing party would be the Muslim Brotherhood, an Islamic group founded in 1928. Over time, the Muslim Brotherhood has periodically embraced and renounced violence, survived numerous crackdowns, and established chapters in countries throughout the Arab world. Its central tenet is that Sunni Islam provides the solution to all problems and that a return to the pure faith will cure social ills. In Egypt in recent years, it has adopted the language of democracy and has sought to collaborate with more secular reform groups. Although the organization is officially banned, its social influence remains substantial, and its members—running independently—scored impressive gains in the parliamentary elections of 2005. The Muslim Brotherhood might evolve, if permitted, into a moderate Islamist party of the type that has held power in Turkey, Indonesia, and Bosnia-Herzegovina, and now, potentially, in Iraq. Less rosy scenarios, however, are also plausible. The Egyptian government insists that the Muslim Brotherhood is preparing to use violence, and that this is why it will not allow the organization to compete for power through nonviolent means. Such is the logic of repression.

Mubarak's intention, no doubt, is to foster a managed opposition that would create a patina of democracy without threatening his own party's hold on power. A population once awakened, however, can prove difficult to control. The idea that Egyptians should have true alternatives to single-party rule is likely to gain strength between now and 2011, when the next presidential elections are scheduled. To minimize pressure for further change, Mubarak will continue to remind U.S. policy makers of his usefulness in other arenas. With the Gaza Strip no longer under Israel's control and the

Middle East situation fluid once again, he will be careful to arrange events that demonstrate his capacity to sway the Palestinians and his role as an elder statesman among Arabs.

Thirty-four years after John Kennedy's speech about freedom, independent Algeria finally held a national multiparty election. The year was 1991; the winning party was Islamist. Western policy makers worried that the party, though empowered through a democratic process, would fail to honor democratic obligations—such as allowing a legal opposition, a free press, and an independent judiciary. When the Algerian army intervened, annulling the results, the first Bush administration was relieved. Former secretary of state James Baker explained:

> When I was at the Department of State, we pursued a policy of excluding the radical fundamentalists in Algeria, even as we recognized that this was somewhat at odds with our support of democracy. Generally speaking, when you support democracy, you take what democracy gives you. If it gives you a radical Islamic fundamentalist, you're supposed to live with it. We didn't live with it in Algeria because we felt the radical fundamentalists' views were so adverse to what we believe in . . . and to the national interests of the United States.

As history reflects, not all democratic elections are won by democrats. In most Arab societies, the largest community-based groups are organized around religion. If democracy were to blossom tomorrow, the election results would be determined more by Muslim leaders than by the small groups of academicians, businesspeople, and professionals who are the most vocal supporters of democratic change. This is certainly the case in the Palestinian Authority and Iraq.

In 2005, I cochaired a bipartisan task force on Arab democracy for the Council on Foreign Relations. My partner was the widely respected former congressman Vin Weber. The task force concluded that if Arabs are able to express their grievances freely and peacefully, they will be less likely to turn to extreme measures and more likely to build open, prosperous societies. That will benefit them and us. We argued further, however, that in promoting democratic institutions, we should bear in mind that sudden change is neither necessary nor desirable. Our goal should be to encourage democratic evolution, not revolution. This caution was not sufficient for one member of the task force, who wrote in dissent that the United States should not focus on elections in the Arab world at all. "Even the most moderate and nonviolent of Arab Islamist parties," he argued, "disagree with American goals on Arab-Israeli issues and would not be willing to accept the kind of influence the United States now exercises in the region." This analysis, based on realpolitik, strikes me as out-of-date. To believe that America can sustain its influence in Muslim countries without supporting free and fair elections is to believe that we can defeat terrorism by acting the way terrorist leaders have predicted. This would be like fighting a battle on ground that will give way beneath our feet; strategically, it does not make sense.

Some analysts fear that democracy would allow Islamist political movements to sweep into power across North Africa, through the Middle East and Gulf, and all the way to southeast Asia. The result would be a formidable bloc of states united in their hatred of Israel, their opposition to America, and their resistance to external pressure regarding terrorism and the production of nuclear arms. Although risk is inherent in democracy, such an outcome is extremely unlikely. Islam has more potential to bring these societies together than communism had, but no single movement is likely to bridge the vast cultural and theological differences within the faith.

The argument made by Mubarak and like-minded Arab leaders is that political parties organized around Islam are uniformly undemocratic and prone to violence. This was the assumption made by the United States after the Algerian election in 1991. It is a view that cannot simply be dismissed. We should, in fact, assume that free elections might result in militant Islamist regimes in some countries. Yet it would be untenable to bar the participation of broadly supported political parties on the basis of an assumption about what some might do. It is all too easy for a repressive government to label anyone who disagrees with its policies a "terrorist." The label can be self-fulfilling: persecution is more often a cause of violence than a solution to it. If democracy is to take root in the Middle East, Islamist parties cannot be excluded out of hand. Through history, many legitimate political parties had their origins outside the law; even movements once associated with terrorism should be encouraged to renounce violence and move into the mainstream.

Those worried about Islamists would be well advised to concern themselves less with trying to ban such parties and more with the challenge of competing against them at the ballot box. In his novel *Snow*, the Turkish writer Orhan Pamuk explained the success of their methods:

As for these Islamists, they go from door to door in groups, paying house visits; they give women pots and pans, and those machines that squeeze oranges, and boxes of soap, cracked wheat, and detergent. They concentrate on the poor neighborhoods; they ingratiate themselves with the women; they bring out hooked needles and sew golden thread onto the children's shoulders to protect them against evil. They say, "Give your vote to the Prosperity Party, the party of God; we've fallen into this destitution because we've wandered off the path of God...." They win the trust of the angry and humiliated unemployed; they sit with their wives, who don't know where the next meal is coming from, and they give them hope; promising more gifts.... We're not just talking about the lowest of the low. Even people with jobs—even tradesmen—respect them, because these Islamists are more hardworking, more honest, more modest than anyone else.

The inclusion of Islamist parties will give them a stake in the democratic process, just as their exclusion would give them a stake in trying to destroy that process. Democracy is valuable because it offers the means to solve the hardest problems nonviolently, through reason, debate, and voting. The hardest problems in the Arab world today revolve around the very issues that most concern Islamist parties: What does Islam demand? How is terror defined? What should young people be taught? How do we balance modern demands with traditional values? It is better to hash these issues out through the give-and-take of democratic procedures than try to solve them through recurring cycles of violence and repression.

Some factions may indeed be determined to prevail by force and terror. Recognizing this, every political party should be required to abide by the rules of democracy, including nonviolence and respect for constitutional procedures, as many Islamist parties have already pledged they

will do.* In the long run, however, the best way to marginal-
ize violent extremists is to make room for as broad an array
of nonviolent perspectives as possible. Nothing will push any
political movement toward the center more quickly than the
need to find policies that attract votes. President Bush, who
knows something about winning elections, put the argument this way: "Maybe some will . . . say, 'Vote for me; I look
forward to blowing up America,' but . . . I think people who
generally run for office say, 'Vote for me; I'm looking forward to fixing your potholes or making sure you've got
bread on the table.' " Tip O'Neill made the same point
another way: "All politics is local."

Arab leaders should know that progress toward democracy
will have favorable consequences for their relations with the
United States and that the reverse is also true. Countries
moving toward democracy should receive special consideration on such matters as trade, investment, and aid; and
Washington should distance itself from governments that
refuse over time to recognize the rights of their citizens.

The United States should support democracy in the
Middle East, just as it does elsewhere around the world and
for the same reasons. I hope, however, that we proceed with
some degree of humility. Democracy is not a gift delivered
either by God or by the United States; it is a system of government that each country may choose to develop at its own
pace and in its own way. In his second inaugural address,
President Bush declared, "From the day of our founding, we
have proclaimed that every man and woman on this earth

---

* According to *Islamism in North Africa I: The Legacies of History* (April
2004), a report by the International Crisis Group, "Islamic political movements in
North Africa no longer condemn democracy as un-Islamic or counterpose the idea
of an Islamic state to the states which actually exist. In fact, they explicitly reject
theocratic ideas and proclaim acceptance of democratic and pluralist principles
and respect for the rules of the game as defined by existing constitutions."

has rights, and dignity and matchless value." He did not add that in the United States for the first 130 years or so, half of those people of matchless value did not have the right to vote; or that for the first seventy-five years, millions were held in chains; or that before the American civilization could be built, another civilization had to be pushed aside.

We should also be realistic about what we expect. To the administration, transforming the Middle East is necessary to keep Americans safe—not an argument the average Arab reformer is likely to use. Arab democracy, if it comes at all, will arrive with the purpose of fulfilling Arab aspirations. It will not change overnight how Arabs look at the world; nor will it spur reconciliation with Israel; nor will it ensure social liberalization. But elections are still a step in the right direction if they lead to genuine political debate. There is a big difference between a society in which opinions depend on "what everybody thinks" and a society in which citizens begin by saying, "Let me tell you what I think."

When I was in government, I often made a suggestion that my colleagues rejected at the time, only to embrace it later when they could claim it as their own. I have also often rejected someone else's suggestion only to accept it after the opportunity for additional thought. Arab leaders cannot be expected to embrace democracy overnight, or if it appears that they are being coerced into doing so. The world can hope, however, that at least some will promote a system resembling democracy, even if they call it something else. When that happens, it will not be as a favor to the West. It will happen because Arab leaders have learned, perhaps the hard way, that as John Kennedy said many years ago, the most powerful force in the world is man's desire to be free.

Sixteen

Islam in the West

———— ⌣⌣ ————

S oon after I became secretary of state, I took a trip around the world. The first five stops were in Europe. Only in Germany was religion an issue, and the religion in question was scientology. The Germans, claiming that scientology was a moneymaking cult, had banned it; the United States (for reasons *not* having to do with Tom Cruise) considered it a valid faith. In 1997, this passed for religious controversy.

The period of such innocence is over. The attacks on the twin towers, the bombings of trains in Madrid, and the explosions on the Underground in London have darkened our outlook. These acts of terror differed in scale but were similar in the passions they evoked and in the images stamped on our minds: smoke, blood-smeared faces, anxious rescue workers, sobbing relatives, candlelight services, and forlorn piles of flowers. As might be expected, the tragedies have brought Europeans and Americans closer together, but in a solidarity soured by bickering. Leaders agree on the goal of preventing further attacks, but not on how best to achieve that. In my travels, I have found many Europeans angry about Iraq and convinced that President Bush's ambivalence about legal due process and his rhetoric of good versus evil do more to create terrorists than to defeat them. Europeans, having lived for a long time with the threat of terrorism from various sources, are also puzzled by the U.S. claim that 9/11 changed everything. For its part, the Bush administration has suggested that some people across the Atlantic do not take the threat seriously enough, pointing especially to the withdrawal of Spanish troops from Iraq shortly after the train bombings in Madrid—an ill-timed move that gave the terrorists precisely what they had sought.

My own experience with bombing in Europe dates back to my earliest years, when I huddled in shelters with my family and neighbors during the battle of Britain. There was no doubt then who was to blame for the terror. The question of responsibility was fiercely debated, however, following the strikes in London in July 2005. Some, including the mayor of London (on the political left) and Tory politician Kenneth Clarke (on the right), attributed the attacks to Britain's involvement in Iraq; others blamed the hate-filled rhetoric of some British-based Muslim clerics. Neither explanation is fully persuasive. The invasion of Iraq certainly made it easier for radical imams to assert that all Muslims are under attack; but a sense of victimization provides no moral excuse for blowing up Underground carriages in London. Fiery preachers should be held accountable for stirring up a hornet's nest, but this doesn't mean that it was smart to give them a stick with which to hit the hive.

The quarreling has evolved into a running controversy about the definition of European values, the boundaries of free speech, and the growing problem of integrating Muslim immigrants. Since 1975, the European continent's Muslim population has tripled because of high birthrates and an influx of workers from North Africa, the Middle East, and south Asia. If these trends continue, Muslims will account for about 10 percent of the population of the European Union (EU) by 2020. Meanwhile, tens of millions of prospective migrants await their chance, restlessly biding their time on the overcrowded streets of Tunis, Rabat, Algiers, and Damascus. As anyone who has spent time recently navigating the sidewalks of such cities as London, Paris, and Berlin can attest, the dam separating Christian Europe from the Muslim East has sprung a leak, altering Europe's culture.

The arrival of immigrants in any society has an impact on the host country's sense of self. In the United States, each successive wave of immigration has generated worries that the American identity would become diluted or lost. The recent rise in Asian and Latino populations has set off just such a volatile reaction; but the adjustment is even harder in Europe, whose countries are less accustomed to absorbing foreigners. The expansion of the EU to the east, north, and south has given fresh flavor to the old query about what it means to be European. Is it solely a question of where you lay your head at night, or is the answer determined by values, customs, and beliefs? As one church leader in Germany has remarked, "The countries of Europe have the same basic culture. We know how to live together with Catholics and Protestants because we have a common belief in Christ and common convictions. But relations with Muslims are quite different. . . . The U.S. is a coming-together of people from many cultures. But traditionally the countries of Europe have had the same form and culture."

I was eleven years old when my family arrived in the United States. Although proud of my European heritage, I had only one ambition in my new home, and that was to fit in. Eager to be seen as a bona fide American teenager, I chewed bubble gum, devoured comic books, and imitated the way my more stylish classmates dressed and talked. It drove me crazy when my parents acted foreign, with my mother telling fortunes and my father so formal that he wore a coat and tie even when fishing. In Europe today, the generational breakdown in many Muslim families is just the reverse. The elders may be more committed to blending in than their children or grandchildren. Young people in Birmingham, Marseilles, and Rotterdam, just as much as those in Cairo and Casablanca, feel called—or pressured by their peers—to assert their Islamic identity by speaking out politically and by wearing the badges of faith: the head scarf, veil, and beard.

The challenge of integration is especially acute in France, the scene of widespread rioting in the fall of 2005, following the accidental electrocution of two Muslim teenagers who were fleeing the police. Young people, many unemployed and living in projects, burned thousands of cars to protest discrimination, vent frustration about harassment, and, as some admitted, "have fun." French authorities responded by invoking a state of emergency for the first time since the Algerian war of independence half a century earlier. Those analyzing the protests blamed the French for acting as if their slogan "Liberty, Equality, and Fraternity" were the reality instead of an ideal. The French secular state does not recognize racial or religious distinctions; thus, there is no basis for policies that might seek to reduce high unemployment among citizens of North African extraction. Conducting a survey on the basis of color or creed is something the Americans or British might do, but not the French. This leaves the recent immigrants in a bind; they are told they are fully French, but they are often treated as second-class citizens when they apply for a job or shop for an apartment or house. To address this, the government has appointed a council to fight discrimination and has begun considering the possibility of some sort of affirmative action

program. That would be, for France, a step both revolution-
ary and sure to be resisted by the country's robust right wing.

Even before the riots in France, European leaders were
increasingly anxious about the inability or unwillingness of
recent migrants to integrate themselves into the life of their
adopted countries. For Muslims in Europe, it is not a question of Islam and the West; their lives reflect the dilemma
and opportunity of Islam *in* the West. The ability of Europe
to translate this reality into something positive is still being
measured.*

I had the opportunity to discuss this challenge in September
2005 at a conference hosted by former president Clinton in
New York. Among those participating was Mustafa Cerić, the
grand mufti of Bosnia. Cerić suggested that many Europeans
have given short shrift to the contributions made by Muslims
and Jews to European history. For centuries, Muslim families
have lived in Central Europe and the Balkans; in the West,
there are millions of second- and third-generation immigrants
who are full members of their communities. It is the large flow
of newcomers that has created an awkward mix. Cerić said
that Muslims need to accept that they cannot expect Islamic
law to govern in a place where they are a minority, but that
Europeans need to accept the right of Muslims to live in equality with others. He proposed a social contract in which
European Muslims would pledge their unequivocal commitment to democratic principles while also asserting their political, economic, and religious rights. Cerić argues that Muslims
should focus on their responsibilities in order to be worthy of

---

* The issues of integration and identity that are addressed in this chapter are
also relevant in the United States, but to a lesser extent. Although exact numbers
are elusive, Muslims probably make up between 1 and 2 percent of the American
population. Of that number, at least one-third are African Americans born in the
United States. The shape and direction of "American Islam" are vibrant subjects
of study and discussion within the religious and academic communities.

freedom and that Europeans must realize that Islam is not alien to their culture but part of it.

Cerić's task is complicated by a combustible political environment in which charges of prejudice are tossed around at the slightest provocation by one side and allegations of radicalism by the other. In September 2005, a Danish newspaper printed a series of cartoons that caricatured the Prophet Muhammad and associated him with terrorism. A wave of protests, some violent, erupted when the offensive cartoons were reprinted elsewhere in Europe and made available on the Internet. The hysteria dramatized both the divide between secular Europe and Muslims, and the eagerness of extremists on all sides to turn hate to their advantage. The publication of the cartoons, though an exercise in free speech, was also an act of bigotry. The protests were equally an exercise in free speech, except for those that turned violent. The whole sad episode, a triumph of emotion over reason, was deeply regrettable. The attitudes that gave rise to it, however, were hardly new.

In 1991, I participated in a *Los Angeles Times* survey entitled "The Pulse of Europe." We were not surprised to find prejudice toward minority groups, but I was still stunned by the extent of ill feeling toward Muslims, especially those who had emigrated from North Africa. During the war in Bosnia, I was further shocked (and depressed) by the attitude of some of my European colleagues who seemed to consider the Bosniak Muslims less civilized than their Serb and Croat tormenters. It has been common in recent years to hear shrill cries of "Europe for the Europeans" and "Foreigners go home." Politicians routinely call for tighter restrictions on immigration while Muslims complain they are being discriminated against, the victims of "Islamaphobia." The recent crisis of the cartoons was preceded by other ugly events—the murder, in 2002, of a Dutch politician who had criticized Islam and in October 2004, of a second Dutchman, this one a filmmaker, who had released what was perceived to be a virulently anti-Muslim film.

Meanwhile, the culture of tolerance, long a source of pride to many Europeans, is being questioned by those who say that too much live-and-let-live leads to a loss of control. Indeed, experts worry that Europe could become the next major breeding ground for terrorists: a place where conspirators can conceal themselves behind the protective wall of legal due process, relatively easy access to social benefits, the tradition of free speech, and the absence of capital punishment. Europe's mainstream Muslim leaders are worried about the same thing. They have tried diligently to grab the microphone away from ideologues whose angry pronouncements earn headlines but embarrass and even endanger the law-abiding Muslim majority.* The presence of extreme elements, however, is uncontested.

In April 2004, the British police uncovered a half-ton cache of ammonium nitrate fertilizer, an explosive ingredient used earlier in terrorist attacks in Bali and Turkey. This discovery led to the arrest of eight Muslim men. Later that year, the Spanish police apprehended a group of Pakistanis allegedly linked to Al Qaeda. Early in 2005, the German and

---

* The bombings in London have also prompted American Muslim leaders to intensify their efforts to prevent violent extremism. According to Salam al-Marayati, executive director of the Muslim Public Affairs Council in Los Angeles: "Before, people thought, 'We have nothing to do with the terrorism, our religion is clear and it should be obvious to everyone else. Now, we can't afford to be bystanders anymore, we have to be involved in constructive intervention. So we're doing it collectively, speaking out with one voice and now telling our children that they have to get it right, they can't be confused and can't give any credence to anybody who comes to them and says there is room for violence."

French police broke up cells recruiting insurgents for Iraq. Operatives of Abu Musab al-Zarqawi's terrorist organization have been arrested in six European countries. British officials estimate that 10,000 to 15,000 Muslims in the United Kingdom are supporters of Al Qaeda and that as many as 600 have received training from violent groups in Afghanistan or elsewhere.

It is frustrating to authorities that the terror suspects do not fit neatly into any demographic profile. Though most are from immigrant families, the perpetrators of the subway bombings were all British-born; one was quite well off, and none had a history of violence. If there is a pattern, it is that recruits experience a sharp change in attitude toward religion. A Muslim who has been drifting through life giving little heed to his faith may suddenly find a new identity through devotion and militance. The British prime minister, Tony Blair, told me, "Part of the Muslim community is just not integrating. Jews, Hindus, Chinese, and the majority of Muslims have integrated, but there are pockets of Muslims dedicated to extremism." Because there is no central authority in Sunni Islam, one does not have to be a religious scholar to preach. "In these neighborhoods, you have someone get up and announce, 'I am an imam and here is a fatwa,' " says Blair. That is why the radical imams can be so dangerous. What they teach is not real Islam but rather a version distorted by politics and the kind of out-of-context Quranic quotations favored by bin Laden. Young Muslims looking for something meaningful to care about can be fooled into thinking they have found it in the call to holy war; they are born again as terrorists.

It doesn't help that prisons in Europe are filled disproportionately with Muslims. In France, they make up a majority of the imprisoned population. Experts in counterterrorism fear that the criminal population is prime territory for the kind of recruitment that Al Qaeda practices.* Few western prisons are equipped to offer sound moral guidance to large numbers of Muslim inmates. European governments are alert to the problem but uncertain how to respond. Some have tried dispersing Muslim prisoners; others argue that this only spreads the danger. In any case, prison space is limited. Another challenge is finding a way to prevent ethnic neighborhoods from degenerating into ghettos. The latter are home to the kind of economically deprived and socially out-of-joint populations that a century ago might have been attracted to the utopian promise of Marxism. People who have left one country only to find the new one inhospitable may feel robbed of any national loyalty and eager to pledge themselves to a more universal cause.

In the face of all this, European leaders have little choice but to reconsider their approach to the balancing act between the imperatives of security and the principles of democracy. The question being asked in both religious and secular circles is whether it is wiser to try to accommodate the customs and values of immigrants or to insist that they fully conform to European rules. Hardliners suggest that dialogue is fruitless because it fails to reach the people most likely to cause trouble; terrorists don't attend ecumenical conferences, nor are they swayed by appeals to shared moral concerns. Safety should come first.

In that spirit, efforts are under way in many countries to expand the authority of the police to spy on and detain sus-

---

* Richard Reid, who boarded a Miami-bound airplane in December 2001 with a bomb in his shoe, converted to Islam in a British jail. Mohammed Bouyeri, the murderer of the Dutch filmmaker Theo van Gogh, became radicalized during a seven-month jail term. Late in 2004, Spanish officials arrested thirteen North African immigrants for planning to blow up the national court in Madrid. The men were small-time criminals who, after meeting in prison, decided to form their own terror group, Martyrs for Morocco.

pected terrorists. Several countries have made it easier to expel extremist preachers and have begun programs to train moderate ones, in the hope of nurturing the development of a European version of Islam. Some countries have begun to finance mosques in order to make them less dependent on sources (such as Saudi Arabia) that counsel Islamic separation rather than social integration. In the Netherlands, Muslim clerics are required to conduct their services in Dutch instead of Arabic. Blair's government has moved to ban groups that have a history of supporting terror and has created a blacklist to block alleged sympathizers from entering Britain and deport those already there. It has also taken steps to outlaw the kind of preaching, articles, and websites that foment terrorism.

Democracy is based on the premise of settling policy differences through a process of open debate. A democratic government that shuts down whole categories of speech will immediately find itself in alien territory, walking the same ground as tyrants. The communists who seized control of Czechoslovakia in the years following World War II would not tolerate dissent; that is why my family ended up in the United States. For centuries, dictators have filled their jails with people whose ideas were judged dangerous, provocative, or likely to incite violence against the prevailing order. More recently, despots in many countries have used the threat of terrorism as an excuse to silence violent and nonviolent opponents alike. The risk in today's Europe (and for that matter, the United States) is that the difference between advocating terrorism and criticizing policy will be blurred, turning the law into a means of stifling legitimate debate.

That risk, however, must be weighed against others, including the possibility that inflammatory words will lead to incendiary actions, a sequence for which there is also much precedent. The old saying about free speech is that it does not extend to yelling "Fire!" in a crowded theater. We are in a crowded theater now, and I think it fair to proscribe public speech that is clearly intended to promote terrorism. I also find myself in agreement with Blair's warning to those who arrive in Great Britain from other countries, whether in search of a political safe haven or economic opportunity. "Staying here carries with it a duty," he said. "That duty is to share and support the values that sustain the British way of life. Those who break that duty and try to incite hatred or engage in violence against our country and its people have no place here." The same caution would be appropriate in the United States.

In saying this, I am placing my faith in the vigor of American and European civil society, an independent judiciary, and democracy itself to protect against abuses of power. The balance we must seek on both sides of the Atlantic is really nothing more than the product of common sense: stopping those who would destroy our system, without ourselves undermining the basic principles that define that system.

The real victory over terrorism will come not through silencing anyone, but through the amplification of more reasoned voices such as that of Mustafa Cerić. In Europe, as elsewhere, the battle that counts most is the one that is being waged for the heart and soul of Islam at every level, within families, neighborhoods, communities, and nations. In this battle, every ally can make a difference and every potential ally should be sought out. For that reason, I worry about the possibility that Europe and the United States will turn their backs on the people and government of Turkey, longtime friends of the West who are in a unique position to help.

•   •   •

The victory of the Allies in World War I destroyed what remained of the Ottoman Empire; from its ashes there emerged something never before seen: a secular Muslim state. The republic of Turkey was created in the image of its first president, Kemal Atatürk, a man of boundless energy intent on building a country both modern and oriented toward the West. Atatürk brashly described religion as "a poisonous dagger directed at the heart of my people." Reacting against the crowd-pleasing dervishes and religious sheikhs of the time, he declared, "I flatly refuse to believe that today, in the luminous presence of science, knowledge, and civilization, . . . there exist, in the civilized community of Turkey, men so primitive as to seek their material and moral well-being from the guidance of . . . [a] sheikh."

Atatürk took a sledgehammer to the foundations of society, abolishing the Islamic caliphate and asserting control over religion on behalf of the state. At his direction, religious schools were closed, the Turkish language was latinized, a western-style constitution was adopted, and the practice of separating the sexes in the classroom and workplace was ended. "We will not catch up with the modern world," he proclaimed, "if we only modernize half the population." In the decades since then, the Turkish military has served as the guardian of Atatürk's legacy, preserving the secular nature of the government. Eager to cement its status as a western country, Turkey began in 1960 to apply for membership in the European Common Market, which later became the EU; it is still knocking on the door.

Like most exclusive clubs, the EU selects its own members. Meddling by American secretaries of state is not welcome. While in office, I nevertheless did my best to nudge my European colleagues in the direction of accepting Turkey. My view, reflected in U.S. policy, was that a prosperous, pro-western Turkey was needed to ensure stability in a sensitive region. I was pleased when, in 1999, the EU finally declared that Turkey was an official candidate. The Turkish government has since been checking the boxes on a long list of changes required for it to meet European norms. It has abolished the death penalty, reformed its judiciary, adopted a new penal code, changed its banking laws, and implemented stronger protections for human rights. Most of the reforms have been implemented under the leadership of the Islamist Peace and Development Party, which has confounded the Islamist stereotype by accepting Atatürk's secular model, moving toward the political center, and generally respecting the rights of Turkey's women and minorities.

Turkey is uniquely important because it is the only member of NATO included in the Organization of the Islamic Conference, representing the world's Muslim states; it is also one of the few Muslim countries to have diplomatic relations with Israel. In the words of the Turkish foreign minister, Abdullah Gul, "At a time when people are talking of a clash of civilizations, Turkey is a natural bridge of civilizations. All we are trying to do is to use our position to bring Islam and the West closer together." Joschka Fischer, at the time Germany's foreign minister, echoed this thought: "To modernize an Islamic country based on the shared values of Europe would be almost a D-Day for Europe in the war against terror." So it seemed a breakthrough when the EU decided in December 2004 to take the next step, declaring that Turkey had made enough progress to warrant the start of formal negotiations. The question is whether these negotiations will lead Europeans to embrace Turkish Muslims or to give them the diplomatic equivalent of a cold shoulder.

When, in June 2005, French and Dutch voters rejected a proposed new constitution for the EU, anti-Turkish sentiment received much of the blame. Although most European leaders have expressed support for Turkey's application, the

majority of their constituents are unconvinced. The process
of enlarging the EU is based on a vision of the continent as
dynamic and outward-looking, but many Europeans would
prefer—in the face of globalization—to hunker down.
Enlargement has already enabled millions of new workers
to compete for jobs. Europeans are reluctant to open their
borders and markets further to Turkey, a country both big
(with 70 million people) and poor (with a per capita income
roughly half that of Poland.)

The difficulties go beyond dollars and euros, however, to a
more fundamental question: whether Turkish culture is compatible with that of the rest of Europe. The disdain toward
Muslims I had encountered during the Bosnian conflict was
also directed toward Turkey. This reflects the realities that
virtually all of Europe has waged war against Turks at some
point; that the Greeks have clashed repeatedly with Turkey
over Cyprus and certain islands in the Aegean; and that
Christians have not forgotten the Turks' massacre of
Armenians during World War I. This history, distant as some
of it is, has instilled enduring prejudice. Prime Minister
Silvio Berlusconi of Italy has boasted about the "superiority"
of European civilization compared with that of the "Islamic
countries." Valéry Giscard d'Estaing, a former president of
France, has declared that "Turkey is not a European coun-
try"; its admission, he says, would mean "the end of the
European Union." Before becoming Pope Benedict XVI,
Cardinal Joseph Ratzinger expressed his opposition to
Turkey's application, saying that "Turkey has always repre-
sented a different continent, in contrast with Europe."

The failure of the European constitution to pass muster
with voters was a traumatic setback for advocates of a larger
EU. There are many who would now like the question of
Turkey's membership to be forgotten. It should not. To push
Turkey away would be a monumental error. It would also be

yet another gift to those seeking to stir up trouble between Muslims and the West.

Assuming that the negotiations do proceed, several principles should be kept in mind. First, the EU and Turkey have already reached an understanding. If Turkey continues its rapid progress toward European standards, it has a right to expect European leaders to endorse its membership. That is the whole rationale behind the negotiating process.

Second, Turkey's European identity should not be questioned. Although the Ottoman Empire was, at times, more than a European power, it was never less than a European power. Turkey still includes regions that are inward-looking, where day-to-day life has changed little in hundreds of years; but since Atatürk, there can be no question that Turkey's primary focus is toward the West.

Third, Turkey's religious identity should not be relevant to its application to join the EU. That principle appears basic, but is by no means clearly understood. Both Europe and Turkey have secular governments. Europe, like the United States, has evolved into a multidenominational society. Just as important, the EU is organized around the norms of western democracy, at the heart of which is religious liberty. It would betray Europe's own values to exclude a country on religious grounds.

Finally, it is unconvincing to argue, as some do, that Turkey's membership would disrupt the cultural harmony of Europe. That line of thinking might have made sense in the days of a Common Market with only half a dozen members, but today's EU, with twenty-five members, is a cultural kaleidoscope. Adding Turkey will not change that.

During the 1990s, the prospect of joining NATO provided a powerful incentive for democratic reform within the newly free countries of Central and Eastern Europe. Instead of resuming historic rivalries, they focused on democratic goals, such as respect for the rule of law, human rights, free enterprise, and civilian control of the military. NATO provided a magnet for positive change, a place where onetime rivals could work together on behalf of peace. The EU has been serving a similar function, but that will continue only if it leaves the door open to new applicants and keeps its mind open in judging those who apply. Says Tony Blair, "No doubt very few countries would vote yes if there were a referendum on Turkish membership today. That's why we have to work to change the perceptions. To qualify, Turkey has come a long way; it would be a mistake now for us to push it in the other direction."

The United States has its own obligations. The decision of the Bush administration to invade Iraq shocked the Turks, 40 percent of whom—according to a survey made in 2005— now see America as their biggest enemy. A best-selling Turkish novel, *Metal Storm*, predicts an American invasion of Turkey, prompting in retaliation the detonation of a nuclear bomb near the White House.

I have traveled to Turkey several times in recent years. The fact that the United States invaded Iraq—Turkey's neighbor—without taking Turkey's perspective into account will not soon be forgotten. That perspective is heavily influenced by the Turks' complicated and inglorious relationship with the Kurds. Turkey is worried that an autonomous Kurdistan inside Iraq will encourage nationalist ambitions within its own Kurdish minority; it is upset that Kurdish terrorists have retained a foothold inside northern Iraq; and it is worried that Iraqi Kurds will out-muscle Iraq's Turkish minority for control of the prized oil-rich city of Kirkuk. Future American policy does not have to mesh perfectly with Turkish policy on these issues, but it would be wise to tread lightly and cooperate where possible, while still insisting on respect for Kurdish rights.

Looking ahead ten years, it seems likely that the dominant power in the Persian Gulf will be Iran, allied with the Shiite majority in Iraq. It would be hard to overstate the importance of Turkey at that point, as a member of NATO, a leader within the organization of Muslim states, a friend to Israel, and a potentially unifying force throughout Europe and the Near East. It would be comparably difficult, therefore, to overestimate the value for Europe and the United States of treating Turkish interests seriously. If the West does not respect a Muslim country such as Turkey that has been so responsive to our concerns, it will be hard to make the case to any other Muslim country that friendship will be rewarded.

Small gestures can sometimes make a big difference. I made this observation to Turkish officials who didn't agree or disagree; they just waited for the subject to change. That subject was the status of the Halki Greek Orthodox seminary on the island of Heybeliada, about an hour's ride by boat from Istanbul. The seminary began operations in 1844 and has been described as "a splendid piece of mid-nineteenth-century architecture—airy, high-ceilinged and with views of the city in every direction." The facility was shut down in 1971, not because it was involved in anything subversive but because its very existence was deemed an affront to the secular rules of the Turkish state. If Muslim institutions were not allowed to operate outside the government's control, why should a Christian seminary be allowed to do so?—or so the thinking went. This policy falls into the category of what Emerson referred to as "a foolish consistency."

Speaking as a friend and also as an American official, I pressed the Turks repeatedly to reopen the seminary as a gesture of goodwill toward the world's 250 million Orthodox

Christians—a move made more meaningful by a curious fact of history: that the center of Orthodox Christianity is not in a Christian country but in Turkey. Not even the Ottoman conquest of Constantinople in 1453 could dislodge the patriarchate—the Orthodox equivalent of the Vatican— from its historic capital.

Along with President and Mrs. Clinton, I had an opportunity to meet with Ecumenical Patriarch Bartholomew at his headquarters in the middle of Istanbul's old city. Istanbul is beautiful, but also noisy and crowded. The patriarchate, by contrast, is serene, mystical, and unassuming. The patriarch himself is a Turkish citizen, an alumnus of both the Halki seminary and the Turkish army reserve. He looks as you might expect a patriarch to look, with a long white beard, medallions, and a cross draped around his neck, and cloaked in a magnificent black robe.

Since he entered office in 1991, Bartholomew has earned praise for his environmental activism and his efforts at interfaith reconciliation. He is an intellectual, speaks seven languages, and is a thoughtful man; but he seemed genuinely puzzled when talking about the Halki seminary. He did not understand who profited from leaving the institution empty, or how the seminary or indeed Turkey's tiny Christian minority could be considered a threat to anyone. On the contrary, the seminary's reopening would surely boost Turkey's prospects for joining the EU, a goal the patriarch fully supports. The government says that it wants to find a solution, but after thirty-five years, that quest should be completed. The fate of a single center of learning would not seem to matter much in the relationship between two civilizations; but in a world such as ours, we should never underestimate what can be accomplished through civilized acts.

Seventeen

Africa: A Race for Souls

———— ᘛᘚ ————

W e are heading—you can see it—toward a clash," said a Muslim leader in Uganda. The United States "will never stop fighting you until you turn away from your religion." "There is a race," said another Ugandan, this one a Christian minister. "Islam is also racing for the soul and the mind of the African." Nowhere is the global religious revival more in evidence than in Africa, where two opposing tides are rising and the information revolution is bringing the exhortations of Christian preachers and Muslim clerics into living rooms and community halls. Muslim countries in the Middle East and North Africa (notably Saudi Arabia and Libya) are pouring money in to educate and indoctrinate Africa's young. New mosques and religious schools are proliferating; instruction in Arabic is increasing; Islam is finding a substantial foothold even in traditionally Christian countries such as Zambia, Rwanda, and Uganda.

Meanwhile, the number of Africans who call themselves evangelical Christians has risen in just three decades from 17 million to an estimated 125 million; overall, there are now more than 350 million African Christians. The region is awash in storefront churches, revival tents, and bumper stickers reading "Jesus Saves." The Bible and related texts have been translated into hundreds of local languages and dialects.* It is anticipated that within twenty years there will be more Christians in Africa than in Europe and North America combined. This expansion has been helped along by missionaries of many nationalities and financed by affiliated churches in the West.

Much of this is good. Faith can provide hope to people who, burdened by the hardships of daily life, might be tempted to despair. Financial contributions—whether from the Middle East or Middle America—can build much-needed schools, clinics, and community centers. The connection established between Africans and U.S. churches can deepen understanding and support for America's perspective on democracy and terrorism, while raising awareness about such abuses as domestic violence and female genital mutilation.

The simultaneous expansion of Islamic and Christian activism also poses risks. In countries where populations are evenly divided, tense rivalries have emerged. In countries where one faith is dominant, the minority often feels intimidated. Africa today is a religious battleground, just as it was an ideological battleground during the cold war. That contest, too, had its positive side. The United States, western

---

* Missionaries have grown skilled at adapting their message to local surroundings. A creed composed for the Masai tribe reads: "We believe that God made good his promise by sending his Son Jesus Christ, a man in the flesh, a Jew by tribe, born poor in a little village, who left his home and *was always on safari* doing good, curing people by the power of God and man, showing that the meaning of religion is love. He was rejected by his people, tortured and nailed hands and feet to a cross, and died. He lay buried in the grave but *the hyenas did not touch him,* and on the third day, he rose from the grave." Cited in Jaroslav Pelikan, *Whose Bible Is It?* Viking, New York, 2005, 215.

Europe, the Soviet Union, and China all financed development in Africa, and each was eager to educate and thereby lure into its camp the rising generation of African elites. Those pluses were outweighed, however, by the lives that were lost when local rivalries escalated into proxy fights in a long list of countries including Chad, Sudan, Ethiopia, Somalia, Angola, Mozambique, and Zaire. As surrogates for communism and the free world slugged it out, arms flooded the region; compliant but autocratic governments were propped up; and essential nation-building tasks, such as instilling a sense of citizenship and creating strong state institutions, were neglected.

Economically and socially, the paramount need in Africa remains what it has been for decades: to build cohesive societies with good governments that can spur development. That task is made harder in almost every case by the ethnic and linguistic diversity so characteristic of Africa. It is further complicated when individuals or groups feel called on to place their religious identity ahead of national loyalty.

The traditional African religions make no such demand. Animistic beliefs are universal and are based on a conviction that God is present in all creatures and objects, and that the spirits of ancestors are also present in the world. Unlike the newer faiths, animistic rites are blended with daily life; there is no enforced separation, as when Christians attend church or Muslims halt other activities to pray; nor are there symbolic confrontations between Bible and Quran, cross and crescent, Arabic and local tongues.

A government trying to organize an army or build a better public school system will find itself stymied if every move must be analyzed for its impact on the competition between Christians and Muslims. This rivalry can become especially bitter when proselytizers shift from celebrating their own faith to denigrating the other. Muslims may dismiss followers of Jesus as polytheists who worship three gods instead of one. Christians may characterize Muhammad as an unworthy figure, warlike, lecherous, and unimpressive compared to the miracle-working Jesus. Although such religious one-upmanship has been practiced since Muslim traders first visited Africa's coasts in the seventh century, in recent years the sniping has grown worse.

Problematic relations between Muslims and Christians may well be aggravated by outsiders—most well-intentioned, some not—who see themselves as having a stake in Africa's internal struggle. There is also a risk that savvy Africans will exploit this outside interest to attract financial and political support for "moral" causes that are actually quite the opposite. It wouldn't be the first time. Funds raised for Islamic charities have often been diverted for political or personal gain; and in the 1980s, the American Christian right backed murderous Mozambican and Angolan rebel groups who had religious pretensions but only selfish interests at heart.

Violence between Christians and Muslims is a problem in many parts of Africa, but it has created particular havoc in Sudan, the continent's largest country, and Nigeria, the most populous. Both countries have much to fight over, including oil. Both are influential—Sudan in Africa's north and east, Nigeria in the west—and each has engaged the interest of the United States.

Although U.S. policy makers are often criticized for neglecting Africa, I visited the continent seven times while I was in government, stopping in almost two dozen nations, including, in the spring of 1994, Sudan. I was anxious because this was my first diplomatic mission to a government we considered hostile. Still, our party was received correctly enough by President Omar al-Bashir, a former military officer who had several years earlier come to power through a coup.

Bashir, in his early fifties, had a mustache and a well-trimmed short beard. He was tough-looking and wielded a wooden staff; he exuded seriousness. However, before getting down to business he presented me with a tall glass filled with a pink liquid that appeared to have the consistency of shampoo. I had often joked that my job as an ambassador was to eat and drink for my country, but this seemed beyond the call of duty. I noticed, moreover, that Bashir was not drinking anything, nor were any of the other Sudanese. Why? It occurred to me that they might actually be trying to poison me. With Bashir watching, I took what I hoped was a convincing sip of the stuff but barely swallowed anything. The taste was sweet, like Pepto-Bismol. To my relief, I didn't keel over.

The substance of my meeting with Bashir was no more satisfying than the refreshments. My purpose had been to convey a warning about Sudan's role in providing a safe haven for terrorists. The warning was not heeded. The following year the government was implicated in a failed attempt to assassinate the president of Egypt. At the time, Sudanese authorities were in the process of trying to turn their country into the regional vanguard of Islamic revolution. Among the terrorists to whom they played host was Osama bin Laden, whose construction company built highways that helped Sudan's military in its fight against southern separatists.

Sudan is one-fourth the size of the United States, stretching from the shores of the Red Sea to the continent's tropical center. The northern half is poor; its inhabitants are mostly Arab Muslim. The south is even poorer and is home to black African animists and Christians, as well as some Muslims.

The fertile land could easily feed all of Sudan and more; instead it is littered with land mines. Since achieving independence in 1956, Sudan has been the scene of almost nonstop civil war. Leaders in the capital, Khartoum, have for decades sought to consolidate political control over the south, in part because of its oil. In the 1980s, they sought religious control as well, through the imposition of sharia law. Southern rebel movements, though themselves divided, have fought for independence or autonomy. The result has been a permanent humanitarian crisis, made worse by dust storms and droughts, and marked by the brutal fighting, which has claimed some 2 million lives. Although all sides have been guilty of killing civilians, Bashir's government has been the primary abuser, blocking food supplies, attacking villages, and driving huge numbers of displaced people into areas where they could not survive.

Seeking ways to help, I met both in Africa and in Washington with those who bore witness to the war's carnage. Their stories of starvation, slavery, religious persecution, torture, and attacks on civilians infuriated me. I was moved by the young Sudanese who presented me with a carving of a black Christ and by groups of American schoolchildren who came to offer prayers. A Catholic bishop, who had been working in the Nuba Mountains, reported the death of more than a dozen first-graders whose school had been intentionally bombed. A spokesman for the government had responded to the tragedy outrageously, saying that the school was a legitimate military target. The bishop asked for my help in seeing that such atrocities did not recur. I was sitting there with all the power of the United States behind me, but had to say I was unsure what more we could do. We had long since imposed military and economic sanctions. We had also made clear to Sudan that if it wanted normal relations, it would have to curb its violations of human rights. In addition, we had provided more than $1 billion in humanitarian relief to the victims of the fighting, and appointed a special envoy to assist negotiations between the government and the south.

The commander of the southern rebels was John Garang. He was fifty-two years old when I first met with him in Uganda, a stocky man with a round bald head and a short salt-and-pepper beard framing his rotund chin. Educated in the United States, Garang had a reputation for beguiling everyone from communist theoreticians to Christian activists; and I was not surprised when he told me precisely what I wanted to hear: he supported peace, respected human rights, was willing to share power, and hoped Sudan would evolve into a democratic country. We knew that Garang's record was far from spotless, and we were not about to get the United States involved militarily in Sudan's civil war. We did, however, see Garang as the only person potentially able to unite the south and thereby put pressure on the government to mend its ways. Garang, a fighter since 1983, had the intelligence and charismatic style of a true leader, and was knowledgeable about economic and military matters alike. His portrait adorned banners and T-shirts all over the south.

The attacks of 9/11 may not have changed everything, but they did scare Sudan's government into seeking improved relations with Washington. Suddenly, Bashir started to be helpful on terrorism and also to negotiate productively, albeit unhurriedly, with Garang. The American envoy, John Danforth, an Episcopal minister and former senator, prodded the north and south relentlessly. Finally, in 2005, the two sides reached a settlement, pledging to merge their armies and share political power and oil revenues. The pact was met with jubilation. An estimated 1 million people jammed the central square in Khartoum to cheer when the pair of longtime enemies—Bashir and Garang—raised their clasped hands as partners in a new government. There was, literally, dancing in the streets.

The ceremony took place on July 9 and coincided with Garang's installation as vice president. This was the high point. Three weeks later, Garang was killed in a helicopter accident. Orators at his funeral compared him to Moses, a leader cut down after the merest glimpse of the promised land. Shocked but putting on his best face, Garang's successor, Salva Kir Mayardit, held hands with Bashir and promised to honor the legacy of his fallen leader by implementing peace.

I am hopeful but not optimistic. There are figures within the Sudanese military who profited under the old arrangements and have no interest in working as partners with the south. They can be counted on to pit various factions in the region against one another, a task that will be easier with Garang no longer around to quell fights. The former rebels will have to heal their own divisions and at the same time develop the administrative skills required to deliver public services. The UN will help, and so will the return from exile of many educated Sudanese, but the country's development needs are boundless. The religious divide will remain an obstacle to unity as Islamist activists seek to expand their influence in the face of resistance from Christians and animists. Even more seriously, the peace agreement does not provide for peace throughout Sudan. It does not extend to the Darfur region in western Sudan, where murderous militias backed by the government have sought to purge non-Arabs at the cost of hundreds of thousands of lives. The government has also continued to provide a safe haven for Uganda's loathsome Lord's Resistance Army. Despite efforts to rehabilitate himself internationally, Bashir still has much to answer for.

Under the peace agreement, national elections are scheduled for 2009. Two years later, the south will be entitled to hold a referendum on whether or not to secede. Although Garang was committed to keeping the country intact, the prospect of secession will entice many of his followers. The United States should do all it can to help the peace settlement take hold and to encourage a broader diplomatic solution that will finally bring an end to the genocide in Darfur and the grotesque violence in northern Uganda. Recognizing that religion cannot be ignored, we must continually make clear that our policies are aimed at helping all Sudanese. We should do what we can to prevent divisive outside forces, whether Christian or Muslim, from making matters worse by their meddling. Instead of trying to do everything ourselves, we should work in partnership with other countries and support the efforts of faith-based mediation groups to bind Sudan together across geographic, racial, and religious lines.

Experience tells us that roughly half the nations emerging from civil war are able to achieve lasting stability; the other half lapse into violence within five years. Reaching peace between the north and the south in Sudan took more than two decades; maintaining that peace—and preventing yet another cycle of suffering—will require an effort at least as concentrated and as long.

The oldest city in West Africa—Kano, Nigeria—is not a place to which American secretaries of state ordinarily venture; that is one reason I went. The world was changing, and U.S. diplomacy needed to make new connections. For almost a millennium, Kano—now a city of half a million people— had been a center of Islam. Since 1804, it had been home to a caliphate established after a series of holy wars. The caliphate's thirteenth leader, Emir Ado Bayero, had served since 1963. In 1999, he was my host.

I met him in his palace. After exchanging greetings, we went into an ornately decorated hall. He invited me to sit on his right, a gesture of respect, before seating himself on a bench covered with lambskin. The emir's elaborate head-dress, with colors representing his village and family, circled his neck and was tied on top. For the benefit of reporters, he made welcoming remarks in the local language (Hausa); then I spoke, in English. We walked out into the courtyard under two huge purple umbrellas and marched through the crowd that had gathered; it parted in front of us like a human Red Sea. Everyone was chanting, though I had no idea what the people were saying. Old men waved rifles aloft; others waved spears. I waved my hand. The emir showed a clenched fist, which I learned was also a sign of respect. We ascended a reviewing stand, where I was treated to the unique spectacle of a durbar: a celebration commemorating the victorious jihad two centuries before and showcasing Kano's rich blend of African and Islamic culture.

The event began with local rulers approaching and paying homage to the emir, accompanied by singers, dancers, jugglers, and stilt walkers. Groups of men then rode by on horseback saluting and holding signs indicating the villages from which they had come. Warriors fired old-fashioned muskets into the air. Medicine men whipped daggers around, touching their eyes, lips, and ears in a routine that made them symbolically immune from harm. Proudly, the emir identified several of the most colorfully costumed horsemen as some of his seventeen sons. At the climax of the ceremony, the warriors lined their steeds up and charged at the reviewing stand. Fortunately, I had been told to expect this and had also been told that the horses would stop in time. They did, just. Impressed and eager to show appreciation, I rose to my feet, beginning to clap before remembering instead to raise my clenched fist.

The durbar festivities and other traditions associated with the caliphate reflect the cultural and religious pride of the Islamic community. The emir is both an embodiment of that pride and someone who transcends the distinction. Within his region and throughout Nigeria, he is respected by Muslims and Christians alike. Such figures must be cherished because Nigeria's population of 128 million is almost equally divided between adherents of the two faiths. As in Sudan, Muslims are dominant in the northern part of the country, Christians in the south. The ability of the two to live in harmony is essential to their nation's future.

Unfortunately, symptoms of trouble showed themselves soon after my visit. Nigerians had just elected as their president, Olusegun Obasanjo, a politician who had, from the perspective of some northern Nigerians, three strikes against him. First, Obasanjo was a southerner; second, he was a born-again Christian; and third, he had campaigned on a pledge to purge the corrupt Nigerian military, most of whose senior officers were Muslims from the north. For these reasons, Obasanjo's victory stirred fear in the northern Nigerian states and led promptly to a reaction. In one of the states, a candidate for governor thought it would be smart to promise that he would protect Muslim interests, if elected, by decreeing Islamic law. The ploy was successful, and the promise quickly fulfilled. Other governors followed suit, and within weeks sharia law was in place in a dozen northern states, including Kano.

Previously, Muslims had been allowed to settle personal matters (such as divorce) in their own courts, whereas criminal matters were handled by civil authorities. The general imposition of Islamic law meant that its rules would be applied more broadly. Muslim leaders justified the action as necessary to prevent corruption, curb lewd behavior, and control crime. Christians, however, felt threatened. They objected to requirements that the Quran be studied and the Arabic language taught in their schools. They opposed the rigorous punishments prescribed (though rarely carried out) by the sharia code and the enforcement of prohibitions against dancing and alcohol. They pointed in vain to the Nigerian constitution, which prohibits any state or local government from adopting an official religion.

In the time since, sensitivities have been rubbed raw, and both Muslim and Christian mobs have been guilty of violence. In Kano itself, the house of a Christian preacher who had been accused of converting Muslims was set on fire, killing the entire family. Widespread fighting broke out in 2002, when a local news columnist suggested with ill-judged enthusiasm that a contestant in a beauty pageant was worthy of marriage to the Prophet Muhammad. There have been hundreds of incidents of mob violence directed against churches and mosques, often triggered by allegations that adherents of one faith had disrespected the other. An estimated 10,000 people have been killed, and thousands more have been displaced. Although the federal government discourages religious incitement, it lacks both the means and the moral authority to enforce its will. Christian leaders continue to accuse Muslims of wanting to drive them completely out of northern Nigeria; Muslims continue to resent Christian efforts to evangelize their population.

The roots of religious strife in Nigeria are, of course, not altogether religious. Like many African countries (including Sudan, and indeed also like Iraq), Nigeria was cobbled together by western powers out of an array of ethnic groups. From the first days of independence, Nigeria's federal government has struggled to assert control over its component regions. For decades, greedy dictators mismanaged Nigeria's economy and plundered its oil income, leaving the population poorer and more cynical. Wherever there are large numbers of impoverished and underemployed people, any spark can ignite a big fire. Further, in Nigeria's central highlands, seminomadic Muslim herders have battled with Christian farmers over grazing rights and access to water for their cattle. (A similar competition for resources caused bloodshed on the American frontier through much of the nineteenth century.) In Nigeria, the strains have been made worse by the combination of little rain and a high birth rate, which has left more people trying to survive on smaller parcels of productive land. While economic strains may be the primary source of the violence, religious differences make it simpler to pretend that the killing is being done for a higher purpose than the right to graze cows or plant corn.

In Sudan, in Nigeria, and elsewhere in Africa, there will continue to be a more general danger: alienated Muslim populations provide particularly favorable recruiting grounds for groups like Al Qaeda. Weak governments, porous borders, and civil conflict create openings for predatory organizations. Islam in Africa has traditionally been of the most moderate variety, but extremist pressures have been coming in from the outside; the radicals swoop in with money to operate mosques and social centers that cater to, and sway the allegiances of, the poor. Traditional Muslim leaders lack the resources to compete and their message is, in any case, less stirring to those in search of excitement. Already, a significant number of Africans have been found among the antigovernment insurgents doing battle in Iraq. The United States has responded by deploying troops to Djibouti as part of an antiterrorist task force for the Horn of Africa. It is also training various military entities in the region in counterterrorism techniques. There is value in this, but also considerable risk. We need to ensure that our strategy is both comprehensive and selective. During the cold war, we sometimes supported anticommunist governments that were in other respects disreputable and wretched to their own people. If we provide aid to military forces that cooperate in fighting Al Qaeda but that are also widely hated, we will strengthen Al Qaeda's appeal.

If we want Africans to help in fighting the kind of terrorism that Al Qaeda practices, we need to assist them in combating the forces that most terrorize them—including disease, a lack of clean water, inadequate schooling, and environmental devastation. If we are going to conduct military training, it should be aimed at helping African security forces to prevent civil strife and genocide, as well as to combat terror. We must also develop a new sophistication in our approach to matters of faith. I wrote earlier about the need for American diplomats to be well versed in the religious beliefs and practices of the countries to which they are assigned. In the past, officers in the foreign service who have been trained in Arabic and Islam have shown a decided preference for assignments in Arab, as opposed to African, capitals. We should have no doubt: highly qualified diplomats are needed in both places.

Songs of Enchantment, by Nigerian writer Ben Okri, begins: "We didn't see the chaos growing; and when its advancing waves found us we were unprepared for its feverish narratives and wild manifestations." Today, we have no such excuse. We can see the chaos growing. God help us if we are not prepared.

Part Three

Final Reflections

Eighteen

The Whole Shooting Match

A n eye for an eye," said Mahatma Gandhi, "makes the whole world blind." In earlier chapters, we have looked at the harm caused by a zero-sum approach to religion in the Middle East, Iran, Iraq, Afghanistan, Europe, and parts of Africa. We could—at the risk of belaboring the point— explore similar issues in such countries as Indonesia, Thailand, and the Philippines in southeast Asia, and the Caucasus and Chechnya in central Asia. We could examine the complex balancing act inherent in U.S. policy toward Pakistan, or the outlook in Lebanon, where Shia and Sunni Muslims and Christians strive for calm in a cauldron long-divided by political, doctrinal, and clan-related issues. Even in North America, where Islam is the fastest-growing religion, there are troublesome questions of cultural acceptance and discrimination reinforced by fears about violent extremism; the terrorists of 9/11 may have been born elsewhere, but they lived and trained in the United States for months preceding the strikes.

Some people might conclude from the ubiquity and intensity of these conflicts that the central challenge in the world today is not how to avoid a clash of civilizations but how to manage a struggle already under way. That is too dark a picture. Al Qaeda and its imitators may want to stir up a global Islamic revolution, but that does not mean they will succeed.

Fear fuels terrorism. Only if fear is allowed to spread can Al Qaeda hope to win lasting support. Surveys have found that Arabs view religious fanaticism as a significant problem both within their own societies and in the West. There is little generalized desire on the part of Muslims to involve themselves in violence. If they agree about anything, it is about the peaceful nature of their faith. Even when the Taliban held power in most of Afghanistan, the movement was recognized diplomatically by only three of the fifty-three Muslim-majority countries. Terror attacks that have killed Muslims in Saudi Arabia, Jordan, Egypt, Turkey, Indonesia and Bangladesh have caused some Muslims who had been sympathetic to Al Qaeda to change their minds.

For its part, the Bush administration, despite major errors in judgment, is not engaged in a religious crusade. The president understands that the best way to defeat Al Qaeda is to deprive it of the sympathy and support it has managed to attract among some Muslims. Most Americans grasp this as well. Few, even among Christian evangelicals, would agree with Pat Robertson that confronting Al Qaeda is at bottom a "religious struggle."* A plurality think Islam is no more likely than other religions to encourage violence.

It is good that relatively healthy attitudes have survived despite a succession of events that have conspired to poison

---

* Robertson told an audience in Jerusalem in 2004: "Ladies and gentlemen, make no mistake—the entire world is being convulsed by a religious struggle. The fight is not about money or territory; it is not about poverty versus wealth; it is not about ancient customs versus modernity. No—the struggle is whether Hubal, the Moon God of Mecca, known as Allah, is supreme, or whether the Judeo-Christian Jehovah God of the Bible is Supreme."

them. The truth is that most Muslims have interests compatible with those of the West, and that Arabs and Americans would both gain from improved relations. Indeed, the United States cannot defeat terrorism without the help of the Arabs; and the Arabs cannot maintain economic health without investment from the West. There is nothing inevitable about holy war.

Even so, there exist dangerous differences of opinion about three emotion-laden issues: first, the composition of a fair and just settlement in the Middle East; second, the legitimacy of the American military presence in in Iraq; and third, the overall nature of U.S. intentions. When these issues are seen in the best light, there are prospects for progress on each front.

After years of violence, the Palestinians and Israelis both have new leaders. With change comes turbulence but also opportunities. The Israelis, under Sharon, came to accept what many once denied—compromise on land is essential to the preservation of a democratic and predominately Jewish state. The Palestinians chose a president, Mahmoud Abbas, who genuinely believes that negotiation, not attempts at intimidation, is the way to fulfill his people's most basic needs and hopes. Although Hamas is now well placed to block progress toward peace, there remains a thirst on both sides to find a permanent solution. Nothing would do more than an Israeli-Palestinian peace settlement to put relations between Arabs and the West on solid ground.

As for Iraq, Arabs' expectations are so low that even modest gains could have a major impact. If the Arab Sunnis in Iraq fully embrace the democratic process, it will be difficult for Arabs elsewhere to continue complaining about American policies. If the insurgency dwindles, it will be easier and safer to withdraw our troops. If we can extricate ourselves voluntarily and within a reasonable period, and if the government we leave behind is legitimate and the country undivided, anger should dissipate and suspicions about our motives should become less intense.

This bundle of "ifs" shows how much has to go right for Arab perceptions to change. The current view in the region, according to one joint study by groups in the United States and Egypt, is that "Americans are arrogant, paternalistic, decadent, unfair, cruel, uncaring, and driven by lust for power and wealth." A second survey found that a majority of Muslims view America as greedy, immoral, and violent. These stereotypes cannot be blamed solely, or even primarily, on President Bush, but they did deepen significantly during his first term. This was not coincidental. In Iraq, particularly, the president knowingly sacrificed international support to pursue a goal he thought right, consciously disregarding the views of many Arabs and Muslims. To the frustration of the State Department, then under Colin Powell, efforts to smooth the way diplomatically were dismissed as unnecessary. The president had the power and the will to press his agenda, for better or worse; part of the worse was the alienation of world opinion.

On taking office in early 2005, Condoleezza Rice declared that "the time for diplomacy is now." Indeed, under her direction the State Department has been more visible in shaping foreign policy than it had been during Bush's first term, and the administration has seemed more interested in working cooperatively with allies and other countries. Even the president, seemingly intent on healing the wounds opened earlier, gave Karen Hughes, one of his most trusted assistants, the job of coordinating outreach to the Muslim world.

At Hughes's swearing-in ceremony, the president said he expected her to make sure that "every agency and department gives public diplomacy the same level of priority that I do." He then outlined a somewhat anemic three-point strategy: enlisting the help of the private sector; responding more quickly to terrorist propaganda; and urging Americans to "study the great history and traditions" of the Middle East. He added that every citizen who "welcomes an exchange student into their home is an ambassador for America." The problem with this rosy sentiment is that the Muslim students who once lined up to get into our universities are now heading elsewhere; for both sides, this is a lost opportunity from which it may take generations to recover. It would contribute much to public diplomacy if we were to find a better balance between legitimate security measures and policies that heighten misunderstanding. Today, many Arabs have the impression that the United States regards all of them as actual or potential terrorists. Some are actually convinced, for example, that to procure a visa for travel to America, Arabs must first agree to be photographed naked, proving that they are not concealing a bomb.

I might scoff at such exaggerated fears if not for the experience of an acquaintance whom I shall call Ahmed.

Ahmed had always felt at home in the United States. He graduated from an American university, served as an official of the American Chamber of Commerce in his country, and had traveled to and from the United States on many occasions. He is someone who knows and likes America and is, as such, an ally in opposing extremism. In August 2005, while en route from abroad to a conference at which I was among the participants, Ahmed was stopped at an airport in the northern United States. With no provocation, he was asked about the well-being of his "friend" Osama bin Laden. He was then kept waiting for hours while he was interrogated in classic good-cop/bad-cop fashion and his luggage and laptop were searched. During the ordeal, a photo of his six-year-old son produced allegations of pedophilia. A copy of Robert Kessler's best-selling book *The CIA War on Terror* led to a series of sarcastic questions about Ahmed's "interest in terror." The agenda for the conference he was scheduled to attend prompted questions about his association with other Arabs. Finally, a CNN transcript that he was carrying, of an old broadcast by Al Qaeda, caused the cancellation of his visa, leaving him no choice but to fly back home. The agents may have thought they were making America safer, but what this and similar incidents really do is make Karen Hughes's assignment that much tougher.

Public diplomacy can achieve little unless the policies it is designed to back up are viable and the audience it is intended to persuade is listening.* On both counts, the outlook will brighten if the best-case scenarios cited earlier in this chapter materialize; if they do not, current problems will worsen. Political and security setbacks in the Middle East, for example, could easily generate new rounds of violence. Iraq could break apart or fail to settle down, emboldening terrorists and causing our troops either to retreat in disarray or remain indefinitely with no promise of ultimate success. The rivalry between the Sunnis and the Shiites could evolve into a combustible regionwide competition. More broadly, the tensions within Islam and among Muslims, Christians, and Jews could escalate further, causing people of all three faiths to lose sight of common values.

The former German chancellor Konrad Adenauer once quipped, "History is the sum total of things that could have been avoided." A generalized confrontation between Islam

---

* One clear example of the connection between policy and popularity was President Bush's decision to order a large-scale American military and civilian relief effort following the tsunami of December 2004 in southeast Asia. The favorability ratings for the United States in Indonesia and India improved dramatically and have remained at a relatively high level.

and the West can and should be avoided; it will be if those with the power to shape events and attitudes keep their wits about them. I offer seven ideas that—if not pillars of wisdom—are at least cautions against foolish mistakes.

First, localize, don't globalize. Al Qaeda yearns for a worldwide stage; we should prevent it from claiming one. The specific issues stirring the pot in Chechnya, Nigeria, the Middle East, Iraq, and other trouble-prone areas vary widely; they should be dealt with separately. That will make each easier to solve, while hindering the terrorists' drive to portray every front as part of a single religious struggle.

Second, remember who the enemy is. There is a cottage industry of western commentators eager to identify "radical Islam" as the new communism. There are Arab leaders who reflexively exploit the fears of their citizens by saying that Islam is under attack by the West. This is nonsense. Neither the West nor Islam is under attack by the other. Both, however, are imperiled by Al Qaeda and the groups it has spawned. We must keep the terms of confrontation as narrow as possible.

Third, don't play with matches. The political climate is already overheated. Every miscalculation of word and deed drives the temperature higher. In theory, modern communications should tamp down emotions by creating a base of commonly accepted facts. In reality, the media often amplify passions by transmitting harmful rumors and shocking pictures (or offensive cartoons) to audiences all too eager to react to them. In the spring of 2005, deadly riots broke out in response to a single unsubstantiated report that American soldiers had desecrated the Quran. To avoid similar incidents, our leaders must exercise extraordinary discipline in what they do and say, while demanding similar caution from their subordinates. This is not, however, a one-way street. Making an insensitive statement or mishandling a holy book is to be condemned, but—as Muslim leaders should be pressed to agree—it does not provide an excuse for violence.

Every effort, in any case, should be made to improve communications. The Bush administration's hostility toward the independent Arab broadcasting network Al Jazeera, for example, is misplaced. Al Jazeera's audience is precisely the one officials of the United States most need to reach. Instead of attacking Al Jazeera, our government should be making its finest spokespersons available to appear regularly on the network's shows.

Fourth, we should develop a common understanding of what terrorism is. In politics, controlling the accepted meaning of words can be as vital as controlling the high ground in combat: hence the effort by some to label certain categories of terrorists as freedom fighters. This effort cannot be allowed to succeed. People who use terror in pursuit of national independence or to resist occupation may be freedom fighters in their own minds, but their motives do not excuse their methods; they are terrorists and should be treated accordingly. I often argued with Arab leaders about this. None of them explicitly justified violence toward civilians, but many considered terror attacks by Palestinians against Israelis to be legitimate elements of a struggle to recover lost lands. The Saudis, for example, sent payments to the families of Palestinian suicide bombers, even issuing press releases about it.* When I protested, they said that the funds were being provided "for humanitarian reasons."

---

* The Saudi embassy in Washington issued a press release in January 2001 claiming that the Saudi Committee for Support for the Al Quds Intifada, chaired and administered by Interior Minister Prince Nayef, distributed $33 million in support of wounded and handicapped Palestinians to the "families of 2,281 prisoners and 358 martyrs." The press release also reported that the committee "pledged a sum of SR 20,000 ($5,333) cash to each family that has suffered from martyrdom."

This view was taken recently by Sayd Mohammed al-Musawi, head of the mainstream Shia World Islamic League in London, who insisted that "there should be a clear distinction between the suicide bombing of those who are trying to defend themselves from occupiers, which is something different from those who kill civilians, which is a big crime." Whatever claim to our consideration this statement might have vanishes in light of the actual record of Palestinian suicide bombers. How is it self-defense to blow up a school bus, a pizza parlor, and a vegetable market?

Violence that is intentionally directed at noncombatants is wrong legally and morally. This principle applies to people who place bombs in public places; to all sides in Iraq and the Middle East; and to individuals, militias, and regular armed forces whether serving a dictatorship or a democracy. It applies, as well, to those who are sure they have God's permission to make an exception. The principle is universal.

This is not to say that the contrast between legitimate and illegitimate uses of force will always be clear. A painful balancing is often required—even in a just cause—between anticipated military gains and possible risks to civilians. Reasonable people may well differ in some situations about who is a combatant and who is not. So, too, the line between self-defense and aggression can become muddied when each side fears attack by the other. Faulty information may also lead to tragic mistakes or to accidents. Clausewitz was right when he wrote that events in war can take on "exaggerated dimensions and unnatural appearance," like the "effect of fog or moonshine."

We can, however, at least be clear about what is clear. There is no excuse for intentionally targeting noncombatants or for not taking into account the danger to noncombatants when military targets are struck. Countries and causes without access to conventional military power have no right to compensate by using unconventional means to spread terror among civilians. Countries with superior military power have no sanction to act with impunity, secure in the knowledge they can escape accountability for their actions. The rules for one apply to all. If Christians, Jews, and Muslims can agree on that, they will find it easier to agree on other matters.*

Fifth, we should talk about the treatment of women in a manner that leads to actual progress. I support the empowerment of women both as a matter of individual human rights and as an essential element of economic and social development. The cause is not helped, however, by ill-informed, smug, or simplistic criticism of Islam. Historically, few societies have cause for pride in their treatment of women. Even today, I am asked by some Muslims whether I would rather see a teenage girl in a burka or in a brothel. Islam neither mandates nor justifies the marginalization of women, but the Quranic distinctions that do exist cannot be ignored by Muslims of either gender, for to them the Quran comprises the actual words of God. Non-Muslims have no right to impose their own standards; nor is there any need to do so. In many Muslim societies, women can and do thrive, although others struggle against the sometimes brutal chauvinism that can be found to a degree in every culture. It is a mistake to disparage Islam or to assume that all is lost under sharia law; a better approach is to fight for the prerogatives that women should have under such law and to focus on the rights of women everywhere to define their roles for themselves.

Sixth, Christians, Muslims, and Jews should realize how

---

* In September 2005, world leaders considered but failed to agree on a definition of terrorism that had been proposed by Kofi Annan. The main issue was whether actions taken to resist occupation should be considered terrorism if they result in the death or injury of noncombatants.

much they have in common. The same forces of globalization and change that raise fears in conservative Muslim societies are also generating anxiety in the West. The same
concern that God's role as a source of law and a guide for living will be lost is felt by the devout in Kansas as much as in
Karachi, in the average Orthodox kibbutz as much as in
Riyadh. Rick Warren, a popular evangelical preacher who is
the author of *The Purpose-Driven Life*, has identified the
peaceful modernization of Islam as a primary international
goal for the next two decades. I agree, but with creationism
once more in vogue in many American communities, I am
uncertain who is qualified to lecture whom about the need
for modernization. Conservative Muslims perceive a war
against Islam; conservative Christians believe that they, too,
are under siege. Religious families on the Arabian Peninsula
and in south Asia do not want Washington telling them
what to teach their children; the same is true of families in
Florida, Alaska, and points in between. Those in many societies who are inclined toward a more secular outlook or who
practice a minority faith worry that the moral views of the
religious majority will be imposed upon them; in the United
States, some fear that the constitutional barrier between
church and state is breaking down. What is most striking
about the relationship between Islam and the West is not
how different we are but how similar. We ought to be able to
understand each other better.

During a telephone interview, I asked Bill Clinton about
this; he said that the question comes down to whether we are
willing to admit that we are not in possession of the whole
truth. That is, he said, "the whole shooting match, the
whole shebang."

"It is OK," he added, "to say you believe your religion is
true, even truer than other faiths, but not that you are in
possession in this life of a hundred percent of the truth." He

quoted the apostle Paul talking about the difference between life on Earth and in heaven: "For now I see through a glass darkly; but then face to face; now I know in part, but then I shall know even as I am known by God."

In a later discussion, at his home in Chappaqua, New York, Clinton told me, "If you accept that you may not know everything, it is harder to feel any kind of joy in hurting others. I guarantee that the people who fly airplanes into skyscrapers do not believe they are seeing through a glass darkly; those who burn down mosques or destroy sacred places do not think they know only in part; the guy who killed Yitzhak Rabin for being a 'bad Jew' was absolutely convinced he knew it all. You can't pretend if you're a person of faith that religion doesn't affect your politics; but if you believe you know all there is to know, then you'll think of others as less holy, less worthy, less deserving of respect. Not that there isn't truth; it's just that we don't know all of it. Most religions teach a lot of the same thing—a kind of spiritual integrity that is good for any society. We'd be a lot better off with an honest dialogue about our differences provided everyone 'fesses up about not knowing the absolute truth."

The Quran has passages that make a point similar to Clinton's quotation from Paul: "Compete with one another in good works; unto God you shall return altogether, and He will tell you the truth about what you have been disputing." Referring to David's killing of Goliath, the Quran advises that "if Allah did not check one set of people by means of another, the earth indeed would be full of mischief: but Allah is full of bounty to all the worlds."

It is no overstatement to suggest that if the future is to be "full of bounty" for any of us, people of different religions and cultures will need to get along. Here education is central. We must explore every means of developing and conveying a more fully shared understanding of the history of the Middle East, relations between Islam and the West, the belief systems of the three Abrahamic faiths, and the whole question of how to differentiate between truth and propaganda or myth. These are hugely contentious issues, requiring input from many sources, and with no single set of "right" answers. A thorough consensus would require so many departures from deeply held beliefs as to be beyond the bounds of reasonable hope. Yet even stormy and inconclusive discussions will build common ground as participants shed their weaker arguments in order to shore up more vital ones. Dialogue alone is no guarantee of peace, but it is better than a status quo in which the various sides are preoccupied with preserving age-old dogmas and chastising those who even suggest revisiting them.

It would be naive to put too much faith in projects that could be grouped under the heading, "Why can't we all just get along?" Ordinarily, the people who participate in such projects don't need persuading, and those responsible for the problems don't participate. The result can be intellectual cotton candy—sweet and pleasing to the eye, but lacking in nourishment. On this set of issues, however, especially at this time, a concentration of energy at every level has value. We may not be able to convert the extremes, but we can make the middle more active, cohesive, and confident.

I am encouraged, therefore, by the fact that intercultural and interfaith efforts have become growth industries at many think tanks and universities. Almost everywhere you look, Christians, Muslims, and Jews—and often people of other faiths—are conferring, signing declarations, strategizing. Among those leading the charge, not surprisingly, is Bill Clinton's Global Initiative, which is rounding up practical commitments for action in four areas, including religion.

The UN's Alliance of Civilizations High-Level Group, sponsored by Turkey and Spain, is striving to promote tolerance by drawing on some of the world's most accomplished minds. An organization called Meaden—whose name comes from the Arabic word for a town square—is fostering a series of online conversations. What, for example, would one ask the parents of a girl in Saudi Arabia, a college student in Pakistan, a Sunni shopkeeper in Iraq, or a teacher in Iran? What would we want them to know about us?

Others rely more on the power of faith. The Cordoba Initiative, which is based in New York and is headed by Feisal Abdul Rauf, a prolific author and imam of a mosque there, is a multifaith, multinational project dedicated to healing relations between Muslims and the United States. It is named for the Spanish city where in medieval times Muslims, Jews, and Christians lived and flourished together. Yale University has joined the National Center for Evangelicals and the government of Morocco in launching a Christian-Muslim dialogue. The Interfaith Youth Core, which is based in Chicago, was started by Dr. Eboo Patel to bring young people of different faiths and nations together to work for social justice. The Seeds of Peace organization continues to give young Arabs and Israelis an opportunity to learn about each other in an environment free from the tension of their homelands.

The hope driving such projects brings to mind a story that was included in an eighteenth-century German drama, *Nathan the Just*. The story is about a special ring that conveys to its owner both the respect of his peers on Earth and the favor of God. The ring was handed down from generation to generation, going always to the most virtuous son (this was, after all, the eighteenth century, so daughters did not figure in the story). The system worked well until in one generation there were three sons of equal virtue. The father solved the problem by arranging for an artisan to make two duplicate rings so perfect that no one could tell the difference between them and the original. As his life ebbed away, the father gave each son a ring and cautioned all three to act as if theirs were the true ring, as indeed it might be. The sons soon fell to quarreling about whose ring was genuine, and the matter was submitted to a judge. With the judge's guidance, they agreed that the only solution was for each son to believe in his own ring and to remain worthy through moral action, while admitting the existence of other possibilities.

In that spirit, we arrive at the seventh and last of my suggestions. Al Qaeda's leaders do not speak factually, but neither do they speak trivially. They concern themselves with transcendent issues of history, identity, and faith. To be heard, the rest of us must address matters equally profound. The three monotheistic religions provide a rich tradition of overlapping principles, ethics, and beliefs. Each places a high value on justice and compassion, points the way toward common ground, offers the opportunity for repentance, and is a religion of peace. Leaders should not hesitate to draw on such values to identify what might best be called the Judeo-Christian-Islamic tradition and to pursue shared objectives. These objectives might include an assault on global poverty as envisioned in the UN's Millennium Development Goals; or the "peace of the brave" that Yitzhak Rabin desired for the Middle East; or the fulfillment of the desire expressed by King Abdullah of Jordan, to see the world's 1.2 billion Muslims become "full partners in the development of human civilization, and in the progress of humanity in our age."

In Aesop's fable, a lion hunts a group of bulls without success, because he always finds them gathered together in a circle. Whichever way the lion approaches, he is met by horns. One day, the bulls quarrel and angrily stomp off to separate pastures. Caught alone, each is devoured. We should all be aware, irrespective of our faiths, that there is in the world today no shortage of prowling lions.

Nineteen

Summoning the
Better Angels

I have long been wary of those who claim to be sure of the truth about the biggest questions. Certainty is not in itself an asset; that depends on whether what one is certain about is actually true. Religion in particular defies attempts at proof. I find it interesting, for example, that some Christian groups have tried to use the scientific method to show that prayer works. They do this by dividing a list of ill people into two halves, then praying for one and not the other. The results of such experiments have, to date, been inconclusive. Is this because God isn't listening or because the best Christians spoil the experiment by secretly praying for both groups? As C. S. Lewis, the chronicler of Narnia, has observed, "Christians and their opponents again and again expect that some new discovery will either turn matters of faith into matters of knowledge or else reduce them to patent absurdities. But it has never happened."

As I grow older, I am reminded of a good Catholic—the friend of a friend—whose chosen epitaph was "I leave the world as I entered it: bewildered." The years have not brought me certainty about religion. I am a hopeful Christian but also an inadequate one, with doubts. I respect other religions because I think they are reaching for the same truth, though from a different angle. The Protestant theologian Paul Tillich wrote, "Doubt is not the opposite of faith; it is an element of faith." I like the sound of that.

Having admitted uncertainty, I can hardly say that fundamentalists must be wrong, but I am fairly sure they are not wholly right. Evangelicals accord scripture a high degree of authority; fundamentalists go beyond that to insist that every word in the Bible is literally true. To believe that of the Bible or of any other holy book is to assume too much about the ability of human narrators to rise above the subjective influences of their time and place. The scriptures are full of politics. To me, that is why the core teachings, not the minutiae, carry the weight of what a religion is about. I am particularly impatient with those who, having cited a few quotations, conclude that women should not be allowed to lead in church or that homosexuality is an abomination to God—who, after all, created homosexuals. As a practical guide to moral life in ancient Israel, a book such as Leviticus may have served well enough; but a piece of writing that accepts slavery, authorizes the sale of one's daughter, prohibits the trimming of beards, and bans the wearing of garments made from two different kinds of thread is neither timeless nor flawless. Jesus was not a fundamentalist, either. He was condemned by Pharisees for working on the Sabbath, sharing meals with a tax collector, and coming to the aid of an adulteress. He broke cultural taboos by conversing with a woman he met at a well and by taking children seriously. He rejected explicitly the doctrine of "an eye for an eye."

If God has a plan, it will be carried out. That is heaven's jurisdiction, not ours. If, however, one believes that creation has given us both life and free will, we are left with the question of what to do with those gifts. That is both a practical challenge and a moral one, and it is what this book has been about.

Religion concerns itself with the hopes and fears of all the years; the terms of American presidents are not so expansive. The policies of the United States government have to be based on what we might hope to accomplish in a finite period on Earth, not on postmillennial expectations. At the same time, what we can accomplish on Earth is mixed up with the different understandings people have of God. As I travel around the world, I am often asked, "Why can't we just keep religion out of foreign policy?" My answer is that we can't and shouldn't. Religion is a large part of what motivates people and shapes their views of justice and right behavior. It must be taken into account. Nor can we expect our leaders to make decisions in isolation from their religious beliefs. There is a limit to how much the human mind can compartmentalize. In any case, why should world leaders who are religious act and speak as if they are not? We must live with our beliefs and also with our differences; it does no good to deny them.

This does not mean, however, that we should inflate the importance of those differences. It is human instinct to organize into groups. For most of us, this sorting process is largely passive. The groups to which we belong are part of our inheritance and culture—a consequence of where we were born and how we were raised. My family's heritage was Jewish, but I was raised a Roman Catholic. If, as a child, I had been sent to temple instead of to church, I would have grown to adulthood with a different group identity. I was born overseas. If not for the cold war, my family would have had no cause to emigrate to the United States and I would never have become an American.

Nature allows us to choose neither our parents nor our place of birth, limiting from the outset the groups with which we will ever after identify. True, some of us will weigh competing philosophies and convert from one religion to another out of spiritual enlightenment or intellectual and emotional conviction. Some will find reason to shift allegiance from one country to another. More often, we remain within the same general categories we dropped into at birth or, as in my case, the categories where events beyond our control have placed us. That is not much of an accomplishment.

Logically, then, our differences should not matter so much. People of diverse nations and faiths ought to be able to live in harmony. However, the gap between what ought to be and what actually is has been a recurring source of drama throughout human existence. Decades ago, Reinhold Niebuhr warned us that the brutality of nations and groups cannot be tamed no matter how hard we try. "Social conflict," he wrote, is "an inevitability in human history, probably to its very end." Good and wise people might seek to prevent catastrophe, he conceded, but they would likely be no match for the fears and ambitions that drive groups into confrontation. It is sobering that Niebuhr arrived at this grim judgment before World War II. He was not reacting to the war; he was predicting it.

If Niebuhr is right, the pursuit of peace will always be uphill. And yet, I cannot accept the view that because our characters are flawed there is nothing we can do to improve the human condition. Decision makers can usefully search for ways to minimize the inevitable social conflicts referred to by Niebuhr—not so much with the aspiration of finding Utopia than with the goal of saving us from even greater destruction. Our inherent shortcomings notwithstanding, we can still hope to create a better future. And we know that the right kind of leadership can do much to prevent wars, rebuild devastated societies, expand freedom, and assist the poor.

I wrote at the start of this book that I wanted to identify ways to bring people together in support of policies that reflect the unifying rather than the divisive aspects of religion. My purpose is not to create a spiritual melting pot in which competing religious claims are reduced to mush; my interest is in solving problems and in responding to a practical political imperative. Technology has made outrages more visible, borders more permeable, weapons more dangerous, and conflicts more costly. In the process of realizing our dreams, scientists have also brought some nightmares closer to reality. The job of our leaders is to foster an international environment in which we can live with as much security, freedom, and justice as possible; this, by its nature, requires communication and cooperation.

President Bush deserves credit for affirming America's place at the rhetorical forefront of promoting democracy. He should be praised for acknowledging political freedom as a potential source of global unity. He has, however, undermined his own capacity to lead through mistakes and omissions that have made many countries less eager to stand with America. Clearly, the narrow vision and heedless unilateralism of the president's first term must not be repeated. We must restore alliances, take every region seriously, and understand that if we want other countries to collaborate on dangers that threaten us, we will need to assist in tackling the perils that threaten them. We must once again become known as a country whose leaders listen, admit mistakes, and work hard at addressing global challenges.

It would help a great deal if Americans from across the political spectrum did indeed come together (as I envisioned in Chapter 7) to push our government to lead on human rights and humanitarian issues. This would do much to restore respect for America and to legitimize our positions on the core security issues of proliferation and terror.

More vital still is the question of how we Americans define our country's international role. Do we see ourselves as subject to the same rules as other nations; or do we see ourselves as entitled to act in any way we see fit? Do we have a responsibility to strengthen international institutions and law, or a duty to remain free from such restraints in "answer to a calling from beyond the stars"? Is our proper role to lead or to dominate?

William Kristol, the neoconservative writer, has asked, "What's wrong with dominance, in the service of sound principles and high ideals?" This is a question Americans asked a century ago when conquering the Philippines. The answer President McKinley claimed to have received from heaven was that we had a mandate to impose our will. Whether or not that was the right reply then, it is the wrong answer today. The policy of dominance is at odds with America's self-image and a poor way to protect our interests. Its application in service to what our leaders believed were "sound principles and high ideals"—applied most obviously in Iraq—has proved to be a deadly drain on American resources, military power, and prestige. Let this be a lesson. American exceptionalism owes its long life not to the power of the United States but to the wisdom and restraint with which that power has most often been exerted—including the use not of military might alone but of all the assets that can contribute to our security and good name.

Looking ahead, we would be well advised to recall the character of wartime leadership provided by Abraham Lincoln. He did not flinch from fighting in a just cause, but he never claimed a monopoly on virtue. He accepted that God's will would be done without professing to comprehend it. He rejected a suggestion that he pray for God to be on the side of the Union, praying instead for the Union to be on the side of God.

Lincoln led a divided country. We must lead in a divided world. To that end, we should blend realism with idealism, placing morality near the center of our foreign policy even while we debate different understandings of what morality means. We should organize ourselves better to comprehend a globe in which religious devotion is both a powerfully positive force and an intermittently destructive one. We should respond with determination and confidence to the danger posed by Al Qaeda and its ilk. And we should make clear not only what America stands against, but also what we stand for.

Half a century ago, in writing about the cold war, my father argued that, whether we are "American individualists or British laborists, conservatives or progressives, socializing democrats or democratic socialists, white, black or yellow—we can all accept that human dignity and respect for the individual" must be the focus of everything. I believe that, too.

Respect for the rights and well-being of each individual is the place where religious faith and a commitment to political liberty have their closest connection. A philosophy based on this principle has the most potential to bring people from opposing viewpoints together because it excludes no one and yet demands from everyone full consideration of the ideas and needs of others.*

Yet the question arises: how can we hope to unite people around a principle—respect for the individual—that is such

---

* Respect for the individual is not, as some say, the opposite of respect for the rights of groups. On the contrary, individuals bring their rights to the groups to which they belong. Thus, freedom from discrimination on the basis of race, gender, or religion is *both* an individual and a group right.

a uniquely western concept? The answer, of course, is that it is not. Hinduism demands that "no man do to another that which would be repugnant to himself." The Torah instructs us, "Thou shalt love thy neighbor as myself." Zoroaster observed, "What I hold good for myself, I should for all." Confucius said, "What you do not want done to yourself, do not do unto others." Buddha taught us to consider others as ourselves. The Stoics of ancient Greece argued that all men are "equal persons in the great court of liberty." The Christian gospel demands, "Do unto others as you would have done unto you." The Quran warns that a true believer must love for his brother what he loves for himself. Finally, the world's first known legal code had as its announced purpose "to cause justice to prevail and to ensure that the strong do not oppress the weak." This is, we might think, the kind of legal system the world should develop now as a gift to the people of Iraq. In fact, it is the law code of Hammurabi, a gift civilization received four thousand years ago from ancient Babylon, now known as Iraq.

In setting down his idea of the true religion, Benjamin Franklin argued that the "most acceptable service of God is doing good to man." We cannot, I suppose, be certain of that, but we can at least make an informed guess that we have been given a conscience for a reason.

According to the poem by Yeats, it is when the best lack all conviction and the worst are full of passionate intensity that things fall apart, the center cannot hold, and anarchy is loosed upon the world.

We live at a time when the worst are indeed full of passionate intensity. The question is whether the rest of us have the courage of our convictions and the wisdom to make the right choices. Wisdom comes from learning, which comes from education. The heart of education is the search for truth. But there are many kinds of truth.

In mathematics and science, knowledge accumulates. Theorems are built on top of theorems and laws on top of laws. We discover that the Earth is round and will never again think of it as flat. We learn that the square of the hypotenuse of a right triangle is equal to the sum of the squares of the other two sides. Through experiments and research, scientists steadily add to our store of knowledge. We are, in this sense, far wiser than earlier generations about how the world works.

In the arenas of global politics and interfaith understanding, however, I am not sure we are any smarter now than we have been in the past.

The twentieth century was the bloodiest in human history. When the new millennium came, we vowed to make a fresh start, but we have not begun well.

I am an optimist who worries a lot. Through almost seven decades of life, I have seen enough examples of altruism and sacrifice to live in astonishment at what humans are willing to do *for* one another; and enough examples of cruelty to despair at what we are capable of doing *to* each other. The contradictions within human nature are inescapable. Liberty is our gift and our burden, carrying with it both the responsibility to choose and accountability for the choices we make.

I cannot write a happy ending to this book. We remain in the midst of struggle. As Bill Clinton reminds us, none of us can claim full title to the truth. We may hope, however, for leadership at home and abroad that will inspire us to look for the best in ourselves and in others. Lincoln, again, coined the perfect phrase, appealing in the aftermath of war to "the better angels of our nature"—summoning our capacity to care for one another in ways that cannot fully be explained by self-interest, logic, or science.

This is why the principle matters so much: every individual counts. If we truly accept and act on it, we will have the basis for unity across every border. We will take and hold the high ground against terrorists, dictators, tyrants, and bigots. We will gain from the contributions of all people; and we will defend and enrich liberty rather than merely consume it. In so doing, we may hope to inch our way over time not toward a glistening and exclusive city on a hill, but toward a globe on which might and right are close companions and where dignity and freedom are shared by all.

Notes

—————— ❧ ——————

ONE: THE MIGHTY AND THE ALMIGHTY

4 *"It is the policy of the United States,"* President George W. Bush, second inaugural address, Washington, D.C., January 20, 2005.

4 *"more than preemptive,"* Jim Wallis, *"God's Politics: Why the Right Gets It Wrong and the Left Doesn't Get It,"* Harper San Francisco, 2005, 149.

5 *"Freedom is God's gift."* President George W. Bush, quoted in *Plan of Attack* by Bob Woodward, Simon and Schuster, New York, 2004, 88–89.

7 *"As matters now stand,"* Michael Novak, *Belief and Unbelief: A Philosophy of Self-Knowledge,* Mentor-Omega/New American Library, New York and Toronto, 1965, 17.

8 *"clash of civilizations,"* Samuel Huntington, "The Clash of Civilizations?" *Foreign Affairs,* Summer 1993, 22–49.

TWO: "THE EYES OF ALL PEOPLE ARE UPON US"

17 *"seems to have been distinguished,"* President George Washington, first inaugural address, New York City, April 30, 1789.

17 *"The government of the United States,"* letter from President George Washington, cited in Barry Kosmin and S. Lachman, *One Nation under God: Religion in Contemporary American Society,* Harmony, New York, 1993, 23.

18 *"Franklin was a particular champion"* [footnote], "Benjamin Franklin's Gift of Tolerance," by Walter Isaacson in Akbar Ahmed and Brian Forst, eds., *After Terror: Promoting Dialogue Among Civilizations,* Polity Press, Malden, Mass., 2005, 36.

18 *"led by a cloud by day,"* Thomas Jefferson, cited in Robert N. Bellah, "Civil Religion in America," *Daedalus: Journal of the American Academy of Arts and Sciences*, Vol. 96, No. 1, Winter 1967, 1–21.

19 *"America is a land of wonders,"* Alexis de Tocqueville, *Democracy in America*, 1835. (Online.)

19 *"Brother, you say there is but one way,"* Red Jacket, quoted in *Lend Me Your Ears: Great Speeches in History*, selected and introduced by William Safire, Norton, New York, 1992, 431–433.

20 *"All men are not created,"* Senator John C. Calhoun, U.S. Senate, June 27, 1848. *Liberty and Union: the Political Philosophy of John C. Calhoun* (1811–1850), Speeches, Part III, Online Library of Liberty, Liberty Fund, 2004.oll.libertyfund.org/Home3/Book.php?recordID=007.

20 *"How little that senator knows himself,"* Senator Charles Sumner, U.S. Senate, May 20, 1856. Wikisource: Speeches. En.wikisource.org/wiki/wikisource:speeches.

21 *"The truth is,"* President William McKinley, cited in John W. Robbins, "The Messianic Character of American Foreign Policy," *Trinity Review*, September–October 1990.

21 *"It seems strange,"* *Public Opinion*, cited in Stuart Creighton Miller, *Benevolent Assimilation: The American Conquest of the Philippines, 1899–1903*, Yale University Press, New Haven, Conn., 1982.

22 *"There is not an imperialist in the country,"* Theodore Roosevelt, cited in Howard K. Beale, *Theodore Roosevelt and the Rise of America to World Power*, Johns Hopkins Press, Baltimore, Md., 1956; and Collier, 1972, 75.

22 *"I do not think there is any such thing,"* Henry Cabot Lodge, cited ibid.

22 *"The March of the Flag,"* quotations are from the version of Beveridge's speech delivered on the U.S. Senate floor on January 9, 1900. *Congressional Record*, 56th Congress, I Session, pp. 704–712.

23 *"The clergymen have all got hold,"* Charles Francis Adams, cited in John W. Robbins, "The Messianic Character of American Foreign Policy, *Trinity Review*, September–October, 1990.

24 *"A prince,"* Niccolò Machiavelli, *The Prince*, Mentor/New American Library of World Literature, 1952, 94.

25 *"The legions,"* President Calvin Coolidge, inaugural address, March 4, 1925.

25 *"As President Ronald Reagan cautioned."* Cited in John W. Robbins, "The Messianic Character of American Foreign Policy," *Trinity Review*, September–October 1990.

25 *"Jefferson wrote,"* letter from Thomas Jefferson to Roger C. Weightman, June 24, 1826, cited in Wikipedia entry for Jefferson, 10.

26 *"We shall fight,"* President Woodrow Wilson, address to a Joint Session of the United States Congress, April 2, 1917.

26 *"These men were crusaders,"* President Woodrow Wilson, Pueblo, Colorado, September 25, 1919.

27 *"pay any price,"* President John F. Kennedy, inaugural address, January 20, 1961.

27 *"We see how seriously,"* Robert Frost, excerpt from "For John F. Kennedy His Inauguration," from *The Poetry of Robert Frost,* edited by Edward Connery Lathem. Copyright 1969 by Henry Holt and Company. Copyright 1961, 1962 by Robert Frost. Reprinted by permission of Henry Holt and Company, LLC.

28 *"as the center of political enlightenment,"* George Kennan to Richard Ullman, "The U.S. and the World: An Interview with George Kennan," *New York Review of Books,* August 12, 1999.

THREE: GOOD INTENTIONS GONE ASTRAY:
VIETNAM AND THE SHAH

32 *"While normally,"* Hans Morgenthau, "We Are Deluding Ourselves in Vietnam," *New York Times Magazine,* April 18, 1965.

33 *"serious danger,"* John Kerry, Class Day address, Yale University, New Haven, Conn., May 1966. (Copied from the original text.)

33 *"the wrong war,"* U.S. Representative Morris K. Udall, "Vietnam: This Nation Is Caught on a Treadmill," *Reveille* magazine, July 1967, 12.

33 *"Each day,"* Rev. Martin Luther King Jr., "Beyond Vietnam," address delivered to the Clergy and Laity Concerned about Vietnam, Riverside Church, New York, April 4, 1967. Reprinted by arrangement with the heirs to the Estate of Martin Luther King, Jr., c/o the Writer's House, as agent for the proprietor, New York, N.Y.

35 *"Being confident,"* President Jimmy Carter, commencement address, University of Notre Dame, South Bend, Ind., May 22, 1977.

38 *"As a result,"* Gary Sick, *All Fall Down,* Random House, New York, 1985, 54–55.

41 *"Westerners, with few exceptions,"* Bernard Lewis, *From Babel to Dragomans: Interpreting the Middle East,* Oxford University Press, New York, 2004, 285.

41 *"For the Carter administration,"* telephone conversation between the author and Jimmy Carter, March 15, 2005.

FOUR: THE QUESTION OF CONSCIENCE

45 *"Cowardice asks the question,"* this quotation appears with slight variations in many places, including "Remaining Awake Through a Great Revolution," a sermon delivered by Dr. King at the National Cathedral in Washington, D.C. on March 31, 1968, less than a week before his assassina-

tion. It is reprinted by arrangement with the heirs to the Estate of Martin Luther King, Jr., c/o Writers House, as agent for the proprietor, New York, N.Y.

47   *"a good deal of trouble,"* Dean Acheson, "Ethics in International Relations Today," *Amherst Alumni News,* Winter 1965; cited in "Morality in Foreign Policy," in Michael Cromartie, ed., *Might and Right after the Cold War: Can Foreign Policy Be Moral?* Ethics and Public Policy Center, Washington, D.C., 1993, 38.

47   *"The interests of a national society,"* George F. Kennan, "Morality and Foreign Policy," *Foreign Affairs,* Winter 1985–1986, 206.

49   *"when he was still a young lawyer,"* J. G. Holland, *The Life of Abraham Lincoln,* Samuel Fowles & Company, Springfield, Mass., 1866, 78–79.

50   *"A country's first priority,"* Michael Walzer, in "Religion and American Foreign Policy: Prophetic, Perilous, Inevitable," Brookings Institution, Washington, D.C., February 5, 2003. (Panel discussion.)

53   *"In my memoir,"* Madeleine Albright, *Madam Secretary: A Memoir,* Miramax, New York, 2003, 146–155.

57   *"anything but honorable,"* Stanley Hauerwas, "The Last Word: What Does Madeleine Albright's Address Say about the Character of Contemporary Christianity?" *Reflections* magazine, Yale Divinity School, Fall 2004, 53–54.

58   *"President Masaryk declared passionately,"* Tomás Garrigue Masaryk, quoted in Josef Korbel, *Twentieth-Century Czechoslovakia: The Meanings of Its History,* Columbia University Press, New York, 1977, 15.

61   *"When Serbia's civilian leaders"* [footnote], Tim Judah, *Kosovo: War and Revenge,* Yale University Press, New Haven, Conn., 2000, 26.

61   *"Havel characterized it in these terms,"* Václav Havel, "Kosovo and the End of the Nation-State," *New York Review of Books,* Vol. 46, No. 10, June 10, 1999.

FIVE: FAITH AND DIPLOMACY

63   *"Twenty times,"* John Adams, quoted from Charles Francis Adams, ed. *Works of John Adams,* Vol. 10, Little, Brown, Boston, Mass., 1856, 254.

64   *"Too many throats,"* I. F. Stone, *The Truman Era,* Random House, New York, 1953, 218.

64   *"there is an assumption,"* Bryan Hehir, responding to Terrorism Forum Series, John F. Kennedy Library and Foundation, Boston, Mass., October 22, 2001. (Transcript.)

65   *"The government, alarmed,"* quotations cited in David Remnick, "The Talk of the Town: Comment, John Paul II," *New Yorker,* April 4, 2005.

67   *"And I'm talking,"* "Religion and Security: The New Nexus," Pew Forum

on Religion and Public Life, Washington, D.C., November 10, 2004. (Transcript of panel discussion.)

69 *"The LRA's professed goal,"* Richard Petraitis, "Joseph Kony's Spirit War." Viewed at http://www.infidels.org/library/modern/Richard_Petraitis/ spirit_war.shtml, January 17, 2003.

75 *"This is an opportunity,"* telephone conversation between Jimmy Carter and the author, March 15, 2005.

76 *"If you're dealing,"* interview with Bill Clinton, Chappaqua, New York, September 27, 2005.

SIX: THE DEVIL AND MADELEINE ALBRIGHT

79 *"just ordinary folks,"* James Dobson on *Larry King Live*, CNN, May 6, 1998.

79 *"Especially in the past twenty-five,"* Jesse Helms, *When Free Men Shall Stand*, Potomac, 1976 (rev. ed. 1994), 16.

81 *"For the past two hundred years,"* Pat Robertson, *The New World Order*, Word, Dallas, 1991, 92.

83 *"our understanding of marriage,"* report of the Independent Women's Forum cited in "Women Riled by 'Gender' Agenda," *Washington Times*, July 24, 1995.

83 *"the biggest threat,"* James Dobson, quoted in Larry Stammer, "Religious Right Challenges 'Anti-Family' Beijing Agenda," *Chicago Sun-Times*, September 10, 1995.

84 *"Hillary Rodham Clinton,"* Concerned Women for America, "Feminism at the Helm of U.S. Foreign Policy," May 12, 1997. (Press release.)

84 *"Satan's trump card,"* James Dobson, quoted in Stammer, op. cit.

86 *"God's plan."* Cited in most collections of quotations by Oliver Wendell Holmes. This is the senior Holmes, father of the Supreme Court Justice.

86 *"We are not,"* Richard D. Land, response to essay "Morality and Foreign Policy," by James Finn in Michael Cromartie, ed., *Might and Right after the Cold War: Can Foreign Policy Be Moral?* Ethics and Public Policy Center, Washington, D.C., 1993, 65.

SEVEN: "BECAUSE IT IS RIGHT"

89 *"Economist Jeffrey Sachs points out"* [footnote], cited in "Can Extreme Poverty Be Eliminated?" by Jeffrey Sachs, *Scientific American*, September 2005, 60.

90 *"Our aim,"* President Harry S Truman, inaugural address, Washington, D.C., January 20, 1949.

90 *"to those peoples,"* President John F. Kennedy, inaugural address, Washington, D.C., January 20, 1961.

91 *"bought a two-million-dollar yacht,"* Ronald W. Reagan, nationwide television broadcast, October 27, 1964. www.Reaganfoundation.org/reagan/speeches/rendezvous.asp.

92 *"It had been my feeling,"* Jesse Helms, quoted in Carl Hulse, "In Memoir, Jesse Helms Says He Was No Racist," *New York Times,* August 31, 2005.

93 *"foreign policy as social work,"* Michael Mandelbaum, "Foreign Policy as Social Work," *Foreign Affairs,* January–February 1996.

93 *"must move humbly and wisely,"* Senator Sam Brownback, cited in Peter Waldman, "Evangelicals Give U.S. Foreign Policy an Activist Tinge," *Wall Street Journal,* May 26, 2004.

96 *"In one village,"* Ambassador Robert A. Seiple, "Trip Notes," Laos, 2005.

96 *"return every man unto his posession,"* Leviticus 25:10.

98 *"We fight against poverty,"* President George W. Bush, cited in Robin Wright, "Aid to Poorest Nations Trails Global Goal," *Washington Post,* January 15, 2005, 18.

101 *"We should rely more,"* Ronald Reagan, remarks to the Oxford Union Society, London, December 4, 1992.

EIGHT: LEARNING ABOUT ISLAM

107 *"massacre of 70,000 Christians,"* Internet Medieval Source Book, Paul Halshall, Fordham University, 1996.

112 *"insist that even,"* Khaled Abou el Fadl, "Conflict Resolution as a Normative Value in Islamic Law," in Douglas Johnson, ed., *Faith-Based Diplomacy: Trumping Realpolitik,* Oxford University Press, New York, 2003, 192.

113 *"hurt no one,"* Prophet Muhammad, cited in Susan Tyler Hitchcock with John L. Esposito, *National Geographic Geography of Religion,* National Geographic, Washington, D.C., 2004, 346.

114 *"It is true,"* ibid.

114 *"Few Westerners,"* Queen Noor, "Security through Dialogue," in Akbar Ahmed and Brian Forst, eds., *After Terror: Promoting Dialogue among Civilizations,* Polity, Malden, Mass., 2005, 122.

116 *"opened the door wide,"* H. G. Wells, *The Outline of History,* Garden City Publishing, Garden City, N.Y., 1920, 581.

117 *"Today, the majority of Muslims,"* "Itjihad: Reinterpreting Islamic Principles for the Twenty-first Century," United States Institute of Peace, Special Report 125, August 2004.

117 *"Some scholars,"* "Revisiting the Arab Street: Research from Within," Center for Strategic Studies, University of Jordan, February 2005, 52.

117 *"I am America."* This quotation is widely attributed to Ali, including on websites maintained by Wikipedia, Brainyquote, and Infoplease.

118 *"There are those who insist,"* President William J. Clinton, address to the parliament of Jordan, October 26, 1994.

119   *"Think not,"* Matthew 10:34.

120   *"Some jurists,"* Khaled Abou el Fadl, op. cit., 194.

NINE: HOLY LAND, BUT WHOSE?

121   *"A letter signed by the British foreign secretary,"* letter from Arthur James
      Balfour to Lord Rothschild, November 2, 1917. Viewed at http://www.
      Yale.edu/lawweb /avalon/mideast/balfour.htm.

122   *"Zionism is rooted,"* David Balfour, cited in Margaret MacMillan, *Paris
      1919*, Random House, New York, 2001, 422.

122   *"Let us not,"* ibid., 380.

123   *"Make the enemy,"* Ibn Saud, cited in Dennis Ross, *The Missing Peace: The
      Inside Story of the Fight for Middle East Peace*, Farrar, Straus, and Giroux,
      New York, 2004, 34. (Ambassador Ross's book provides an excellent history
      of the Arab-Israeli dispute, along with the definitive account of efforts to
      arrive at a negotiated solution.)

123   *"I will take no action,"* letter from President Roosevelt, cited in interview
      with Hermann F. Eilts, *Frontline*, PBS, June 23, 2003.

124   *"Begin gave thanks and prayed,"* prayer of Menachem Begin, June 1967,
      published in *Jerusalem Post* Internet edition, September 13, 1998.

129   *"Jerusalem is for us,"* Saladin and Richard the Lionheart are quoted in
      James Reston, Jr., in *Warriors of God: Richard the Lionheart and Saladin in
      the Third Crusade*, Doubleday, New York, 2001, 230–231.

130   *"Fight in the cause of God,"* Quran 2:190–191.

131   *"the Redemption of the whole world,"* Rabbi Eleazar Waldman, quoted in
      Karen Armstrong, *The Battle for God*, Knopf, New York, 2000, 286.

131   *"the idea of Greater Israel,"* Leon Wieseltier, "The Fall," *New Republic*,
      September 5, 2005.

132   *"Asked if he had acted,"* Sarah Coleman, "Incitement Campaign Fueled
      Rabin's Assassin, Book Says," *Jewish Bulletin of Northern California*,
      August 20, 1999.

132   *"wildly overestimate,"* Craig R. Charney and Nicole Yakatan, "A New
      Beginning: Strategies for a More Fruitful Dialogue with the Muslim
      World," Council of Foreign Relations, May 2005. (Special report.)

132   *"Another recent survey,"* Center for Strategic Studies, University of Jordan,
      "Revisiting the Arab Street: Research from Within," February 2005, 63.

133   *"A best-selling series,"* "Left Behind": books by Jerry Jenkins and Tim
      Lahaye, published by Tyndale House.

140   *"the reasonable man,"* George Bernard Shaw, *Man and Superman: A
      Comedy and a Philosophy—Maxims for Revolutionists*, University Press,
      Cambridge, Mass., 1903; Bartleby, New York, 1999.

141   *"In that day,"* Isaiah 19:24–25. For a provocative essay on this passage, see
      Manfred T. Brauch, "Choosing Exclusion or Embrace: An Abrahamic

Theological Perspective," in Robert A. Seiple and Dennis R. Hoover, eds., *Religion and Security: The New Nexus in International Relations*, Rowman and Littlefield, Lanham, Md., 2004.

142 *"draw on the springs,"* Yitzhak Rabin, Prime Minister of Israel, ceremony commemorating peace between Israel and Jordan, Aqaba, Jordan, October 27, 1994.

142 *"If the enemy inclines,"* Quran 8:61.

TEN: "THE GREATEST JIHAD"

143 *"Cry aloud,"* I Kings 18:27.

144 *"God continues,"* Jerry Falwell, quoted in John F. Harris, "God Gave U.S. 'What We Deserve,' " *Washington Post,* September 14, 2001.

144 *"clear victory,"* transcript of a videotaped meeting between Osama bin Laden and an unidentified Saudi sheikh, released by the Pentagon on December 13, 2001. The quotations cited are of those of the sheikh.

144 *"If thou shalt indeed obey,"* Exodus 23:22.

145 *"Faith is a fine,"* Emily Dickinson, "Faith Is a Fine Invention." Viewed at http://www.poetseers.org/themes/poems_about_faith.

146 *"I see no sign,"* Remarks of the author, House of Hope Presbyterian Church, Saint Paul, Minnesota, September 30, 2001.

148 *"a group of sixty academics,"* "What We're Fighting For: A Letter from America," February 2002.

148 *"When Gore Vidal,"* Gore Vidal, "The Enemy Within," *Observer* (London), October 27, 2002.

148 *"the only punishment,"* Alice Walker, quoted in the *Village Voice,* October 9, 2001.

149 *"In February 1998,"* "Jihad against Jews and Crusaders," statement issued by the World Islamic Front in the names of Shaykh Usamah Bin-Muhammad Bin-Ladin, Ayman al-Zawahiri, amir of the Jihad Group in Egypt; Abu-Yasir Rifa'i Ahmad Taha, Egyptian Islamic Group; Shaykh Mir Hamzah, secretary of the Jamiat-ul-Ulema-e-Pakistan; and Fazlur Rahman, amir of the Jihad Movement in Bangladesh, February 23, 1998.

149 *"Bin Laden is not entitled,"* United Press International, "Taliban Annuls Bin Laden Fatwas against U.S.," June 17, 1999.

151 *"a torrent of donations,"* CBS News report, July 6, 1999.

151 *"Saladin,"* Henri Gouraud, cited in James Reston Jr., *Warriors of God: Richard the Lionheart and Saladin in the Third Crusade,* Doubleday, New York, 2005, xvii.

152 *"It may be,"* Quran 60:7–8.

ELEVEN: "GOD WANTS ME TO BE PRESIDENT"

156   *"At some point,"* President George W. Bush, cited in Bob Woodward, *Bush at War,* Simon and Schuster, New York, 2002, 81.

156   *research indicates,* Robert A. Pape, "Blowing Up an Assumption," *New York Times,* May 18, 2005.

156   *"Within two years,"* Pew Global Attitudes Project, Pew Research Center for the People and the Press, surveys released in June 2003 and June 2005.

157   *"An advisory panel of the State Department,"* Glenn Kessler and Robin Wright, "Report: U.S. Image in Bad Shape," *Washington Post,* September 25, 2005.

158   *"You know he is the wrong father,"* quoted in Bob Woodward, *Plan of Attack,* Simon and Schuster, New York, 2004, 421.

158   *"I believe God,"* interview with Richard Land, director of the Southern Baptist Convention, "The Jesus Factor," *Frontline,* National Public Broadcasting, April 29, 2004.

159   *"Why callest thou,"* Mark 10:18.

159   *"right as God,"* President Abraham Lincoln, Second Inaugural Address, Washington, D.C., March 4, 1865.

159   *"I say this,"* remarks of the author at Yale Divinity School, March 30, 2004.

160   *"sing* Kumbaya," Jed Babbin, former deputy undersecretary of defense, on Sean Hannity's show, "Is Albright Right That Iraq Is Making the World Hate Us?" March 31, 2004.

160   *"GOP stands for,"* Leon Mosley, quoted by Michelle Crowley, "Press the Flesh," *New Republic,* September 13–20, 2004, 11.

160   *"the shield of God,"* Thomas Edsall, "College Republicans' Fundraising Criticized," *Washington Post,* December 26, 2004, A5.

160   *"When America was created,"* Vice President Richard Cheney, speech to Republican National Convention, New York, September 1, 2004.

160   *"Like governments before us,"* President George W. Bush, speech to Republican National Convention, New York, September 2, 2004.

160   *"You better know what you believe,"* President George W. Bush, remarks in Westlake, Ohio, October 28, 2004.

TWELVE: IRAQ: UNINTENDED CONSEQUENCES

163   *"It makes a great difference,"* Augustine of Hippo, Michael W. Tkacz, and Douglas Kries, trans., and Ernest L. Fortin and Douglas Kries, eds., "Against Faustus the Manichaean XXII," in *Augustine: Political Writings,* Hackett, Indianapolis, Ind., 1994.

163   *"will make things better,"* President Bush, quoted in Bob Woodward, *Plan of Attack,* Simon and Schuster, New York, 2004, 332.

163 *"even if there were an adequate rationale,"* remarks by the author at Columbia University, New York, March 4, 2003.

164 *"Frankly, they have worked,"* Secretary of State Colin Powell, press conference in Cairo, Egypt, February 24, 2001.

165 *"The Methodist bishop,"* quoted by Susan B. Thistlewaite, "Just and Unjust Wars in the Christian Tradition: What Does History Teach Us?" Sermon delivered at Saint Peter's United Church of Christ, Elmhurst, Ill., February 23, 2003.

165 *"Petros VII,"* Susan Sachs, "Petros VII, Top Patriarch Who Sought Religious Dialogue, Dies," *New York Times*, September 13, 2004.

165 *"military action,"* Executive Committee, World Conference on Religion and Peace, "The Crisis in Iraq: The Need for Common Security, Common Responsibility, and Common Action," February 14, 2003.

165 *"A Protestant network,"* Jim Wallis, *God's Politics: Why the Right Gets It Wrong and the Left Doesn't Get It*, Harper San Francisco, 2005, 45–55.

166 *"Absence of evidence,"* Donald Rumsfeld, U.S. secretary of defense, press briefing at the Pentagon, Washington, D.C., August 5, 2003.

167 *"Bush wanted,"* memo from Matthew Rycroft to Sir David Manning (both foreign policy advisers to Prime Minister Tony Blair) concerning a meeting with the prime minister on the subject of Iraq, July 23, 2002. The memo, labeled "Secret and Strictly Personnel," was made public by the *Sunday Times* of London in the spring of 2005.

169 *"Our armies,"* Sir Frederick Stanley Maude, Proclamation of Baghdad, March 19, 1917. www.lib.byu./rdh/wwi/1917/procbaghdad.html.

174 *"The first step,"* Aparisim Gosh, "Inside the Mind of an Iraqi Suicide Bomber," *Time* magazine, July 4, 2005.

174 *"Mustafa Jabbar,"* Somini Sengupta, "The Reach of War," *New York Times*, July 10, 2004.

175 *"For this reason,"* For a provocative article on this episode, see Seymour Hersh, "Did Washington Try to Manipulate Iraq's Election?" *New Yorker*, July 18, 2005.

176 *"In a meeting,"* meeting between the author and King Abdullah of Jordan, Washington, D.C., March 15, 2005.

178 *"Iraq will become the center,"* Kyle Fisk, quoted in Katharine T. Phan, "Evangelical Missionaries Rush to Win Iraq as Middle East Mission Base," *Christian Post*, June 2, 2004.

179 *"The way the preachers arrived,"* Bishop Jean Sleiman, quoted in Caryle Murphy, "Evangelicals Building a Base in Iraq," *Washington Post*, June 23, 2005.

181 *"The terrorist threat to America,"* President George W. Bush, address to the nation, Washington, D.C., March 17, 2003.

THIRTEEN: CONFRONTING AL QAEDA

185   *"Islamic cultural values."* These conclusions are derived from a study conducted in Jordan, Syria, Egypt, Lebanon, and the Palestinian Authority: "Revisiting the Arab Street," Center for Strategic Studies, University of Jordan, February 2005.

185   *"Sweden, for example,"* Osama bin Laden, statement released by Al Jazeera television, October 29, 2004. English.aliazeera.net/NR/exeres/79CGAF22-98FB-4AIC-B21F-2BC36E87F61F.htm.

185   *"In 2004, one of the Defense Department's own advisory boards,"* report of Defense Science Board, cited in Michael Getler, "What Readers Saw and Didn't See," *Washington Post,* December 5, 2004, B6.

185   *"the holy attack,"* quotation from a jihadist website, cited in Susan B. Glasser, "'Martyrs' in Iraq Mostly Saudis," *Washington Post,* May 15, 2005, 1.

186   *"the frequency of suicide bombings,"* remarks of Dr. Bruce Hoffman, an expert on terrorism for the Rand Foundation at a panel discussion: "Suicide Terrorism: How Should the United States Combat This Growing Threat?" sponsored by the Center for American Progress, Washington, D.C., August 25, 2005.

186   *"Oh Mujahid brother,"* quotation from the inaugural issue of *Muaskas al-Battar* ("Camp of the Sword"), published by the Saudi Arabian branch of Al Qaeda, cited in Steve Coll and Susan B. Glasser, "Terrorists Turn to the Web as Base of Operations," *Washington Post,* August 7, 2005.

186   *"When terrorists spend their days and nights,"* President George W. Bush, speech to FBI Academy, Quantico, Va., July 11, 2005.

187   *"According to an assessment by the CIA,"* Douglas Jehl, "Iraq May Be Prime Place for Training of Militants, CIA Report Concludes," *New York Times,* June 22, 2005, A10.

187   *"What we are now awaiting,"* Claude Moniquet, quoted in Roula Kalaf and Jonathan Guthrie, "Europe's Radical Young Muslims Turn to Violence," *Financial Times,* July 11, 2005.

188   *"We lack metrics,"* Defense Secretary Donald Rumsfeld, "The Global War on Terrorism," October 16, 2003. (Memo to the senior Defense Department staff.) www.Foxnews.con/story/0,2933,100917,00.html.

189   *"On one front,"* Colonel Charles P. Borchini, USA (Ret.), forum transcript, "Religion and Security: The New Nexus in International Relations," Pew Forum on Religion and Public Life, Washington, D.C., November 10, 2004.

190   *"The critical problem,"* report of Defense Science Board, cited in Thom Shanker, "U.S. Fails to Explain Policies to Muslim World, Panel Says," *New York Times,* November 24, 2004.

191   *"an offense to God,"* Archbishop Giovanni Lajolo, interview with Italian press, May 11, 2004, cited in "Abu Ghraib Torture and Prisoner Abuse," Wikipedia.

193   *"The barbarous custom,"* Napoleon Bonaparte, letter to Berthier, November 11, 1798. Viewed at http://www.military_quotes.com/Napoleon.htm.

195   *"Where Are the Men?"* Neil MacFarquhar, "Lebanese Would-Be Suicide Bomber Tells How Volunteers Are Waging Jihad in Iraq," *New York Times,* November 2, 2004, A10.

195   *"Bin Laden and,"* National Commission on Terrorist Attacks against the United States, *The 9/11 Commission Report,* Norton, New York. 2004, 362.

196   *"Al Qaeda's leading,"* ibid., 251–252.

196   *In Yemen since 2002,* Brian Michael Jenkins, "Strategy: Political Warfare Neglected," *San Diego Union-Tribune,* June 26, 2005.

197   *"If you study terrorism,"* Hamoud al-Hitar, quoted in James Brandon, "Koranic Duels Ease Terror," March 7, 2005, Interfaith Cooperation blog. Viewed at http://daga.dhs.org/icp/blog.html.

197   *"Communism was not defeated,"* Václav Havel, *The Art of the Impossible: Politics as Morality in Practice,* Knopf, Toronto and New York, 1997, 90.

FOURTEEN: THE SAUDI DILEMMA

201   *"I am scared,"* Mona Eltahawy, "The Wahhabi Threat to Islam," *Washington Post,* June 6, 2004, B7.

201   *"My kingdom will survive,"* Ibn Saud, quoted in Sandra MacKey, *The Saudis: Inside the Desert Kingdom,* Norton, 2002, 371. (Updated edition.)

201   *"We are part of this world,"* King Fahd, statement issued by government of Saudi Arabia, May 20, 2004. www.Saudiembassy.net/Reportlink/Extremism-Report-January-2005.pdf.

203   *"un-Islamic,"* Ayatollah Khomeini, quoted in Fawaz A. Gerges, *America and Political Islam: Clash of Culture or Clash of Interests?* Cambridge University Press, Cambridge, 1999, 44.

204   *"transformed Saudi Arabia into the ultimate welfare state."* Information drawn from remarks of Charles W. Freeman, former U.S. ambassador to Saudi Arabia, at a New Republic Symposium on Public Policy, "Political Reform in Saudi Arabia: Examining the Kingdom's Political Future," Washington, D.C., October 2, 2003.

204   *"The country's oil revenues,"* Jad Mouawad, "Saudis Shift toward Letting OPEC Aim Higher," *New York Times,* January 28, 2005, C1–2.

206   *"no one with known links,"* National Commission on Terrorist Attacks against the United States, *The 9/11 Commission Report,* Norton, New York, 2004, 330.

206   *"some 210 Islamic centers,"* Statistics are from King Fahd's official website, www.kingfahdbinabdulaziz.com.

208   *"The managing editor of one daily paper,"* Khaled Batarfi, "The Problem Lies with Those Who Misinterpret History in Order to Serve Self-Interest," Middle East Research Institute, Special Dispatch Series, No. 830,

December 17, 2004. (Dr. Batarfi is the managing editor of the Saudi
Arabian daily *Al Madina*.)

208   *"It is a certain fact,"* Abdel Rahman al-Rashad, "A Wake-Up Call: Almost
All Terrorists Are Muslims," *Arab News*, September 9, 2004.

208   *"a global crime perpetrated,"* Crown Prince Abdullah, International
Conference on Counter-Terrorism, Riyadh, Saudi Arabia, February, 2005.
www.Saudiembassy.net/2005news/statements/StateDetail.asp?cIndex=498.

209   *"a poll conducted privately,"* survey cited in Fareed Zakaria, "The Saudi
Trap," *Newsweek*, June 28, 2004.

209   *"It should be no surprise,"* Susan B. Glasser, " 'Martyrs' in Iraq Mostly
Saudis," *Washington Post*, May 15, 2005, A1.

211   *"I had a chance during my visit,"* conversation with Crown Prince
Abdullah, Riyadh, Saudi Arabia, February 22, 2005.

212   *"he has allocated $3.3 billion,"* Edward S. Walker, "Islam's Battle within
Itself," *Baltimore Sun*, October 12, 2005.

213   *"a sort of oily heart,"* Max Rodenbeck, "Unloved in Arabia," *New York
Review of Books*, October 21, 2004. (Rodenbeck is characterizing a general
perception.)

FIFTEEN: ARAB DEMOCRACY

215   *"The most powerful force,"* Thurston Clarke, Senator John F. Kennedy, cited
in *Ask Not: The Inauguration of John F. Kennedy and the Speech That
Changed America*, Holt, New York, 2004, 83.

215   *"rash intervention,"* ibid, 83.

216   *"stability cannot be purchased,"* President George W. Bush, address to the
National Endowment of Democracy, Washington, D.C., November 6, 2003.

218   *"Surveys have found that Arab and Muslim populations,"* Pew Global
Attitudes Project, "Views of a Changing World," June 2003.

219   *"the election system,"* King Fahd, cited in John L. Esposito, *The Islamic
Threat: Myth or Reality?* Oxford University Press, New York, 1999, 242.

220   *"To be a secularist,"* Abdou Filali-Ansary, "Muslims and Democracy,"
Journal of Democracy, July 1999.

221   *"If one were to ask if Muslims,"* Seyyed Hossein Nasr, University Professor of Islamic Studies, George Washington University, cited in Osman
bin Bakar, "Pluralism and the 'People of the Book,' " in Seiple, Robert A.
and Dennis R. Hoover, eds., *Religion and Security: The New Nexus in
International Relations*, Rowman and Littlefield, Lanham, Md., 2004.

222   *"The U.S. and U.K.,"* Prime Minister Ateif Ebeid, cited in David Remnick,
"Going Nowhere," *New Yorker*, July 12 and 19, 2004.

224   *"When I was at the Department of State,"* "Interview with James A. Baker
III," *Middle East Quarterly*, Vol. 1, No. 3, September 1994, 83.

225   *"Even the most moderate,"* dissent by F. Gregory Gause III to Council on

Foreign Relations Independent Task Force Special Report No. 54 (co-chaired by Vin Weber and Madeleine K. Albright), "In Support of Democracy: Why and How."

226 *"As for these Islamists,"* Orhan Pamuk, *Snow*, Knopf, New York, 2004, 26.

228 *"Maybe some will ... say,"* President George W. Bush, cited in Michael Hirsch and Dan Ephron, "Can Elections Modify the Behavior of Islam's Militant Groups Fighting Occupation?" *Newsweek*, June 20, 2005.

228 *"From the day of our founding,"* President George W. Bush, inaugural address, Washington, D.C., January 20, 2005.

SIXTEEN: ISLAM IN THE WEST

233 *"The countries of Europe,"* Dr. Gerhard Ludwig Müller, cited in Elyse Schneiderman and Caroline Vazquez, "Immigration and Its Discontents," *Yale Globalist*, October 2004, 13.

237 *"The bombings in London"* [footnote] *Voice of America*, editorial, "Muslim Leaders Confront Terrorism," September 13, 2005.

237 *"the Spanish police apprehended,"* Elaine Sciolino, "Spain Continues to Uncover Terrorist Plots, Officials Say," *New York Times*, March 13, 2005, 11.

237 *"German and French police broke up cells,"* Elaine Sciolino, "France Seizes 11 Accused of Plotting Iraq Attacks," *New York Times*, January 27, 2005, A8.

238 *"Operatives of Abu Musab al-Zarqawi's terrorist organization,"* Craig Whitlock, "In Europe, New Force for Recruiting Radicals," *Washington Post Foreign Service*, February 18, 2005.

238 *"British officials estimate,"* counterterrorism officials cited anonymously, ibid.

238 *"Part of the Muslim community,"* interview with Prime Minister Tony Blair, London, October 17, 2005.

238 *"In these neighborhoods,"* ibid.

241 *"Staying here carries with it a duty,"* Tony Blair, quoted in Irshad Manji, "Why Tolerate the Hate?" *New York Times*, August 9, 2005. (Op-ed article.)

242 *"I flatly refuse to believe,"* Kemal Atatürk, quoted in Margaret MacMillan, *Paris 1919*, Random House, New York, 2001, 370.

243 *"At a time when people,"* Abdullah Gul, quoted in Amer Tahiri, "Turkey's Bid to Raise Its Islamic Profile and Court Europe May Backfire," *Arab News*, October 6, 2004.

243 *"To modernize an Islamic country,"* Joschka Fischer, quoted in David Masci, "An Uncertain Road: Muslims and the Future of Europe," Pew Forum on Religion and Public Life, Pew Research Center, December 2004.

244 *"a per capita income,"* *World Development Indicators,"* World Bank, 2003.

244 *"Prime Minister Silvio Berlusconi,"* The quotations from Berlusconi and Giscard d'Estaing are cited in Masci, op. cit.

244 *"Turkey has always represented,"* Cardinal Joseph Ratzinger, cited in Ian

Fisher, "Issue for Cardinals: Islam as Rival or Partner in Talks," *New York Times,* April 12, 2005.

246 *"No doubt very few countries,"* interview with Prime Minister Tony Blair, London, October 17, 2005.

246 *"40 percent of whom,"* survey cited in Karl Vick, "In Many Turks' Eyes, U.S. Remains the Enemy," *Washington Post,* April 10, 2005.

247 *"a splendid piece,"* Vincent Boland, "Faith, Hope, and Parity," *Financial Times Weekend,* August 27–28, 2005.

SEVENTEEN: AFRICA: A RACE FOR SOULS

249 *"We are heading,"* Andrew Rice, "Evangelicals v. Muslims in Africa," *New Republic,* August 9, 2004.

249 *"There is a race,"* ibid.

261 *in Nigeria's central highlands,* Somini Sengupta, "Where the Land Is a Tinderbox," *New York Times International,* June 16, 2004, A4.

262 *"We didn't see the chaos growing,"* Ben Okri, *Songs of Enchantment,* Cape publishing, London 1993.

EIGHTEEN: THE WHOLE SHOOTING MATCH

266 *"Surveys have found,"* Center for Strategic Studies, University of Jordan, "Revisiting the Arab Street: Research from Within," February, 2005, 46. (Study.)

266 *"Robertson told an audience"* [footnote], Pat Robertson home-page online, www.PatRobertson.com/speeches.

266 *"A plurality think Islam,"* survey, Pew Forum on Religion and Public Life, Pew Research Center for the People and the Press, July 2005.

268 *"according to one joint study,"* "An Arab-American Relationship for the Twenty-First Century," Report of the Middle East Institute in Washington, D.C.; and the Al Ahram Center for Political and Strategic Studies in Cairo, with the Support and Participation of the Ford Foundation, March 2005.

268 *"A second survey,"* Pew Global Attitudes Project, "Unfavorable Image of U.S. Is Largely Unchanged," Pew Research Center for the People and the Press, Washington, D.C., June 2005.

268 *"every agency and department,"* President George W. Bush, U.S. Department of State, September 9, 2005.

269 *"Some are actually convinced,"* Craig R. Charney and Nicole Yakatan, "A New Beginning: Strategies for a More Fruitful Dialogue with the Muslim World," Council on Foreign Relations, May 2005.

272 *"The Saudi embassy in Washington"* [footnote], cited in Jessica Stern, *Terror in the Name of God: Why Religious Militants Kill,* HarperCollins, New York, 2003, 49.

273 *"there should be a clear distinction,"* Sayd Mohammed al-Musawi, quoted

in Mona Eltahawy, "After London, Tough Questions for Muslims," *Washington Post*, July 24, 2005.

273   *"Clausewitz was right,"* Carl von Clausewitz, *On War*, 1832, cited in Wikipedia entry for "Fog of War."

275   *"It is OK,"* telephone conversation between the author and Bill Clinton, August 17, 2005.

276   *"For now, I see through a glass darkly,"* I Corinthians 13:12.

276   *"If you accept that you may not know everything,"* interview with Bill Clinton, Chappaqua, New York, September 27, 2005.

276   *"Compete with one another,"* Quran 5:48.

276   *"if Allah did not check,"* Quran 2:251.

279   *"full partners in the development of human civilization,"* message of King Abdullah, Amman, Jordan, November 9, 2004. Additional information for last item under chapter 18 (Abdullah citation): www.kingabdullah.jo/body .php?page_id=464&menu_id=&lang_hmkal=1.

NINETEEN: SUMMONING THE BETTER ANGELS

281   *"Christians and their opponents,"* C. S. Lewis, *The World's Last Night* (ch. 6), cited in Clyde Kilby, ed., *A Mind Awake: An Anthology of C. S. Lewis*, Harcourt, 1968, 226.

282   *"Doubt is not the opposite,"* Tillich's aphorism appears in numerous collections of quotations, including Brainyquote, Tentmaker Quotes, and Use Wisdom online.

284   *"Social conflict,"* Reinhold Niebuhr, *Moral Man and Immoral Society*, Scribner, 1932.

286   *"answer to a calling,"* President George W. Bush, speech to Republican National Convention, New York, September 2, 2004.

286   *"What's wrong with dominance,"* William Kristol, cited in Jim Wallis, *"God's Politics: Why the Right Gets It Wrong and the Left Doesn't Get It,"* Harper San Francisco, 2005, 138.

288   *"most acceptable service,"* Benjamin Franklin, *The Autobiography of Benjamin Franklin*, Washington Square, New York, 1975, 99.

288   *"According to the poem by Yeats,"* William Butler Yeats, "The Second Coming." *Selected Poems and Two Plays of William Butler Yeats*, Collier Books, New York, 1962, 91.

Acknowledgments

In the spring of 2004, I was invited to address the Yale Divinity School. Clyde Tuggle, a friend and an alumnus of the school, had initiated the idea. Since leaving government, I had spoken to groups of almost every description, and I am not usually at a loss for words, but I was unsure what would interest a hall full of aspiring ministers and theologians. Rule one in any speech is to start off on a light note, so I dredged up the only story I knew featuring both God and a former secretary of state:

A man dies and goes to heaven. At the pearly gates, he tells Saint Peter how happy he is to be there because he had always wanted to meet Henry Kissinger. Peter replies that Dr. Kissinger is still alive and not expected for some time. Disappointed, the man enters Heaven but soon rushes out very excited. "Saint Peter," he exclaims, "Henry Kissinger *is* in there; I just saw him. He is pacing around with his hands behind his back muttering about the Middle East." Peter shakes his head sadly, "No, I'm afraid you're wrong. That wasn't Kissinger; that was God. He just *thinks* he's Henry Kissinger."

A story, however, takes one only so far. For publicity purposes, Yale wanted to know in advance the title of my remarks. That is when this book, *The Mighty and the Almighty*, was truly born. I prepared the speech and delivered it to a positive reception but realized at the time that I had merely skimmed the surface of a subject of boundless importance and depth.

When I was in college, I had reported for the school newspaper and dreamed about a career in journalism. *The Mighty and the Almighty* gave me a chance to play reporter. I began by interviewing two people uniquely qualified to discuss religion and U.S. foreign policy, former presidents Jimmy Carter and Bill Clinton. Both men have hectic schedules, but both still took time to share with me insights that have immeasurably enriched this book. I especially want to thank President Clinton for doing me the honor of writing such a superb introduction to this book. I am grateful, as well, to Prime Minister Tony Blair, King Abdullah of Saudi Arabia, King Abdullah of Jordan, and former president Václav Havel of the Czech Republic for allowing me to discuss this project with them and for giving me the benefit of their experience and thoughts.

Early in my career, I came to appreciate the truism that a little knowledge is a dangerous thing. In writing this book, I knew that I would be touching on volatile subjects. I worried that I might mischaracterize religious beliefs, get part of the history wrong, offend people unintentionally, or fail to raise obvious issues. In other words, I needed help. For that, I turned to old friends and new. Bob Seiple, former U.S. ambassador for international religious freedom, was the first to review a draft of this text with an expert's eye. I am grateful to him for supporting this project so strongly and for his many helpful suggestions. Ambassador Seiple and I do not see every issue the same way, but we agree fully on the close connection between knowledge of religion and the protection of international security.

I turned next to Imam Abdul Feisal because he is a wise man and could read the draft from a Muslim perspective. He responded to my request for help by clearing his calendar, reading the entire book, commenting in depth on every chapter, correcting my punctuation, and extending a blessing to me and my loved ones—all within four days. He, too, will not agree with everything in these pages, but because of his contributions it is a far better volume (and more grammatical) than it otherwise would have been.

Hard as it was for me to believe, Rabbi David Saperstein, director of the Religious Action Center of Reform Judaism, matched Imam Feisel in the energy and care with which he reviewed the draft. His page-by-page comments on issues large and small were uniformly helpful if not always decipherable. The memo he attached, thankfully typewritten, contained a wealth of superb suggestions. I am deeply in his debt.

During the eighteen months of this book's evolution, I have become a skilled and diligent picker of brains, ruthlessly tapping the best ones I know. Among those who have willingly (or at least politely) succumbed to this treatment are Zbigniew Brzezinski, my former boss at the National Security Council; Reverend Susan Thistlewaite of the Chicago Theological Seminary; the scholar Elaine Pagels of Princeton University; Senator Sam Brownback of Kansas; Walter Isaacson, president of the Aspen Institute; Fareed Zakaria; Vin Weber, chair of the National Endowment for Democracy; Reverend Donald Argue, former president of the National Association of Evangelicals; Father Alexander Karloutsos of the Greek Orthodox

Archdiocese of America; Dr. Richard Land of the Southern Baptist Convention; M.K. Rabbi Michael Melchior, Israel's deputy minister for the Israeli Society and World Jewish Community; Dr. Mustafa Cerić, the Grand Mufti of Bosnia; John Podesta, president of the Center for American Progress; and Douglas Johnston, president of the International Center for Religion and Diplomacy.

Given my other activities, I also needed help with research. As I have walked by his office over the past year, I have watched as the pile of books on Bill Woodward's desk has grown until it became a mountain range whose peaks are labeled with such names as Armstrong, Novak, Neibuhr, Esposito, Benjamin, Weigel, Wallis, Reston, MacKey, Ross, and King James. In the crevices are crumpled think-tank studies, ripped-out news clippings, a letter from a woman in New Jersey explaining about Satan, and—from a man who had done work on my farm—a brochure entitled "Are You Going to Heaven?" Bill, who was my speechwriter while I was in government, did much of the hardest work on this book, helped with the writing, pushed me to think more deeply, and contributed many ideas of his own.

Elaine Shocas, formerly my chief of staff at the State Department, provided invaluable assistance through her repeated careful readings of the manuscript and her thoughtful suggestions and advice. Elaine helps me decide what to say and, even more important, what *not* to say.

In the course of preparing my memoir, *Madam Secretary,* I had my first experience—a humbling one—of working with that subspecies of magician known as a professional editor. It was my luck to get the best in the business and to have him back now for a second go. Richard Cohen, a marvelous author in his own right, is expert at rearranging sentences (and whole chapters), deleting excess verbiage, and finding the right tone. It didn't hurt that he had spent some time in a Benedictine monastery when younger and helped me avoid at least one unintentional act of heresy. I am pleased to be able to count Richard and his talented wife, Kathy Robbins, among my good friends.

Others who deserve thanks for reading and providing perceptive comments on the draft include my brother and sister, John Korbel and Kathy Silva; Ambassador Wendy Sherman, a partner in the Albright Group and my counselor while at the State Department; Evelyn Lieberman, former undersecretary of state for public diplomacy; Ambassador Dennis Ross; Jamie Rubin, former State Department spokesman; Susan Rice, former assistant secretary of state for Africa; Toni Verstandig, former deputy assistant secretary of state for Near East affairs; Suzy George, my present chief-of-staff; Jamie Smith, my director of communications; and Thomas Oliphant, columnist for the *Boston Globe*. I should also single out Dan Consolatare, who, in the initial stages of this project, helped creatively both in research and in the suggestion of themes. My colleagues Carol Browner, Jim O'Brien, Diana Sierra, Margo Morris, Amy McDowell, Laurie Dundon, Drew McCracken, and Anna Cronin-Scott provided the much-needed—and much-appreciated—daily support.

It is no secret that I went to HarperCollins because of one man—Jonathan Burnham. As senior vice president and publisher, Jonathan has advised me, anchored me, and guided me during the writing of this book. In my memoir published in 2003, I described him as "that rarity, a man both elegant and modest." He may not be infallible, but you could not prove it by me; he has yet to steer me in any direction except the right one.

I am grateful to Jane Friedman, president and CEO of HarperCollins; and Michael Morrison, president and group publisher, Harper/Morrow Division, for welcoming me so warmly into the HarperCollins family. They and every member of this legendary publishing house have provided a remarkable level of encouragement, and I thank them all. Tim Duggan, executive editor, has shepherded me through every stage of the editing and production with his good counsel, good company, and patience. I have been fortunate to work again with the creative vice president and associate publisher Kathy Schneider and all the members of the sales force—a talented group whose enthusiasm is contagious. Vice president and art director Roberto de Vicq has produced a wonderful design for the book—not an easy task when the Almighty is involved. Tina Andreadis, vice president and director of publicity, has worked very hard to make the book a success. I particularly want to thank Caroline Clayton and Allison Lorentzen of HarperCollins for their assistance no matter what the hour. Timothy Greenfield Sanders is an extraordinary photographer; a session with him is a grand adventure. I thank him for again doing the best he could with the material before his lens.

For over thirty years, Bob Barnett has been a close personal friend, political comrade, and legal counsel. He has advised me well, as they say, in good times and in bad. I thank him and his talented colleague, Deneen Howell of Williams and Connolly, LLP, for guiding me in my newest career as an author and through the fascinating maze of the publishing world.

I cannot conclude these acknowledgements without expressing appreciation to all the members of what has become a large family for their companionship, support, and love. With them in my life, I know I am truly blessed.

Index